TERRA PACIFICA

Sherman and Mabel Smith Pettyjohn Distinguished Lectures in Pacific Northwest History, Department of History, Washington State University, Pullman, Washington—

Paul W. Hirt, ed., *Terra Pacifica: People and Place in the Northwest States and Western Canada* (1998)

David H. Stratton, ed., *Washington Comes of Age: The State in the National Experience* (1992)

David H. Stratton, ed., *Spokane and the Inland Empire: An Interior Pacific Northwest Anthology* (1991)

William H. Goetzmann, *Looking at the Land of Promise: Pioneer Images of the Pacific Northwest* (1988)

David H. Stratton and George A. Frykman, eds., *The Changing Pacific Northwest: Interpreting Its Past* (1988)

John W. Reps, *Panoramas of Promise: Pacific Northwest Cities and Towns on Nineteenth-Century Lithographs* (1984)

TERRA
PACIFICA

PEOPLE AND PLACE IN THE
NORTHWEST STATES AND WESTERN CANADA

EDITED BY PAUL W. HIRT

WSU PRESS

Washington State University Press
Pullman, Washington

Washington State University Press
PO Box 645910
Pullman, WA 99164-5910
Phone 800-354-7360; FAX 509-335-8568
©1998 by the Board of Regents of Washington State University
All rights reserved
First printing 1998

Library of Congress Cataloging-in-Publication Data
Terra Pacifica : people and place in the northwest states and western Canada
  / edited by Paul W. Hirt.
        p.   cm.
     Includes bibliographical references (p.   ).
     ISBN 0-87422-163-3 (hdb. : alk. paper). — ISBN 0-87422-162-5
  (pbk. : alk. paper)
     1. Northwest, Pacific—History.   I. Hirt, Paul W., 1954-   .
  F851.T29   1998
  979.5—dc21   97-49181
                                                                        CIP

Contents

Acknowledgments

THIS VOLUME IS THE PRODUCT of collaboration in the fullest sense of the word. Thanks are due first to the Pettyjohn family which supplied Washington State University with the Sherman and Mabel Smith Pettyjohn Endowment to support scholarship in Northwest history. This endowment provided the financial support for WSU's Pettyjohn Distinguished Lecture Series and for a variety of history symposia, which have resulted in six books on Northwest history published by the WSU Press since 1984. This volume is the sixth in that series. Without the generous support of the Pettyjohn family, none of this would have been possible.

Second, the distinguished authors in this volume deserve thanks for their fine contributions. Nine of the ten authors came to WSU as Pettyjohn Distinguished Lecturers. All ten authors were chosen for their prominence in the profession and for the quality of their scholarship. The speakers deserve thanks not only for providing these original essays, but also for agreeing to spend a full week at WSU as lecturers interacting with students, faculty, and members of the community. Many of these Pettyjohn lecturers also gave the keynote addresses at annual Pacific Northwest history conventions. All of us at WSU are grateful for their generosity and cooperation at the time of their presentations, as well as subsequently during the editorial revisions for this book.

The editing of this book was a joint effort between myself and Glen Lindeman at the WSU Press. Mr. Lindeman, who earned a graduate degree in history from WSU, has served as one of the primary editors at the Press for nearly a decade. He is responsible for bringing to fruition dozens of books and is one of the region's most valued experts on Northwest history. His careful reading, proficient editorial pen, and vigilant fact-checking greatly improved this volume.

When I arrived at WSU in the Fall of 1993, I inherited the position of Pacific Northwest historian from retiring Professor David H. Stratton. Professor Stratton had orchestrated the Pettyjohn Distinguished Lecture Series since its inception in 1980. He also helped organize several Northwest history symposia which, together with the Lecture Series, resulted in the five previous Pettyjohn books published by the WSU Press. Half of the

Pettyjohn lectures in this current volume were originally presented under Professor Stratton's direction. Without his efforts, there would be no sixth book in the Pettyjohn series. For his prolonged, good-natured dedication to the Lecture Series, to Northwest historical scholarship, to the History Department, to WSU, and to the state of Washington we owe him more gratitude than can be expressed.

Several other WSU History Department faculty members provided the organizational energies for a number of post-1993 Pettyjohn lecturers' visits: John Kicza arranged for David J. Weber's visit in 1994, Orlan Svingen organized Donald Worster's coming in 1995, and Margaret Andrews arranged both Quintard Taylor's visit in 1996 and the invitation to Kenneth S. Coates who came in 1997. Of course, behind the scenes there have been history department staff members who did as much work as the faculty in making arrangements for visiting lecturers. Diane Triplett and Pat Hawkins both provided invaluable and essential support over the past ten years, while Rich Lewis provided significant word processing support for this volume. Thanks go to all of these people for helping make the Pettyjohn Distinguished Lecture Series and the resulting publications such a success.

Paul W. Hirt
Pullman, Washington
January 1998

Foreword
Terra Pacifica

Paul W. Hirt
(Washington State University)

IT IS RARE FOR SUCH A distinguished collection of scholars to be assembled
together in one small volume such as this, and rarer still that so many
nationally renowned scholars would focus their intellectual energies on the
history of the Pacific Northwest. This unique accomplishment was made
possible by the Sherman and Mabel Smith Pettyjohn Endowment which
has sponsored Washington State University's Pettyjohn Distinguished Lecture Series since 1980. The endowment is dedicated to promoting Northwest history through teaching, research, and public outreach. The lecture
series and the publications it has spawned have been a crucial part of that
mission. All of the contributors to this volume except one came to WSU as
Pettyjohn Distinguished Lecturers.

This is the sixth book published by the WSU Press showcasing scholarship supported by the Pettyjohn Endowment. Each volume stands as a
milestone in the interpretation of Northwest history. Three of the five previous publications were collections of essays like this one; all of them have
been used on occasion as supplemental reading for courses in Pacific Northwest history. We intend for this volume to serve the same purpose. The
essays included herein are highly readable and provocative, and they provide an in-depth look at important events and issues in the region's history
that broad historical surveys usually do not furnish.

Among the previously published collections of Pettyjohn essays, one
focused on Spokane and the Inland Empire, another concentrated on the
history of Washington State in celebration of its centennial in 1989, while
the third focused on Northwest historiography—interpreting the region's
past. The fourth collection, which you hold in your hands, stands apart
from the others in that it offers a uniquely expansive view of the Northwest with three essays that include western Canadian history, two of them

written by Canadian historians. This volume is also unique in the way it approaches the region's history from so many different vantage points: from a micro view of a farm family in the Snake River Plain, to a macro view of the Pacific Northwest's position in world history. Running through all these essays is a concern for "people and place." Some chapters emphasize the human dimension of history, the personal stories and experiences of everyday people; while others focus on location, geography, the interaction between nature and culture, regional identity, and the shifting alliances that bind a region together and connect it to the wider world. This interesting mix of approaches to the region's history makes this collection of essays especially versatile and instructive.

The first section of essays addresses the question of perspective. One hundred and seventy-five years ago the Northwest—as residents of Washington, Oregon, and Idaho now think of it—did not exist. There was no international boundary and no political states, just overlapping congeries of native and non-native peoples from many different tribes, ethnicities, and nations interacting socially, commercially, politically, and religiously. As currently conceived, "the Northwest" is a product of a relatively short period of human history and a relatively narrow cultural perspective. It may not exist—as we now know it—a hundred years from now as a result of the increasing globalization of information, trade, and political systems. The popular and quasi-futurist promotion of "Cascadia"—made up of Oregon, Washington, British Columbia, and Alaska—portends a possible future. If we hope to fully understand our region's past and present, or prepare for its future, we must recognize that regional identity is constantly evolving and that developments in the Northwest are inextricably tied to broader national and global events.

These insights inspired the essays in the first section that we have grouped under the title, "Regions, Nations, and Global Relations." David J. Weber opens with an overview of the period in Northwest history beginning not long after European nations had discovered the so-called "New World." Professor Weber paints a vivid picture of that crucial stage of early exploration and contact between natives and newcomers; a stage of the region's history when several European nations staked competing claims to lands along the Pacific coast while establishing sometimes cooperative and sometimes competitive relationships with indigenous peoples while in pursuit of commercial opportunities. At this time, the "Northwest coast region" included everything from San Francisco to the Bering Straits. It was a time in which global economic relations drove various competing European nations to explore, claim, and establish outposts in this vast Indian-populated region in a struggle for commercial dominion. The Spanish sailing up from the south and the Russians directing their attention down from the north established claims to the region in the late 1700s and were the first Europeans to explore many of the safe harbors and sounds along the coast. Eventually, Spain pulled back to California and Russia retreated to Alaska, leaving the British and the new American nation to contend over what is now Oregon, Washington, Idaho, and the coterminous parts of Montana and Wyoming located west of the continental divide, as well as much of the vast Province of British Columbia. Professor Weber examines the Spanish "moment" in Pacific Northwest history, largely from the perspective of Spain itself, giving students of the region's history a unique vantage point from which to comprehend this important early contact period.

By the second decade of the 1800s, the English-speaking nations had squeezed out their European rivals, and by the 1850s and 1860s a regional identity and a regional literature were forming among the growing non-Indian population. The second essay in this section, by Richard W. Etulain, investigates this regional literature from its earliest representations to the present. His is an inward looking analysis that seeks to identify a distinctive regional literature born and bred in the distinctive Northwest environment. He identifies the major authors and dominant characteristics of the region's literary tradition, suggesting that creative writing in the Northwest has passed through three different phases since the mid-nineteenth century, with each phase connected to historical and cultural developments within the region.

At the same time, Professor Etulain opens the door to a broader view of the Northwest. His recent book, *Re-imagining the Modern American West: A Century of Fiction, History, and Art* (Tucson: University of Arizona Press, 1996) assesses western regional literature—from Mexico to Canada, from the Missouri River to the Pacific—in terms similar to the essay contained here. He finds, as in the Northwest, that the literary tradition of the whole American West passed through the same three stages: from "frontier" novels and popular tales, to "regional" literature, to what he calls a "postregional" literature. This parallelism between the Northwest and the more encompassing American West reminds us that while the Northwest may be regionally distinct, it is also a part of a larger "West," which is in turn part of a larger nation, which is ultimately connected to neighboring nations and to a global community.

This theme of the Northwest's connection to the wider world is explored in all four of the remaining essays in section one. Patricia Limerick's essay on the significance of the Hanford nuclear facility in Richland, Washington, places the history of Hanford within the larger context of the development of the American West as a whole. Hanford, she says, is a preeminent emblem of the modern world, yet its history repeats the classic patterns of the supposedly bygone era of nineteenth-century "westward expansion." Hanford followed the familiar nineteenth-century social displacement scenario, as Indians and farmers were removed to make way for the sprawling nuclear reservation. It replayed the treatment of deserts in western history as "wastelands"; a place to exile marginal populations (Indians), and a place to dump the wastes and byproducts of industry in the nuclear age. Hanford also fits the classic western boom/bust economic pattern, with its "ruins and relics of lost times." Finally, she says, like western history in general, we find in the history of Hanford a troubling "disparity between what people said and what they did," leaving observers today questioning our cherished national myths and raising issues of government honesty and accountability.

Like Limerick's essay on Hanford, Donald Worster's "Two Faces West" also places the Northwest within the context of the unfolding history of the American West as a whole, and then makes interesting comparisons between it and the history of the Canadian West. After the Oregon Treaty of 1846 established the current international boundary, the U.S. and Canada proceeded to develop in sometimes similar and sometimes divergent ways. The border at the 49th Parallel arbitrarily divides a continent and a people, yet there is much the regions of the two countries have in common. Comparing similarities and differences between the American Northwest and western Canada is one of the most effective means of illuminating both nations' histories. In a comparative framework, we can see what is distinctive to a region or nation and what is not. Conversely, a comparative framework allows us to trace connections and common patterns of development that would not be visible in a study of a single place.

Comparative history is a difficult and risky enterprise, but well worth the effort. In his essay, Worster examines and critiques the concept of "development"—a word with profound connotations that appears regularly in speech and print in both Canada and the U.S., yet a word most people take for granted, employing it without much thought to its origins or implications. "Development," especially as used in historical narratives, has generally implied progress, improvement, the advance of civilization, and the creation of wealth and material comforts. This positive spin on the idea of development tells only one side of the story, however. Worster carefully examines what he calls "the development myth" from all sides, emphasizing its problems and biases. What one group sees as "development," for example, another group may experience as decline—as in the conflict between proponents of Northwest dams and advocates of Northwest salmon. Moreover, most development activities carry with them economic, environmental, and social costs. It is necessary, Worster says, to weigh all the costs and repercussions of development against its promises. Even more to the point, Worster questions whether the concept of "development"— with all its cultural baggage—should serve as an organizing framework for interpreting history or as a principle for making policy in the modern world.

Just as Worster blends economic and cultural analysis in his bi-national critique of the development myth, Gerald Friesen combines the economic and the cultural in his essay on recent free trade agreements between the U.S. and Canada. Professor Friesen is a Canadian, so he provides a welcome north-of-the-border perspective. The trade agreements themselves are of less concern to Friesen than their social, political, and historical implications. He paints a vivid portrait of the Canadian perspective—especially that of western Canada—regarding its southern neighbor, the United States. Thus, like Worster, he provides an illuminating comparative history that addresses both nations and their relationships.

Also like Worster, Friesen examines what is similar in the two nations' experiences as well as what is different. Through a review spanning early European settlement and relations with aboriginal peoples, to the industrial-capitalist revolution of the late nineteenth century, to the globalization of business, markets, and communications in the modern era, Friesen considers the potential merging of Canada and the U.S. into an integrated political economy, and examines the reasons why Canadians in particular have feared this looming possibility for most of the country's history. Growing globalization, Friesen asserts, has put both regional and national loyalties and identities in a state of flux. Canadians must be prepared for change, he warns; but, likewise, Friesen wisely suggests that Americans south of the border should study and assimilate Canadian history and culture more fully in preparation for the inevitable debates and negotiations surrounding cultural exchange and the evolving economic integration promoted by the Free Trade Agreements.

The final essay in this section on "Regions, Nations, and Global Relations" is by Professor Kenneth S. Coates who, like Friesen, is a Canadian.

Professor Coates started out as a regionalist specializing in western Canadian history, but grew fascinated with western Canada's relationship with Alaska and the American Northwest. Later he began investigating New Zealand's history and comparing frontier (early contact) history in Canada, the U.S., and New Zealand. After working in comparative history for a while, he expanded his horizons even more into the exciting new field of world history. Professor Coates caps off this section by discussing how global events have affected regional history in the broader Northwest and how regional events in turn have influenced history in distant parts of the world. His observations underscore the significance of connections—within and between regions and across national boundaries—and the importance of perspective, the standpoint from which one views and interprets history. Looking inward upon the Northwest as well as outward to the wider world provides us with the clearest sense of who we are and how we came to be.

The theme of section two is "Natives and Newcomers." These essays focus inward on the region, with particular attention paid to social history. Professor Julie Roy Jeffrey, best known for her pioneering 1979 book, *Frontier Women*, revisits the famous story of Narcissa and Marcus Whitman and their Protestant mission to the Cayuse Indians in the Walla Walla Valley, 1836 to 1847. The Whitmans, among the first missionaries to come to the Northwest and the first family to travel the Overland Trail to Oregon, hold a revered place in the historical iconography of the region, in part because of their martyrdom. The Whitman story is one of the most often recounted, even if not the best understood, of the "pioneer" tales of the Northwest. Professor Jeffrey places this familiar tale under new light. As a leading scholar of western women, she provides an intimate view of Narcissa Whitman throughout her decade-long residency at the Waiilatpu mission, illuminating how Narcissa's expectations and perceptions were shaped by nineteenth-century missionary culture and nineteenth-century white middle-class gender roles. Without understanding Anglo-American Protestant missionary culture and female status at that time, we cannot understand the Whitmans or their relationship with the Cayuse Indians or the tragic demise of the mission.

Another of Professor Jeffrey's objectives is to complicate the Whitman story a bit. Because the Whitman tragedy is one of the seminal events of the "contact era," when Europeans first encountered Northwest natives and attempted to settle on their lands, it becomes essential that historians offer a complex interpretation, detailed enough to match the complexity of real life during that volatile transition period. Consequently, Jeffrey's portrait of Narcissa Whitman is not only rich in its assessment of the protagonist, but also rich in its portrait of her relationship with her husband Marcus and to the Cayuse Indians. Indeed, Jeffrey often steps out of her focus on Narcissa to offer an equally empathetic view of the Cayuse perspective. The result is a sensitive portrait that leaves readers sympathetic to the missionaries *and* to the Indians, and leaves the issue of fault for the slayings ambiguous enough to stimulate critical thinking and debate.

John R. Wunder's essay offers a detailed survey of the legal status and rights of Indians, particularly in the Pacific Northwest, as they have evolved since the founding of the American nation. Citing key laws and legal decisions that affected or defined Indian rights and citizenship—including those that denied Indian rights—Wunder recounts in moving terms the often shameful history of discrimination and dispossession that Indians experienced at the hands of the American legal system. The story is complex, however, because the record is mixed; native peoples have successfully fought for recognition and rights over time and have won some important battles, especially during the twentieth century. Still, there has been some significant backsliding and resistance, which leaves us wondering how much real "progress" has been achieved.

Professor Wunder explains in detail contemporary legal battles as well as their legal precedents and historical contexts. Most importantly, Wunder reviews all the key disputes over Northwest Indian rights that appear in today's news: fishing and hunting rights, water rights, mineral and land use issues, tribal right to tax, sovereignty, tribal court jurisdiction, family and parental rights, and religious freedom. It is an impressive review that provides an invaluable context for understanding many of today's ongoing conflicts between Native Americans and non-natives.

The third essay in this section is by Washington State University's award-winning historian, Susan H. Armitage, who helped inaugurate the field of western women's history over two decades ago. Besides editing two outstanding published collections of essays on women in the American West, Professor Armitage also has extensively researched women's experiences in the Pacific Northwest. Her essay in section two is one of her most recent interests focusing on a pioneer farm family in the Snake River Plain of southern Idaho, where government-supported irrigation projects around the turn of the century were opening up desert lands to would-be farmers by damming rivers and diverting waters to "make the desert bloom." Through a close reading of Annie Pike Greenwood's diaries, Professor

Armitage examines personal life and community formation among the "pioneer" irrigation farmers who tried to make a living on often marginal lands with little capital and dependent on water provided by bureaucrats and engineers. It is a story of both dreams and disillusionment, of community building and community disintegration. Personal stories like these help illuminate the broad discussions of economic development found in section one.

The final essay is by Professor Quintard Taylor, a western historian who is America's leading scholar on African-Americans in the West. His essay examines black migration to the Pacific Northwest in the crucial years during and immediately after World War II, when the black population in the region increased at an unprecedented pace due to the attraction of war-industry jobs in cities like Portland and Seattle. The burgeoning black population of the 1940s had to contend with housing and work-place segregation, discrimination and intimidation, a lack of police protection, denial of basic civil rights, consignment to relatively low paying and low status jobs, exclusion from or segregation in most labor unions and industries, and a generally hostile reception among the predominantly white population. Nevertheless, blacks moved to the Northwest in unprecedented numbers, finding jobs and better wages in the war-industries. Although life was difficult, many blacks found that the Northwest offered better opportunities than the places they had left in the East and South. They also found that conditions were not uniform throughout the Northwest: Seattle offered relatively better jobs and conditions than Portland. Moreover, the "war emergency" offered African-Americans—as well as other minority groups—unprecedented opportunities to challenge and incrementally break down racial barriers in the workplace. Professor Taylor carefully traces efforts to improve black access to good paying jobs. Unfortunately, as women found too, economic gains made during the war often proved difficult to retain after the war.

Race relations in the Northwest were not cleanly divided along a black/white fault line. The Northwest always has had a multicultural population and it has only grown more so in the late twentieth century. Professor Taylor makes an especially valuable contribution to regional scholarship with his examination of African-American relations with not only whites, but other ethnic/racial groups as well—particularly the various Asian-American groups. His exploration of the cautious, but sometimes fruitful, cooperation between blacks, Asian-Americans, and whites in community organizations such as the Oregon Committee for Equal Rights, and in labor unions, like the International Association of Machinists, provides a fresh perspective on race relations.

Whether one is interested in race, gender, culture, environment, economics, law, or politics, this volume has something useful to offer. Students of Northwest history will benefit from the stimulating insights and interpretations of these distinguished scholars for years to come.

Section One
Regions, Nations, and Global Relations

I

The Spanish Moment in the Pacific Northwest [1]

David J. Weber
(Southern Methodist University)

IN 1929, ON A HILLTOP in Vancouver along the stretch of scenic coast called Spanish Banks, the government of Canada placed a plaque that read in part:

> Near this place, Captain George Vancouver on the 22nd June 1792 met the *Sutil* and *Mexicana* under Captains Galiano and Valdes—the last Spanish exploring expedition in what is now the BC [British Columbia] coast. The commanders exchanged information, established mutual confidence, and continued exploration together. It was dawn for Britain, but twilight for Spain.

More than half a century later, in 1984, King Juan Carlos and Queen Sophia of Spain spent several days in Vancouver. In anticipation of their visit, the Historic Sites and Monuments Board of Canada removed the plaque and replaced it with a new one designed to give no offense to Iberian sensibilities. The Board had thoughtfully removed the words "dawn for Britain, but twilight for Spain." [2]

That story would surprise most Americans, but not because it illustrates the way in which present-day agendas reshape our understanding of the past. Americans would more likely be surprised at the notion that Spaniards operated in the neighborhood of Vancouver. As one scholar recently put it: "Today's general public remains little aware of Spain's once significant presence along the coastlines and near the shores of modern Oregon, Washington, British Columbia, and Alaska." [3]

Spaniards did, of course, reach the Pacific Northwest, preceding all other European powers in exploring the coastlines of Oregon, Washington, and British Columbia. Spanish subjects, many of them Mexican-born, also planted the first non-Indian settlements in the region—short-lived posts on Vancouver Island and at the entrance to the Strait of Juan de Fuca. The Spanish empire, then, extended to the Pacific Northwest both in theory and in practice, since Spain claimed that coast by right of Papal donation, discovery, and first occupancy.

At first blush, Spain's momentary presence in the Pacific Northwest may seem unworthy of attention. Spain, after all, is no longer around. Indeed, by the time Anglo-Americans reached the Northwest Coast in consequential numbers, England was our chief competitor, not Spain. Why then, concern ourselves with the nation that lost? That question was posed clearly by a reviewer of my recent book—a study of Spain's activities in all of North America. "Usually," Nicholas Lemann wrote in the pages of the *Atlantic Monthly*, "the history of an undertaking is written only if it went well." Lemann did not think Spain's story went well at all. "As a colonial power in what is now the United States, Spain was a complete failure," Lemann wrote. "Spain's substantial efforts," he added, "never amounted to anything." Mr. Lemann liked my book, but thought my narrative failed because Spain failed and thereby prevented me from arranging historical events along, what he called, "a rising arc of portentousness."[4]

Spain clearly failed to win contests with England, France, Russia, or the United States for control of North America, but failing to win is not tantamount to "complete failure." It is interesting and instructive to see how Spain played the game—what it did and how and why it lost—just as watching the rerun of a sporting event might hold the attention of a fan who already knows the final score, but missed the game the first time around. Indeed, few stories, be they of sports teams, nations, or individuals, follow "a rising arc of portentousness." Sooner or later, we all lose the game.

♣ ♣ ♣

When Americans contemplate Spanish activity in what is now the United States—if they contemplate it at all—it is the sixteenth-century "age of exploration" that comes most readily to mind. Americans who are unlikely to know the name of any Spaniard in the New World in the seventeenth or eighteenth centuries recognize the names of sixteenth-century *conquistadores*, whom they associate with high adventure—Ponce de León, Francisco Vázquez de Coronado, and Hernando de Soto. And scholars, no less drawn to high adventure than the general public, have devoted a disproportionate amount of writing and research to that age of exploration.[5]

While *conquistadores* swarmed across much of the Sunbelt in the sixteenth century, the Pacific Northwest lay just beyond their horizon, shielded by stormy seas, contrary currents, and chance. Spanish mariners did, however, reach the southern border of Oregon. Sailing for the viceroy of New

Spain, as Mexico had come to be called, Juan Rodríguez Cabrillo set out from the Pacific port of Navidad in June 1542 with three small ships and orders to explore northward. Viceroy Antonio de Mendoza had instructed Cabrillo to seek evidence of rich cities and to find the strait through the continent that Spaniards imagined must exist and even knew by name— the Strait of Anian. Cabrillo's orders also required him to follow the coast all the way to China; Spanish officials imagined the two continents were joined at their northern extremities.[6]

As the European discoverer of San Diego and other points along the shoreline of Southern California, Cabrillo is well remembered, but his journey took him beyond Southern California. A veteran conquistador from Andalusia, who had survived battles against well-trained Aztec armies while fighting alongside Hernán Cortés, Cabrillo slipped on a rock on Santa Catalina Island and died from his injury shortly after the New Year in 1543. The chief pilot, Bartolomé Ferrer, took command and pointed the expedition's three small ships north. In the area of the present California-Oregon boundary, at 42° latitude, a shortage of supplies and a tempest "with a sea so high that [the sailors] became crazed," forced him to abandon plans to continue to China.[7] He turned back to Mexico. He had probably reached the high water mark of purposeful Spanish exploration on the Pacific coast for the next two centuries—unless one believes the controversial account of Juan de Fuca's visit to the strait that bears his name.[8]

Although Cabrillo and Ferrer had failed to locate the Strait of Anian or rich civilizations, they did explore some 1,200 miles of California's coastline, and they did establish a Spanish claim to the Pacific Coast of North America that no European power challenged seriously for over two centuries. They also made exceptional navigational notes that later mariners would use to good effect, added to the growing doubts that a waterway through North America connected the Atlantic and Pacific, and contributed evidence that Asia and North America, not joined at that latitude, might be two separate continents.

The Cabrillo-Ferrer voyage of 1542-43 occurred just three decades after the first Spaniard touched foot on what would become the shores of the United States—that is, when Ponce de León reached Florida in 1513. Between 1513 and 1543 Spaniards had completed a remarkable reconnaissance of the coastline of what would become the United States—up the Atlantic to Maine, around the entire Gulf of Mexico, and along the Pacific to the 42° parallel. Inland by 1543, De Soto and Coronado had explored much of what we call today the Sunbelt. As a result, the contours of the continent began to appear on European maps and Carlos V could indulge himself in the common European conceit that discovery gave him a strong claim to lands actually held by a variety of native peoples. Even at this early date, Mr. Lemann's assertion that Spain's efforts in North America "never amounted to anything" seems to collide with the evidence.

But Spaniards had little motive to return to North America, much less venture into the unknown northerly latitudes of what are now Oregon, Washington, and British Columbia on the Pacific. The northern reaches held little attraction for a people who had stumbled upon the wealth of the Aztec and Inca empires. Moreover, conventional wisdom suggested that precious metals abounded in hot rather than cold countries, and the tropics yielded other valuable commodities, including sugar and spices not susceptible to cultivation in northern latitudes. As Peter Martyr, the Italian humanist in the Spanish court of Carlos V, explained:

> But what need have we of what is found everywhere in Europe? It is towards the south, not towards the frozen north, that those who seek their fortune should bend their way; for everything at the equator is rich.[9]

▲ ▲ ▲

Following the great reconnaissance of the early sixteenth century, Spain concentrated on building colonies in lands farther south—closer to mineral wealth and tractable Indian laborers. Spain might have forgotten the Pacific coast of North America had it not been for the growth of a valuable trade between New Spain and the Philippines. Prevailing winds propelled Spanish vessels from Mexico to the Philippines, but returning home proved impossible until Andrés de Urdaneta discovered the trick in 1565. Thereafter, galleons returned to Mexico from Manila by sailing north into Japanese waters, then picking up westerlies in those latitudes that took them to the California coast—sometimes as high as Cape Mendocino—and running south with the winds and current to Acapulco.

The long California coast now took on importance. The scurvy-ridden crews on returning galleons needed a place to take on fresh water, fruit, and vegetables after crossing the Pacific, and Spain needed to challenge Dutch and English pirates who lurked in quiet coves along the coast, awaiting treasure-laden galleons. Thus, Spain began a search for a suitable place to establish a base in California—a search that culminated with the voyage of Sebastián Vizcaíno, an energetic merchant with long experience in the Pacific trade and in Baja California.

In 1602-03 Vizcaíno accurately mapped the California coastline as far as Cape Mendocino and bestowed new names on it, replacing those left sixty years before by Cabrillo, whose charts had apparently been forgotten.[10] With few exceptions, Vizcaíno's names remain unchanged. Vizcaíno recommended that Spain occupy the bay that he named for the conde de Monterrey, the viceroy who sponsored his expedition. In retrospect, it seems a curious decision because California had two bays manifestly superior to Monterey. One, San Diego, Vizcaíno judged too far south of the landfall of ships returning from Manila; it also seemed to lack sufficient wood and game. The second, San Francisco, had simply eluded Vizcaíno—as it would other mariners since it is not clearly visible from the sea.

If Spaniards had established a permanent settlement on Monterey Bay early in the seventeenth century, as Vizcaíno recommended, it would have brought them within convenient sailing distance of the Pacific Northwest. But in 1607 a new viceroy, the marqués de Montesclaros, shelved plans to build an outpost on the California coast. Rather than repel foreign interlopers and protect the Philippine trade, Montesclaros decided that a Spanish base would attract English and Dutch smugglers who would come to trade (as they did in the Caribbean and on the Florida coast). California's security, Montesclaros believed, resided in its inaccessibility, and the passage of time confirmed his judgment. Finally, he did not believe that the benefits of building a base fifteen- to twenty-days' sail from Acapulco would justify its costs. The lives of sailors were apparently not worth the high price.

In the decades that followed, Spanish officials occasionally tried to resurrect the California project. A port far up the Pacific coast would not only support the Manila trade, but would serve as a supply base for New Mexico, where Spain had established a permanent colony in 1598 (Spaniards did not fully appreciate the distance between Santa Fe and San Francisco until the late eighteenth century). The idea, however, failed to advance beyond the talking stage. Spain did not occupy the coast of what is today the American state of California until 1769—over a century and a half after Viceroy Montesclaros declared such a plan impractical.

There is no firm evidence that Spaniards deliberately explored the Northwest Coast during that century and a half, although some returning galleons might have accidentally approached the region or made landfall. One galleon, perhaps the *San Francisco Xavier* sailing in 1707, crashed at Nehalem Beach, thirty-five miles south of the mouth of the Columbia. Its cargo included over sixty tons of beeswax destined to become candles for the altars, homes, and mines of New Spain. The castaways—the first European subjects known to have come ashore in the Pacific Northwest—lived long enough among Indians to leave descendants. Nehalem Indians and others salvaged beeswax from the wreck well into the nineteenth century.[11]

Through most of the colonial era, then, Spaniards had no compelling reason to explore or settle in the Pacific Northwest. Pointing to Spain's rational calculations would seem sufficient to explain its absence from the region, but American historians who have often approached the past with an anti-Spanish bias have suggested a simpler explanation—Spanish lethargy. Historian Oscar Winther, for example, contrasted English settlement of the Atlantic coast with Spain's neglect of the Pacific Northwest. "From the founding of Jamestown to the close of the French and Indian War," Winther wrote, "the Spanish remained relatively inactive."[12] Winther chose to overlook Spain's considerable activity elsewhere in North America—in Florida, Texas, and New Mexico—as well as in Mexico, Central America, and South America.

Spain's "relative inactivity" ended, as Winther put it, when "two nerve-racking nightmares . . . contrived to disturb the Spanish *slumbers*."[13] Russian and English threats to Spanish claims to the Pacific Coast of North America aroused the "suspicious Spaniards," Winther wrote. Had he been describing Englishmen or Americans, one suspects that Winther might have referred to them as "vigilant" or "alert" rather than "suspicious." Whatever adjective we apply, however, the defensive measures that Spain took against its European rivals brought Spaniards into Upper California and the Pacific Northwest in the last half of the eighteenth century.

♠ ♠ ♠

The architect of Spanish expansion to California was José de Gálvez, who served as a nearly omnipotent royal inspector in New Spain from 1765 to 1770. In the 1760s, Gálvez regarded both England and Russia as threats to Spanish claims. Gálvez feared that English vessels would soon enter the Pacific from the north if England's well-publicized search for the Northwest Passage succeeded, and he correctly predicted that Englishmen pushing westward from Canada and the Mississippi would find their way to California. The threat from Russian fur traders seemed still more immediate. In 1759 a book by a Spanish Franciscan, José Torrubia, had appeared in Italy with the alarming title, *Muscovites in California*.

Fired by his own considerable ambition, the energetic Gálvez began on his own initiative to lay the foundations for Spanish expansion to the northwest of New Spain. In 1768, when reports of Russian activity on the California coast prompted Madrid to order him to secure Monterey Bay, Gálvez was already prepared to move swiftly.

With the founding of Spanish missions and presidios at San Diego and Monterey in 1769 and 1770, Spain moved closer to the Pacific Northwest. In 1773, a new viceroy, Antonio María Bucareli, became convinced of a renewed Russian threat to California and the need to occupy the extraordinary Bay of San Francisco, which Spaniards had sighted in 1769 from a high point on the San Francisco Peninsula. The cautious Bucareli moved by land and sea to meet the Russians. First, he granted permission to a frontier presidial officer, Captain Juan Bautista de Anza, to blaze an overland trail from Sonora to Monterey. Second, he sent vessels beyond San Francisco to search the coast for foreigners and for sites for further Spanish defensive settlements.

Strapped for officers, men, and ships, Bucareli entrusted the naval exploration to a mere pilot, Juan Pérez, and to a single vessel that would double as a supply ship, the frigate *Santiago*. In January 1774, Pérez set out from the mosquito-infested port of San Blas on a voyage whose destination the viceroy hoped to keep secret, but that quickly became known as "going to Russia." After dropping supplies off at San Diego and Monterey, Pérez set his course far from the continent, then beat his way north into waters no European had sailed before. Near the present-day Canadian-Alaskan boundary at about 54° 40', Pérez made landfall. From there, he cruised south for a closer look at the coastline of what is now British Columbia, Washington, and Oregon. He could not, however, comply with his orders to inspect the coast carefully in search of foreigners, or to stop frequently to perform acts of possession. Bad weather, crippling scurvy, and fear of the cold, uncharted coastal waters forced him to stay far from shore.

These failures notwithstanding, Pérez did, however, establish Spanish claims to the Northwest Coast and identify a number of key places, including Nootka Sound off Vancouver Island, which would soon become a point of international contention, and Mt. Olympus, which he christened "Cerro Nevado de Santa Rosalía."[14] A half century later, American heirs to Spain's claims to the Pacific Northwest would use Pérez's voyage to assert 54° 40'—the present southern boundary of Alaska—as the northern boundary of the Oregon Country.[15]

Soon after Pérez's return, however, Spanish mariners ranged well beyond 54° 40'. In 1775, in conjunction with Juan Bautista de Anza's successful plan to move colonists by land over 1,000 miles from Sonora to San Francisco Bay, Viceroy Bucareli ordered another maritime reconnaissance. This time he dispatched three vessels from San Blas, each commanded by young naval lieutenants recently transferred from Spain specifically to reconnoiter the northern reaches of the California coast in search of Russians and sites for future Spanish bases. One vessel, the California supply ship *San Carlos*, commanded by Juan de Ayala, explored San Francisco Bay—the first non-Indian vessel to enter the Golden Gate and demonstrate its navigability.[16] Two other ships, the *Sonora* under Juan Francisco de la Bodega y Quadra and the *Santiago* commanded by Bruno de Hezeta, continued northward. Against great odds the heroic Bodega y Quadra pushed his ailing crew and the tiny, leaky *Sonora* up the Alaskan coast to 58° 30', near present-day Juneau, taking possession of the coast for Spain at four points, including a place on Prince of Wales Island that still bears the name of the viceroy, Bucareli Sound.

But the same difficulties that had plagued Juan Pérez (who now served as pilot on the *Santiago* and was one of the many sailors to die of scurvy on the expedition), hindered both Bodega and Hezeta from making careful charts that would document their accomplishments and thereby establish an indelible Spanish claim to the coast. Hezeta, for example, made the first known European sighting of the mouth of the Columbia River, which appeared on subsequent maps as the "Entrada de Hezeta," but his failure to explore the river itself, coupled with the lack of publicity about the expedition, made his discovery easy for other nations to ignore. Seventeen years later, the American Robert Gray entered the river and named it Columbia for his ship. The name stuck, even on Spanish maps, and helped strengthen American claims to the Pacific Northwest.

♣ ♣ ♣

Spain had made this rapid thrust up the Pacific, planting settlements from San Diego to San Francisco and exploring into present Alaska, at the same time that it tried to block British expansion in the South Pacific. From Patagonia through the Straits of Magellan, to the islands of Juan Fernández, Easter Island, and even Tahiti, where two Spanish missionaries had failed dismally to convert natives, Spain sought to anticipate British attempts to establish South Pacific bases in the late 1760s and early 1770s. Its treasury badly overextended and chronically short of ships, crews, arms, and equipment, Spain could not realistically defend the Pacific with force. Instead, Spain tried, in the words of its secretary of state, to avoid constructing "costly defended posts, but . . . [to] give signs that the land is ours."[17] (In today's lexicon we might term this an attempt through semiotics to substitute a virtual reality for real settlements.)

Although Spanish officials continued to invoke a royal decree of 1692 that forbade foreigners from entering the Pacific without Spanish permission and required that violators be treated as enemies, the 1780s saw Spain's already limited ability to defend the Pacific decline even further as its priorities shifted.[18] In South America, the great revolts of Tupac Amaru in Peru and the *comuneros* in New Granada forced Spain to turn its attention inward; in North America, the rebellion of the British colonies gave Spain an opportunity to avenge itself against its recent humiliation in the Seven Years' War, and to regain the Floridas.

In North America, Spain took the side of the rebellious Anglo-American colonists, diverting its resources away from California and the Pacific Northwest into the fight against England. Spain drove Britain out of the lower Mississippi Valley and off the northern shores of the Gulf of Mexico. Spain's little-known victories at Baton Rouge, Natchez, Mobile, and Pensacola, not only facilitated American independence but enabled Spain to extract the Floridas from Britain at the end of the war in 1783.

These victories in southeastern North America came at a cost, however, to Spain's position in the Southwest. Spain lost control of the vital Yuma crossing of the Colorado River—an essential link on Anza's trail that connected California by land to Sonora and the rest of New Spain. Quechan Indians, whom Spaniards knew as Yumas, had driven Spanish missionaries and soldiers away in 1781, the same year that Spanish forces defeated the British at Pensacola. Spain never again made a serious effort to regain the Yuma crossing. Initially, war with Apaches and other tribes took priority over the Yumas, and after Spaniards brokered a peace with Apaches in the mid-1780s, projects to reopen the Sonora route failed to get off the drawing board because Spain had more pressing concerns on the edges of the expanding Anglo-American frontier. For the remainder of the Spanish era, California depended upon the sea as its sole source of supplies and immigration. This stunted its growth and halted Spanish expansion beyond San Francisco to the Pacific Northwest.

Spain's position throughout the hemisphere suffered as leadership at the highest levels shifted to new and less able hands with the deaths of José de Gálvez and Carlos III in 1787 and 1788. Under the phlegmatic Carlos IV (1788-1808), Spain staggered into several decades of catastrophic decline. In 1789, within a year after Carlos IV came to power in Spain,

Parisians stormed the Bastille and seized his Bourbon cousin, Louis XVI. Carlos IV's ill-advised effort to reverse the direction of the regicidal French Revolution represented the beginning of Spain's eclipse—an eclipse that saw it go to war with England, as well as France, and cost it nearly all of its American empire.

One of Spain's first setbacks in North America occurred in the Pacific Northwest. There England forced Spain to surrender its exclusive claims to the region as a result of an episode at an obscure spot on Vancouver Island—Nootka Sound.

The troubles at Nootka originated with the 1778 visit of the celebrated Captain James Cook, whose landing at Nootka on his third and final voyage, according to recently discovered evidence, was deliberate rather than coincidental. Cook knew even before leaving London in 1776 that Juan Pérez and the *Santiago* had met friendly Indians at the latitude of Nootka in 1774.[19] There, Cook found more than friendly Indians. Cook's report told of fortunes to be made by marketing the silky pelts of Northwest Coast sea otter in Canton. Published in 1784, that report brought merchant vessels from several nations scrambling to the otter-rich coastal waters off present Oregon, Washington, and British Columbia.

Alarmed by these new intrusions, the viceroy of New Spain, Manuel Antonio Flores, on his own initiative, sent Captain Esteban José Martínez in 1789 to warn foreigners away from this region, which Spain claimed by right of discovery. Viceroy Flores ordered Martínez to establish a base at Nootka Sound—then believed to be on the North American mainland. The viceroy had evidence that Russians or Englishmen might occupy this spacious harbor, and he also foresaw that Americans might try to establish themselves on the Pacific "above our possessions of Texas, New Mexico, and the Californias," and thus "obtain the richest trade of Great China and India."[20]

When Esteban Martínez arrived at Nootka Sound in early May of 1789, he found American and British vessels already riding at anchor. More continued to arrive. One British trader, Captain James Colnett, professed to carry orders from George III to take possession of the region on the strength of Captain Cook's discoveries. Captain Martínez objected strenuously, noting that Juan Pérez had discovered Nootka in 1774, four years before Cook; Martínez knew that for a fact since he had served under Pérez on that voyage. Martínez and Colnett began to discuss their differences amicably, but in Martínez's cabin the morning after a late night of drinking "freely," as Colnett put it, the two headstrong men lost their tempers. Even without the aid of an interpreter, Martínez understood the meaning of what sounded to him like "Gardem España [God Damn Spain]." Although he had received instructions to avoid words and actions that "might bring about a clash," Martínez arrested Colnett, seized two British ships and their crews, and sent them to Mexico.[21]

The incident at Nootka grew into an international crisis. Hoping to gain commercial concessions from Spain, English officials whipped up latent anti-Spanish sentiment and threatened war. Spain in turn appealed to its French ally for help, but the French Revolution had begun and the French National Assembly had little enthusiasm for past alliances made by monarchs. Spain, then, declined to play its weak hand with Britain. At the Escorial in October 1790, Spain capitulated to British demands. In this so-called Nootka Convention, Spain agreed to share the Pacific Northwest with Britain, return British property seized at Nootka, and make reparations. Appeasement averted an almost certain and potentially disastrous war for Spain, but its relinquishment of exclusive sovereignty of a portion of America's Pacific coast also marked the beginning of its slow withdrawal from North America.

The significance of this setback is clearer in retrospect than it was to contemporaries, for Spain did not immediately abandon its interest in the Pacific Northwest. From distant New Orleans in the early 1790s, the barón de Carondelet, the governor-general of Spanish Louisiana, envisioned an overland route up the Missouri River to "near Nootka Sound," where Spain would establish a settlement "to prevent the English or the Russians from establishing themselves or extending themselves on those coasts."[22] He offered a large cash prize to the first Spanish subject to reach the Pacific from the Missouri. Carondelet's project represented part of a larger plan to block the advance of Canadian-based British fur traders all along the Upper Missouri—to prevent them from extending their smuggling operations into New Mexico, Louisiana, or invading Spanish Upper Louisiana in time of war. Anticipating Thomas Jefferson's outfitting of the Lewis and Clark expedition, a group of merchants in Spanish St. Louis (the nerve center of Upper Louisiana or the Illinois country) formed the Missouri Company and sent three exploring parties toward the Pacific between 1794 and 1796. The most successful of them apparently reached the Mandan villages in present North Dakota, but failed to connect St. Louis to the Pacific Northwest.

Meanwhile, Spaniards had continued to explore the Pacific Northwest by sea. In 1791 and 1792, teams of Spanish scholars and artists examined the region's native peoples, topography, flora, and fauna, as part of the brilliant five-year, round-the-world scientific expedition that Alejandro Malaspina had begun from Cádiz in July 1789. Among their achievements, these last explorers Spain would send to the Pacific Northwest made a careful reconnaissance of the Strait of Juan de Fuca "to decide once and for all," as Malaspina put it, if a strait connected the Pacific and Atlantic. The idea of the mythic Strait of Anian had surfaced again.[23]

Spain maintained political as well as scientific interests in the coast north of California. Although the Nootka Convention granted England rights to the Pacific Northwest, it had not given England exclusive rights or precluded Spaniards from also settling in the region. Nor had the Nootka Convention set a clear northern boundary for Spanish California. England claimed that the Convention permitted its subjects to range freely down the coast to San Francisco Bay, the northernmost Spanish settlement. Spain, however, hoped to place California's boundary farther north, at the Strait of Juan de Fuca. Toward that end, in 1792 Spain established a short-lived settlement, Núñez Gaona, at Neah Bay, commanding the entrance to the Strait of Juan de Fuca on what is today the Washington State side. The first white settlement in the continental United States west of the Rockies and north of San Francisco (the Spanish settlement of Santa Cruz de Nootka was the first white settlement west of the Rockies in what is today Canada), Núñez Gaona consisted of "a Cross upon the beach, and . . . about 10 Houses and several good *Gardens*," in the words of one English visitor. Spaniards also built a small barracks with four cannons atop it and some corrals before they abandoned the place in the autumn of 1792, when Spain's negotiations with Britain over Nootka fell apart.[24]

In the summer of 1792, English and Spanish negotiators had traveled to the busy base of Santa Cruz de Nootka to work out the details of the Nootka Convention. They had failed. Although his position was weak, Spain's negotiator, Juan Francisco de Bodega y Quadra, a hospitable and cunning diplomat as well as a courageous mariner, charmed his worthy opponent, George Vancouver, into a stalemate. Negotiations shifted back to European drawing rooms, where Spain finally surrendered its *exclusive* claim to the region, and both sides agreed to leave unresolved the question of California's northern boundary. On March 23, 1795, ceremonies at Nootka brought the quarrel to a formal end, with both sides abandoning the site—to the relief of the Mexican-born soldiers who had suffered from a cold, damp climate, a poor diet, and isolation.[25]

Spain had lacked the resources and the muscle to appropriate more than scientific knowledge in this remote corner of the Pacific. Possession, as Spain had discovered elsewhere, no longer resided in papal bulls, claims to prior discovery, or to scrupulous attention to acts of possession that included the erection of wooden crosses and the burying of bottles sealed with tar.[26] Sovereignty had come to depend on occupancy, and occupancy depended on economic development. Capable officers close to the scene had proposed ways to use private companies to compete for a share of the profits that foreigners reaped from the sea otter trade, but Spanish officials failed to heed this advice. Bureaucratic obstacles to entrepreneurial activity, an essentially reactive policy, and ongoing crises in the mother country left a vacuum in the Pacific Northwest that Spain would never fill.

Although a declining Spain never planted another settlement in the Pacific Northwest, it continued to claim the right to do so. Finally, under pressure to cede Florida to the United States for some advantage, or lose it entirely, Spain renegotiated its North American boundaries. In 1819, Spain and the United States agreed on a new transcontinental boundary that saved Texas for Spain and created a large buffer zone between New Mexico and American territory, but that cost Spain its claim to the Pacific Northwest. In the 1819 agreement, Spain surrendered its claims to territory north of the 42nd parallel, today's California-Oregon border, to the United States.

▲▲▲

Spain lost the international struggle for the Pacific Northwest, leaving little trace of its presence. Beyond the tiny military and naval bases at Nootka and Neah Bay, it never extended its towns, ranches, fortifications, or missions north of San Francisco Bay.[27] In the six-year existence of Santa Cruz de Nootka itself, Spanish Franciscans made no serious effort to replace native religion with Christianity—a rare case where missionization was not part of the process of Spanish expansion.[28] Nor did Spain make a serious effort at colonization. It would not strain the analogy to argue that Santa Cruz de Nootka was a Potemkin village—a theater set, with an all-male cast numbering between 200 and 250, raised by a vastly overextended empire to fool European powers into believing that Spain had achieved sovereignty through occupancy.[29] As in the South Pacific, Spain could only afford the appearance of occupancy.

When Spain withdrew from its most northerly outpost in the empire in 1795, much of the physical evidence of its presence vanished along with its non-Indian inhabitants. Following orders, soldiers tore down the wooden chapel, houses, and other structures prior to their departure. Nootka Indians rebuilt Yuquot, one of their summer villages, on the site.[30]

In written records, too, the activities of Spaniards along the Northwest Coast became hazy, hidden by a fog of Spanish secrecy. As historian Hubert Howe Bancroft noted over a hundred years ago, Spain's failure to publish the results of the great exploring expeditions of 1774-75—by Pérez, Hezeta, and Bodega y Quadra—meant that "the Spanish discoverers lost much of the honor due them."[31] The loss of honor extended even to Spain itself, where an authoritative encyclopedia published in Madrid in the 1960s credited James Cook rather than Juan Pérez with the discovery of Nootka Sound.[32]

Even the voluminous work of Alejandro Malaspina's scientific expedition disappeared into Spanish archives and remained largely unpublished until the twentieth century.[33] That misfortune resulted from chance rather than from Spain's penchant for secrecy. Celebrated on his return to Spain, Malaspina was arrested and exiled within a year, accused of intrigue and in such disgrace that some writers feared to mention his name. One of Malaspina's friends and the promoter of his expedition, Antonio Valdés for whom Valdez, Alaska, is named, observed that Malaspina was "a good mariner, but a very bad politician."[34]

Unable to gain easy access to Spanish sources, early historians of the Pacific Northwest, with few exceptions, relied on Hispanophobic English accounts of Spanish activities in the region and satisfied themselves with stereotypical or superficial analysis.[35] As the author of one survey of the history of the state of Washington concluded, Spain slighted the Northwest coast because "Spaniards had accustomed themselves to thinking only of gold and silver as important natural resources."[36] (That generalization would have applied to the sixteenth century, but not to the eighteenth). With similar acumen, the same author analyzed Spain's failure to stay at Neah Bay: "Neither the fur trade nor the northern climate appealed to the Spaniards," she wrote, "so that maintaining a post there was too much of an ordeal for them."[37] (Spain did not engage seriously in the Pacific fur trade, and soldiers from Mexico disliked the cold, damp climate at Nootka, among other things, but if the Spanish Crown had sufficient power to enforce its claim to the region by maintaining a colony there, Spanish soldiers would have endured the "ordeal.")

Most early historians acknowledged Spanish primacy in the area and chronicled Spain's role in the Nootka Sound controversy, but concentrated on the Anglo-American dramatis personae.[38] For Anglocentric writers, Spaniards generally did not figure among the "Pioneers of the Pacific Coast"—a title they reserved for the likes of Francis Drake, James Cook, George Vancouver, Simon Fraser, and John McLouglin.[39]

On the Northwest coast, visiting Spaniards did not even make good villains. Spaniards at Nootka and Núñez Gaona did not try to conquer Indians, bring them into mission compounds, or subject them to systems of forced labor. Moreover, Spaniards in the region during the Enlightened eighteenth century operated under restrictions imposed by their government, in contrast to American and British fur traders, who, historian Christon Archer has pointed out, "operated well beyond the ordinary constraints and laws that governed in their own societies."[40] English trader John Meares, for example, plundered Nootka villages of winter stores in 1788 and robbed Indian fishermen of their catch at gunpoint.[41] One Spanish observer deplored the treatment of Indians by both British and American fur traders:

> Impiously, they rob these unfortunates and they force them with superiority of arms to give their furs . . . or to defend their possessions at the cost of their lives and the ruin of their temples and houses.[42]

In contrast, Spanish officers carried orders to treat Indians respectfully and went to such lengths to fulfill those orders that Christon Archer has calculated that "Indians [in the Pacific Northwest] suffered less from the presence of Spain than they did from any of the other nations there to make profits from the fur trade."[43]

Archer made that judgment in an important article published in 1973, a year that marked a sea change in Anglo-American historical sensibility toward Spaniards in the Pacific Northwest, because that same year also saw the publication of Warren L. Cook's magisterial book, *Flood Tide of Empire: Spain and the Pacific Northwest, 1543-1819*. The years since have brought a surfeit of studies of Spain's scientific legacy in the region, cresting in the years leading up to and during the bicentennial of Malaspina's round-the-world voyage (1989-94). Some of those new studies narrate the story of Spanish scientific exploration,[44] others contain transcriptions or translations of primary sources,[45] and still others provide guidance to sources[46] or describe exhibitions that have made many of the expedition's artifacts and artistic representations available for the first time.[47]

As a result of this astonishing array of new work brought to light from Spanish archives, Spaniards in the Pacific Northwest seem likely to be remembered as collectors of knowledge rather than as conquerors of Indians. Spanish scientists, rather than priests or soldiers, have become the most celebrated symbol of Spain's presence in the Pacific Northwest. These scientists, Spanish historian Mercedes Palau has noted somewhat extravagantly,

> risked their lives individually and collectively, setting an example of vigor and courage in the service of their country. . . with no attempt made to seek economic benefits.[48]

As we now know, Iberian scientists under Carlos III produced incomparable written and graphic representations of natives and native life, just before Europeans and their diseases began to take their toll on Indian lives, and of flora and fauna before the large-scale importation of European biota transformed the natural world in this corner of the continent. Indeed, Spaniards documented the region in much greater detail than they did any other part of North America, including such bastions of Spanish settlement as California, New Mexico, and Florida. The explanation for this paradox lies in the fact that the Pacific Northwest remained primitive and exotic to Europeans in the late eighteenth century, luring government-funded scientists and artists who could reach it by sea.

Given the current scholarly literature on this time and place, one can no longer sustain the argument that the activities of Englishmen and Anglo-Americans overshadow those of Spaniards. The Spanish moment in the Pacific Northwest, however, remains little known outside a small circle of specialists. One need only consult recent general histories of the region to see that Spanish explorers continue to receive cursory treatment compared to their English and Anglo-American counterparts. Few historians tell their readers that Spaniards established the first non-Indian settlement on the coast of present Washington, that Spanish subjects discovered the Columbia seventeen years before Robert Gray investigated it, that the United States benefited from Spain's achievements after Spain withdrew from the region, or that Spanish scientists left a significant record of the human and natural geography of the region.[49] Even stories of extraordinary human interest, such as the Spaniards' relationship with the principal Nootka chief Maquinna, or the lurid, such as Spanish inquiries into native prostitution and cannibalism, remain more obscure than they would if they had involved Anglo-American observers.[50]

Such oversights and emphases are consistent with our larger reconstruction of the American past. The United States has always been a multi-ethnic society, but in American popular culture and in most general histories America's past has been understood as the story of English America rather than as the stories of the diverse cultures that comprise our national heritage. The Spanish colonial origins of the United States, then, remain to be woven into the fabric of American history—into classrooms, textbooks, and our national consciousness. This is true not only for the Northwest, but even for the Southwest, where Spaniards left their most enduring mark on what is now the United States.

It also appears, however, that a reshaping of our nation's story is well underway, even without the visit of the king and queen of Spain to serve as a catalyst. Growing interest in environmental and Indian history has renewed interest in Spanish sources because those sources provide a graphic baseline for measuring historic change in places like the Pacific Northwest. Then, too, the shift of national political and economic power toward the South and West, and the growth of America's Latino population, has made the Anglocentric, New England version of American history increasingly obsolete. Even in the Pacific Northwest, where the modest Latino population (itself the subject of scholarly inquiry and increased public awareness) has gone from 2 percent in 1970 to slightly over 4 percent in 1990, anything less than a more inclusive story may no longer ring true.[51] Whether or not Spain's story in North America follows "a rising arc of portentousness," and regardless of whether Spain won or lost, a fuller and fairer understanding of our nation's fascinating multiethnic and multinational past requires that we know how, when, and where Spain played the game. And the "when" and "where," we should remember, extended well beyond North America. The Spanish moment in the Pacific Northwest represented a small fraction of over 300 years of Spanish activity throughout much of the western hemisphere.

Notes

1. This essay, prepared for the 1994 Pettyjohn Lecture at Washington State University, derives in part from my book, *The Spanish Frontier in North America* (1992), and is published here with permission from Yale University Press. Sources not noted in this essay can be found in that book. I use the term North America in this essay to mean the areas of the present-day United States and Canada. I use *Spaniard* as a political and cultural term, not a racial category, with full awareness that many of the Spaniards who explored or occupied the Pacific Northwest were Mexican-born mestizos. For careful reading of this manuscript, and useful suggestions, I am grateful to Christon Archer of the University of Calgary, Janet Fireman of the Los Angeles County Natural History Museum, Heather and Gordon Forward of Dallas, and Carlos Schwantes of the University of Idaho.

2. Told by B. Guild Gillespie in her preface to *On Stormy Seas: The Triumphs and Torments of Captain George Vancouver* (Victoria, BC: Horsdal and Schubart, 1992). I am grateful to our friends Gordon and Heather Forward, Vancouver expatriates, for calling this episode to my attention.

3. Booknote by Bernard L. Fontana in the *Southwest Mission Research Center Newsletter* (June 1993):31.

4. Nicholas Lemann, "A Failed Dominion," *Atlantic Monthly* 270 (November 1992):149-50.

5. Michael C. Scardaville, "Approaches to the Study of the Southeastern Borderlands," in *Alabama and the Borderlands from Prehistory to Statehood*, R. Reid Badger and Lawrence A. Clayton, eds., (Tuscaloosa: University of Alabama Press, 1985), 185-88.

6. Cabrillo has long been incorrectly identified as a Portuguese mariner sailing for Spain—a notion so well established that it probably will continue to survive in the literature.

7. [Andrés de Urdaneta's summary of the expedition's log], "Relation of the Voyage of Juan Rodriguez Cabrillo," in Herbert E. Bolton, ed., *Spanish Exploration in the Southwest, 1542-1706* (New York: Charles Scribner's Sons, 1908), 37.

8. For an analysis of the Fuca story, see Warren L. Cook, *Flood Tide of Empire: Spain and the Pacific Northwest, 1543-1819* (New Haven: Yale University Press, 1973), 22-29.

9. Peter Martyr, *De Orbe Novo: The Eight Decades of Peter Martyr D'Anghera*, F.A. MacNutt, ed. and trans., 2 vols. (New York: G. P. Putnam's, 1912), 2:419.

10. One of Sebastián Vizcaíno's vessels, the *Tres Reyes*, apparently passed Cape Blanco, in present southern Oregon—beyond the area that Cabrillo-Ferrer attained, but no good charts resulted and, indeed, it may have been blown in that direction accidentally. See W. Michael Mathes, *Sebastián Vizcaíno and Spanish Exploration of the Pacific Ocean, 1580-1630* (San Francisco: California Historical Society, 1968), 98, 104, 107.

11. Cook, *Flood Tide of Empire*, 31-40. For more speculative but interesting scenarios, see J. Neilson Barry, "Spaniards in Early Oregon," *Washington Historical Quarterly* 23 (January 1932):25-34.

12. Oscar Osburn Winther, *The Great Northwest: A History* (1st ed., 1947; rev. ed., New York: Alfred A. Knopf, 1950), 22.

13. *Ibid.*, 22. Emphasis mine. Historian Joseph Schafer sounded a similar note of Spanish somnolence: British and Russians "roused the Spaniards of Mexico to undertake new schemes of conquest, settlement, and exploration." Joseph Schafer, *A History of the Pacific Northwest* (1st ed., 1905; rev. ed., New York: Macmillan, 1918), 11.

14. The two quotes in this and the previous paragraph, "Ir a la Russia" and "Cerro Nevado," are in Salvador Bernabeu Albert, "Juan Pérez, Navegante y Descubridor de las Californias (1768-1775)," in José Luis Peset, ed., *Culturas de la costa noroeste de América* (Madrid: Turner, 1989), 286-87.

15. Herbert K. Beals, ed. and trans., *Juan Pérez on the Northwest Coast: Six Documents of His Expedition in 1774* (Portland: Oregon Historical Society Press, 1989), 41.

16. One of the ship's boats was actually the first vessel to enter the bay.

17. The marqués de Grimaldi to Viceroy Bucareli, 1773, quoted in Christon I. Archer, "Spain and the Defense of the Pacific Ocean Empire, 1750-1810," *Canadian Journal of Latin American and Caribbean Studies* 11, no. 21 (1986):25. Archer, "Spain and the Defense of the Pacific," 20-23, 34-35.

18. See, for example, the royal cédula of November 25, 1692, invoked by Viceroy Caballero de Croix on July 31, 1788, cited in Christon I. Archer, "Review Article [Frederic W. Howay, *Voyages of the 'Columbia' to the Northwest Coast, 1787-1790 and 1790-1793*]," *BC Studies* 93 (Spring 1992):74, and Archer, "Russians, Indians, and Passages: Spanish Voyages to Alaska in the Eighteenth Century," *Exploration in Alaska*, Antoinette Shalkop, ed., (Anchorage: Cook Inlet Society, 1980), 134.

19. Dagny B. Hansen, "Captain James Cook's First Stop on the Northwest Coast—By Chance or by Chart?," *Pacific Historical Review* 62 (November 1993):475-84.

20. Flores to Secretary Antonio Valdés, Mexico, December 23, 1788, quoted in Cook, *Flood Tide of Empire*, 130. The Nootka Crisis has been the object of considerable study. Christon I. Archer, "The Transient Presence: A Re-Appraisal of Spanish Attitudes toward the Northwest Coast in the Eighteenth Century," *BC Studies* 18 (Summer 1973):3-32, noted the anti-Spanish bias in much of the literature, and offered a fine corrective. Also in 1973, Cook's more balanced work appeared; it remains the indispensable starting point. Derek Pethick, *The Nootka Sound Connection: Europe and the Northwest Coast, 1790-1795* (Vancouver, BC: Douglas and McIntyre, 1980), adds nothing new to the story.

21. For the heavy drinking, see Cook, *Flood Tide of Empire*, 169, 175; for "Gardem España," see p. 172; for Martínez's instructions, see p. 132. For Martínez's sometimes "irrational" behavior, see Christon I. Archer, "The Political and Military Context of the Spanish Advance into the Pacific Northwest," in Robin Inglis, ed., *Spain and the North Pacific Coast: Essays in Recognition of the Bicentennial of the Malaspina Expedition, 1791-1792* (Vancouver, BC: Vancouver Maritime Museum, 1992), 14, who argues, however, that Martínez exercised "logical defensive thinking" on this occasion.

22. Carondelet to the duque de Alcudia, New Orleans, January 8, 1796, in A.P. Nasatir, ed., *Before Lewis and Clark: Documents Illustrating the History of the Missouri, 1785-1804*, 2 vols. (St. Louis: St. Louis Historical Documents Foundation, 1952), 2:388.

23. The quote is from Malaspina's instructions to the commanders of two vessels sent to the Pacific Northwest in 1792, in John Kendrick, ed. and trans., *The Voyage of the SUTIL and MEXICANA, 1792: The Last Spanish Exploration of the Northwest Coast of America* (Spokane, WA: Arthur H. Clark, 1991), 41.

24. Cook, *Flood Tide of Empire*, 350-51, 382-86. The quote is from "John Boit's Log of the Second Voyage of the 'Columbia,'" in *Voyages of the "Columbia" to the Northwest Coast, 1787-1790 and 1790-1793*, Frederick W. Howay, ed., (Massachusetts Historical Society, 1941), 416. The port was named in 1790 for Admiral Manuel Núñez Gaona of the Spanish navy.

25. Christon I. Archer, "Retreat from the North: Spain's Withdrawal from Nootka Sound, 1793-1795," *BC Studies* 37 (Spring 1978):20, 28-30, 32.

26. See, for example, the instructions to Juan Pérez of 1773, summarized in Archer, "The Political and Military Context of the Spanish Advance," 12-13.

27. The one "Spanish" mission to the north of San Francisco Bay, at Sonoma, was founded in 1823 when independent Mexico governed California.

28. By 1791 Franciscans had converted only seventeen Indians at Nootka, but these were outcasts whom Spaniards had purchased. Archer, "Spain and the Defense of the Pacific," 36; Archer, "Retreat from the North," 20-22.

29. Archer, "The Transient Presence," 11, and Luis Navarro García, "Política indígena de España en el noroeste," in Peset, ed., *Culturas de la costa noeste*, 209-22, make this argument. Navarro García also offers several explanations for the Franciscans' failure to attempt conversions.

30. Archer, "Spain and the Defense of the Pacific," 32-33, 34, corrects the assertion by Cook (*Flood Tide of Empire*, 423) and others that natives in search of iron nails tore down the village.

31. Hubert Howe Bancroft, *History of the Northwest Coast*, 2 vols. (San Francisco: History Company, 1886) 1:166. For a sense of how far Bancroft had come, see Robert Greenhow's scholarly *History of Oregon and California* (Boston: Charles C. Little and James Brown, 1844), a serious work of scholarship, but one hindered by scanty sources.

32. Archer, "The Transient Presence," 8, n. 19, and Christon I. Archer, "The Spanish Reaction to Cook's Third Voyage," in *Captain James Cook and His Times*, Robin Fisher and Hugh Johnston, eds., (Vancouver, BC: Douglas and McIntyre, 1979), 99.

33. The great exception was the *Relación del viaje hecho por las goletas Sutil y Mexicana en el año 1792*, 2 vols. (Madrid: 1802). The papers of the Malaspina expedition have recently appeared in a splendid edition. See below, n. 45.

34. Quoted in Emilio Soler Pascual, *Antagonismo político en la España de Godoy: la conspiración Malaspina (1795-1796)* (Alicante: Instituto de Cultura "Juan Gil-Albert"/ Diputación de Alicante, 1990), 72. For explanations for Malaspina's disgrace, none fully accepted, see also Donald C. Cutter, *Malaspina and Galiano: Spanish Voyages to the Northwest Coast* (Seattle: University of Washington Press, 1991), 113, 137-38, and Eric Beerman, *El diario del proceso y encarcelamiento de Alejandro Malaspina (1794-1803)* (Madrid: Editorial Naval, 1992).

35. Archer, "The Transient Presence," 3, notes some exceptions.

36. Mary W. Avery, *Washington: A History of the Evergreen State* (Seattle: University of Washington Press, 1965), 72.

37. *Ibid.*, 79.

38. See, for example, Joseph Schafer, *A History of the Pacific Northwest* (1st ed., 1905; rev. ed., New York: Macmillan, 1918), 20, and George W. Fuller, *A History of the Pacific Northwest with Special Emphasis on the Inland Empire* (1st ed., 1931; 2nd ed., rev., New York: Knopf, 1938), 45-48; Sidney Warren, *Farthest Frontier: The Pacific Northwest* (New York: Macmillan, 1949), 2; Winther, *The Great Northwest*, 21-25; Dorothy O. Johansen and Charles M. Gates, *Empire of the Columbia* (New York: Harper and Row, 1967) 1-62; Lloyd Spencer, *A History of the State of Washington*, 4 vols. (New York: American Historical Society, 1937); Ephraim W. Tucker, *History of Oregon* (1st ed., 1844; Fairfield, WA: Ye Galleon Press, 1970), 13-15; Charles H. Carey, *General History of Oregon through Early Statehood* (1st ed., 1922; 3rd ed., Portland, OR, Binfords and Mort, 1971), 17-33, 62-68, 89-90.

39. Agnes C. Laut, *Pioneers of the Pacific Coast: A Chronicle of Sea Rovers and Fur Hunters* (Toronto: Glasgow, Brook, 1915).

40. Archer, "Review Article," 81.

41. *Ibid.*, 74-75.

42. "Apuntes . . . de los salvajes habitantes del Estrecho de Fuca," Secundino Salamanca, 1792, ms., quoted in Christon I. Archer, "The Voyage of Captain George Vancouver: A Review Article," *BC Studies* 73 (Spring 1987):60.

43. Archer, "The Transient Presence," 23. See, too, Christon I. Archer's later superb articles: "The Making of Spanish Indian Policy on the Northwest Coast," *New Mexico Historical Review* 52 (January 1977):45-70; "Seduction before Sovereignty: Spanish Efforts to Manipulate the Natives of the Northwest Coast," in Robin Fisher and Hugh Johnston, eds., *From Maps to Metaphors: The Pacific World of George Vancouver* (Vancouver:

University of British Columbia Press, 1993), 127-59; and Archer, "Spain and the Defense of the Pacific," 31-36.

44. The splendid narrative of Cook, *Flood Tide of Empire*, puts the work of these scientists in the largest context and offers guidance to sources as of 1973—including the important pioneering work of Henry Raup Wagner. Cutter, *Malaspina and Galiano*, is the best single volume treatment. Mercedes Palau, "The Spanish Presence on the Northwest Coast: Sea-going Expeditions, 1774-1793," in Francisco Morales Padrón, et al., *To the Totem Shore: The Spanish Presence on the Northwest Coast* [World Exposition, Vancouver, 1986, Pavilion of Spain] ([Madrid]: Ediciones El Viso, 1986), 38-89, is the best short introduction in English (and the bibliography in *To the Totem Shore* is comprehensive and up to date). Derick Pethick, *First Approaches to the Northwest Coast* (Seattle: University of Washington Press, 1979), traces European voyages to 1792 in short compass and contains a good bibliography. For a more recent popular account, see John Kendrick, *The Men with Wooden Feet: The Spanish Exploration of the Pacific Northwest* (Toronto: NC Press, 1986). Among recent detailed accounts of the scientific expeditions in the larger context, see especially Juan Carlos Arias Divito, *Las Expediciones Científicas Españolas durante el siglo XVIII* (Madrid: Ediciones Cultura Hispanica, 1968); Iris H.W. Engstrand, *Spanish Scientists in the New World: The Eighteenth Century Expeditions* (Seattle: University of Washington Press, 1981); Fermín del Pino Diaz, ed., *Ciencia y contexto histórico nacional en las expediciones ilustradas a América* (Madrid: Consejo Superior de Investigaciones Científicas, 1988); and Salvador Bernabeu Albert, "Viajes marítimos y exploraciones científicas al Pacífico Septentrional, 1767-1788" (6 vols.; Ph.D. diss., Universidad Complutense de Madrid, 1989). More focused on the Pacific Northwest are the essays in Peset, ed., *Culturas de la costa noroeste* and Inglis, ed., *Spain and the North Pacific Coast*.

45. The first-hand accounts in English published in recent years include José Mariano Moziño, *Noticias de Nutka: An Account of Nootka Sound in 1792*, Iris Wilson [Engstrand], ed. and trans., (Seattle: University of Washington Press, 1970). Recent titles in Spanish include Alejandro Malaspina, *Viaje científico y político a la América Meridional . . . Diario de viaje de Alejandro Malaspina*, Mercedes Palau, ed., (Madrid: Ediciones El Museo Universal, 1984), and most impressively Alejandro Malaspina et al., *La expedición Malaspina, 1789-1794*, 7 vols. (Madrid: Ministerio de Defensa, Museo Naval, and Lunwerg Editores, 1987-94).

Primary sources regarding Spanish expeditions prior to the surge of scientific interest have also appeared recently: Herbert K. Beals, ed. and trans., *For Honor and Country: The Diary of Bruno de Hezeta* (Portland: West Imprints, Oregon Historical Society Press, 1985), Beals, ed. and trans., *Juan Pérez on the Northwest Coast*, Kendrick, ed. and trans., *The Voyage of the SUTIL and MEXICANA, 1792*, and Salvador Bernabeu Albert, ed., *Juan Francisco de la Bodega y Quadra: El descubrimiento del fin del mundo (1775-1792)* (Madrid: El Libro de Bolsillo Alianza Editorial, 1990).

These Spanish scientists visited the California coast, too, and the first-hand accounts published in English include Donald C. Cutter, *Malaspina in California* (San Francisco: John Howell Books, 1960), and Cutter, *California in 1792: A Spanish Naval Visit* (Norman: University of Oklahoma Press, 1990).

46. Mercedes Palau, *Catálogo de los dibujos, aguadas y acuarelas de la expedición Malaspina, 1789-1794* (Madrid: Museo de América, 1980); Carmen Sotos Serrano, *Los pintores de la expedición de Alejandro Malaspina*, 2 vols. (Madrid: Real Academia de la Historia, 1982); Dolores Higueras, *Catálogo crítico de los documentos de la expedición Malaspina*, 3 vols. (Madrid: Museo Naval, 1985); Blanca Sáiz, *Bibliografía sobre Alejandro Malaspina . . .* (Madrid: Ediciones el Museo Universal, 1992).

47. Exhibition catalogues include *La expedición Malaspina, 1789-1794: Viaje a America y Oceania de las corbetas "Descubierta" y "Atrevida"* (Madrid: Ministerio de Cultura and

Ministerio de Defensa, 1984) and [Mercedes Palau, ed.], *El ojo del tótem. Arte y cultura de los indios del noroeste de América* (Madrid: Biblioteca V Centenario, 1988); John Kendrick and Robin Inglis, *Malaspina and Galiano on the Northwest Coast, 1791-1792* (Vancouver, BC: Vancouver Maritime Museum, 1991). Several books cited above, such as Cutter's *Malaspina and Galiano*, were published in conjunction with exhibits.

48. Mercedes Palau, "The Spanish Presence on the Northwest Coast: Sea-going Expeditions, 1774-1793," in Morales Padrón, et al., *To the Totem Shore*, 39.

49. An exception is Gordon B. Dodds, *The American Northwest: A History of Oregon and Washington* (Arlington Heights, IL: Forum Press, 1986), 19-21, 24, and his less balanced *Oregon: A Bicentennial History* (New York: W.W. Norton, 1977), 12-25. More typical are: Norman H. Clark, *Washington: A Bicentennial History* (New York: W.W. Norton, 1976), who confines his brief discussion of the age of maritime discovery to George Vancouver; Robert E. Ficken and Charles P. LeWarne, *Washington: A Centennial History* (Seattle: University of Washington Press, 1988), 8-9; Carlos A. Schwantes, *The Pacific Northwest: An Interpretive History* (Lincoln: University of Nebraska Press, 1989), 38-46; Edward Nuffield, *The Pacific Northwest: Its Discovery and Early Exploration by Sea, Land, and River* (Surrey, BC: Hancock House, 1990), 62-67, 98.

50. Cutter, *Malaspina and Galiano*, 61-63, 100-03.

51. For the population in 1970 (105,311 out of 5.5 million in Washington and Oregon), see Richard W. Slatta, "Chicanos in the Pacific Northwest: A Demographic and Socioeconomic Portrait," *Pacific Northwest Quarterly* 70 (October 1979):156-57. For 1990 Hispanic population figures for Washington (4.41 percent) and Oregon (3.97 percent) see Courtenay M. Slater and George E. Hall, eds., *County and City Extra: Annual Metro, City, and County Data Book* (Lanham, MD: Bernan Press, 1992).

II
Inventing the Pacific Northwest: Novelists and the Region's History

Richard W. Etulain
(University of New Mexico)

EARLY IN 1927 A JOB PRINTER in The Dalles, Oregon, issued a brief pamphlet, *Status Rerum*, attacking several northwestern writers as producers of "a vast quantity of bilge," as creators of an "interminable avalanche of tripe." In the same year Montana editor H.G. Merriam transformed his campus literary magazine, *Frontier*, into a major outlet for regional literature. Throughout the West, in the midlands, in the Southwest, and in the Pacific Northwest, a new wave of regionalism flooded over the section, baptizing numerous writers and editors alike. Indeed, in the decade stretching from the early 1920s through the early 1930s, the West and Pacific Northwest experienced a rising tide of regionalism in the works of historians, novelists, and painters. Although this flood of new regional writings did not erode away earlier, long-popular depictions of the Pacific Northwest as frontier, the deluge did supply a new way of viewing the region, one that continued to gain strength in the next generation.[1]

Nearly two decades later another series of events helped to transform the fiction of the Pacific Northwest. Beginning during World War II and continuing into the mid-1950s, novelists, as well as historians and artists, furnished a third perspective, depicting the Pacific Northwest neither as solely a frontier nor as a region, but as a new postregion. If these postregional interpretations, strengthened by new occurrences and additional followers during and after the disruptive 1960s, did not supplant previous descriptions of a pioneer or regional Northwest, they provided another vista by which to view its history. The Pacific Northwest was no longer a region tied entirely to frontier or colonial outlooks, but one that now spawned new ethnic voices, feminist and revisionist viewpoints, and even hinted at pacesetting perspectives.

Two turning points, then, approximately a generation apart and strongly linked to two world wars, help to chart the literary history of the twentieth-century Pacific Northwest. Although these shifting waves frequently rippled into one another, they never succeeded entirely in washing away evidences of earlier points of view. Together, these shifting and competing fictional interpretations of the Northwest as frontier, region, and postregion illustrate the major transformations characterizing its regional literary history.[2]

Three books published between 1890 and 1910 illustrate the perils and possibilities novelists faced in utilizing Pacific Northwest history in their fiction. The most frequently reprinted Northwest novel of the nineteenth century, Frederic Homer Balch's *Bridge of the Gods* (1890) dramatizes one of those dilemmas: that is, how could a fictionist produce a novel from a regional history that seemed so brief and thin? Meanwhile, eastern artist and author Mary Hallock Foote's *The Desert and the Sown* (1902) represents those early novels comparing the East and West and depicting the Pacific Northwest as an untamed wilderness with a nascent society. The third author of the triumvirate, B.M. (Bertha Muzzey Sinclair Cowan) Bower, the only woman to produce dozens of stylized Westerns in the early twentieth century, illustrates writers satisfied to restrict regional history and culture to the formula Western, thereby following the format of Owen Wister's *The Virginian* and Zane Grey's yearly Westerns. These writers epitomize still other contemporary novelists who characterized the Pacific Northwest as a frontier of new lands and new peoples. None of these three was a regionalist; they were little interested in demonstrating how a settled place shaped character and outlook. Those emphases came in the next generation.

The *Bridge of the Gods* has attracted as much attention as any Pacific Northwest novel published before the 1920s, but, unfortunately, most of this commentary is romantic and sentimental nonsense. No one has ventured even a brief analytical essay entirely on the novel itself. A few biographical backgrounds help to explain the content and approach of Balch's novel.[3]

The only life-long regional resident of the first crop of Northwest novelists, Balch obtained but six months of formal education. He thirsted after knowledge and reading materials, however, and one boyhood chum remembered Balch's incessant bookishness—he was, "a reader and writer from the beginning." Just before he was eighteen, Balch wrote to noted Oregon jurist Judge Matthew P. Deady, asking for a loan of several historical volumes. Impressed by Balch's desire for an education, the judge sent the young man a multivolume world history as a gift. Thanking Deady in an effusive if naive letter of gratitude, Balch revealed he had already read hundreds of pages in the new series. He then compared these books with the writings of Edward Gibbon and T.B. Macauley, whose *History of England* he considered "the most splendid model of historical composition."[4]

Before completing the *Bridge of the Gods* a decade later, Balch also plowed through several historical works focusing on the Pacific Northwest, including the writings of Lewis and Clark, Washington Irving, Ross Cox, and H.H. Bancroft (Frances Fuller Victor). Particularly interested in Indian life and lore of the region, Balch devoured historical sources on those subjects and visited nearby native sites to study existing artifacts and to interview elderly Indians. As he wrote *Bridge of the Gods* he attempted to graft these historical materials onto a romance framework that owed much to earlier American and British authors. Even if Balch's novel is badly flawed and its literary sins stain many pages, the work is interesting historically—for what it reveals about a pioneer novelist's attempts to deal with the early history of the Pacific Northwest.

Summarized briefly, *Bridge of the Gods* depicts the improbable call of the Reverend Cecil Gray, New England minister, to serve as a missionary to the Indians of the Northwest at the end of the seventeenth century. His vision of a giant land bridge over a massive western river and the natives' need for Christianity draws him across the great wilderness separating the two ends of the continent. Eight years after his arrival, Indians of the Pacific Coast gather along the banks of the Columbia in an attempt to fashion a sprawling confederacy. Days after Cecil comes to the assembly, he meets and falls in love with Wallulah, the half-Indian and half-Asian daughter of the great Chief Multnomah. In a final series of catastrophes, an immense earthquake destroys the bridge of the gods and helps bring about the death of Cecil, Multnomah, and Wallulah. Although the projected Indian confederacy collapses and the romance between the white minister and Indian princess fails, the author asserts that the Gospel seeds Cecil plants bear fruit among subsequent generations of Indians.

Balch's novel obviously suffers from several large shortcomings. The young minister/novelist seemed unable to decide what kind of novel he wanted to write and how he could use the earlier history of the Pacific Northwest. Devotedly interested in producing a novel about the Northwest similar in form and mood to what Nathaniel Hawthorne and Sir Walter Scott had done for New England and Scotland, Balch also endeavored to base his fiction on the best published historical and field research

dealing with his region. Mixing these disparate ingredients, Balch produced a hybrid: part romance, part Local Color description, and part historical research. Unable to blend these parts into a smoothly wrought whole,
he additionally marred his novel with frequent authorial intrusions, in which
he tried to validate the historical authenticity of his materials. Unfortunately these encroachments not only destroy the mood and tone of his
romance, they also betray his hesitancy about fictionalizing the region's
history. Moreover, these intrusions sometimes reveal Balch's ambivalences
about his own life. Ought he to remain a minister, was fiction writing an
abandonment of his religious call? The closing preachments in the novel
undercut its artistic qualities even as they suggest the author's unresolved
dilemmas concerning his occupation.

In other ways *Bridge of the Gods* is a notable adumbrative work, illustrating other elements of Northwest fiction typical of the early twentieth
century. Like other western writers treating a new frontier, Balch emphasizes the key themes of newcomers confronting (and sometimes conflicting with) new lands and peoples. His missionary hero, like most protagonists
in early Northwest novels, comes into a new country inhabited by natives
about whom he feels ambivalent. Cecil—and his creator—reacts realistically, though frequently in crudely ethnocentric terms, to Indians of the
Pacific Coast; Wallulah, Multnomah, and other natives are treated sympa-
thetically, but usually in sentimental and excessively romantic terms. Here,
then, is the outsider hero arriving in a new setting, trying to make sense of
the contemporary and the historical occurrences that shaped that present-
day world. As Owen Wister did with his greenhorn narrator a dozen years
later in *The Virginian* (1902), Balch shows Cecil Gray sensitive to the new
terrains and inhabitants he encounters. Viewing the Pacific Northwest
through the eyes of a newly arrived immigrant became a favorite fictional
technique and a notable theme in many early novels about the region.[5]

Some of the ingredients of *Bridge of the Gods* appear in Mary Hallock
Foote's *The Desert and the Sown*, but Foote's uses of history and her reactions to wilderness Idaho set her work apart from the content and tone of
Balch's novel. A New Yorker of Quaker heritage, Foote first came west in
1876 to join her engineer husband in California. After brief stays there
and in Leadville, Colorado, the Footes moved to the Boise area, where
they resided for nearly ten years, before resettling in California.[6]

A talented artist, a person of Victorian sentiments, and a woman inextricably linked to her Hudson River valley origins, Foote once wrote that
she loved her West best when she was in the East. Similarly tied to the

cultural and literary outlooks of her good friend Richard Watson Gilder, editor of *Century Magazine*, Foote produced more than a dozen novels and numerous stories and sketches, many of which married a Local Color West to romance stories. Frequently utilizing mining settings or the experiences of western engineers, as she did in *The Led-Horse Claim* (1883), *John Bodewin's Testimony* (1886), and *Coeur d'Alene* (1894), Foote nearly always dealt with the present, although she allowed events of the past to shape—even bruise—her characters.[7]

In *The Desert and the Sown*, Foote furnishes the story of an eastern family tested in semicivilized Idaho of the late nineteenth century. Eventually a wife and son discover that their husband and father, long thought dead in backcountry Idaho, is very much alive. A series of contrived, fortuitous circumstances bring the man back to life—to reappear in Idaho and then again in New York state.

Embedded in this shaky plot are several interesting comparisons between the East and West as well as revealing glimpses of Foote's alien perspectives on the Pacific Northwest. Frontier Idaho not only intimidates polite company; it also plays host to unsavory men. When a dangerous stationkeeper threatens the wife's virtue, Foote comments: "You hear it said that in the West the toughest man will be chivalrous to a woman if she is the right sort of woman. I'm afraid that is a romantic theory of the Western man." Another character asks: "would you like to live" in the West? It's fascinating, the questioner answers, but he adds "I should want to be sure there was a way out." In noting the differences between Idaho and upstate New York, Foote writes:

> No region could have offered a more striking contrast to the empty plains. Moya [the novel's heroine] felt shut in with old histories. The very ground was but moulding sand in which generations of human lives had been poured, and the sand swept over to be reshaped for them.[8]

For Mary Hallock Foote, as it was for dozens of easterners in her fiction, the West was primarily a backward, distant, and provincial place to be endured while one's heart remained elsewhere. In the *Desert and the Sown* the characters suffer much in Idaho, receive little from it, and eventually return east. Yet they are not able to recover there either; the dead hand of the Idaho past seems still at their throats. Not so much about a pioneer, open, and yet crude place different from the storied "historical" East, Foote's novel instead, like so much of her fiction, clearly reflects her distaste for and fear of the frontier. But, in her later life, as well as in subsequent writing,

Foote gradually exhibited more accommodation to and satisfaction with her newly adopted West.

The novels of B.M. Bower provide another example of the uses of history in early Pacific Northwest fiction. As a producer of dozens of Westerns, she has been, similar to Zane Grey, Max Brand, Luke Short, and Louis L'Amour, the target of numerous critical forays dismissing the Western as mindless subliterature. Some of these criticisms are justified; Bower and other writers did churn out hundreds of Westerns often with superficial protagonists and predictable plots.[9] Yet her treatment of history is nonetheless worthy of attention.

Bower spent nearly all of her life in the Far West, coming as a child to Montana from Minnesota and living as an adult in Idaho, Oregon, California, and the Southwest. As a Montana schoolteacher and ranch wife, she knew intimately the cattlemen's frontier on which she drew for so many of her Westerns. The first and best-known of her novels, *Chip, of the Flying U* (1906), illustrates her emphases.[10]

The plot line is a familiar one. A young woman from the East (Ohio) comes west to her brother's Montana ranch and gradually falls in love with the cowpuncher Chip. Newly graduated from medical school, Della Whitmore ("Little Doc") is intoxicated with the West, but, like Molly Wood in *The Virginian*, worries that civilization in Montana is wafer-thin. Although Chip and Little Doc initially refuse to admit their feelings for one another, their hearts eventually win out. Unfortunately, neither the characters nor the setting is extraordinary. Bower peoples her Western with a standard-gauge hero, heroine, sidekick ("Weary"), and something of a mealy-mouthed villain. The Montana ranch setting is nondescript Western, with towns and society more than a few miles up the trail to the east.

Chip delivers a few differences, however. The hero, often said to be modeled after Montana painter Charlie Russell, does remind one of the sagebrush artist, in his painterly talents and in his night rider mannerisms. Less culturally rich than *The Virginian*, especially in that novel's comparisons of East and West, Bower's Western nonetheless authentically treats range work, humorously deals with the bunkhouse gang (the Happy Family cowpunchers who gallop through the pages of her later works), and plays with gender differences more than does Wister's novel.

Echoing many Westerns of the early twentieth century, *Chip* is not so much historical as contemporary, not so much vertical as horizontal. Indeed, the pasts of the hero and heroine are brief and vague, although Chip has "lit out" for the frontier because of a "comfortless past. He could just remember his mother—and he preferred not to remember his father, who was less kind to him than were strangers. That was his past" (132-33). Bower's setting is Montana in the present, with little or no mention of a recent closing frontier or the carving out of new settlement. History, then, plays a minor role here: action, adventure, and ranch romance dominate the big sky spaces. Following most writers of Westerns and unlike contemporary northwesterners Homer Balch, Mary Hallock Foote, and Eva Emery Dye, Bower emphasizes nonhistorical details. As we shall see, more than a few novelists of the Pacific Northwest have marched down a similar path.

That most early Pacific Northwest novelists depicted a frontier in which newcomers faced and reacted to unfamiliar terrain and new peoples is not surprising. Contemporary historians, painters, and other novelists emphasized parallel themes. Frederick Jackson Turner and Frederic Logan Paxson, for example, stressed the influential roles of the physical environment and Indians in shaping immigrants coming to the frontier. Similar patterns emerge in the art of Frederic Remington and Charles Russell whose western canvases repeatedly limn eye-catching encounters between soldiers, cowboys, and Indians—often against spacious and dramatic natural backdrops. At the same time, such writers as Hamlin Garland, Jack London, and Zane Grey likewise novelized a frontier West in which incoming farmers, miners, and ranchers confronted demanding and sometimes coercive environments. In utilizing several of these themes, Northwest novelists were clearly of their times.[11] But new developments were appearing on the horizon.

🌲🌲🌲

Taking root in the 1920s and flowering in the 1930s, a bounteous crop of regional writing transformed the western literary landscape between the wars. Prefigured by the earlier regional work of historian-philosopher Josiah Royce, nature writer and feminist Mary Austin, and novelist Willa Cather, regionalists in the twenties and thirties abandoned earlier frontier themes and centered on a newly emerging region endeavoring to establish and understand its own cultural identity. Along the way, these regionalists began to create a new past for the American West.[12]

In the Pacific Northwest, two events in 1927 signaled the arrival of the regionalists. In that year, novelists James Stevens and H.L. Davis, in an inspired long evening of collaboration, concocted a brief pamphlet entitled *Status Rerum: A Manifesto, Upon the Present Condition of Northwestern*

Literature, Containing Several Near-Libelous Utterances, Upon Persons in the Public Eye, a vicious attack on college teachers of poetry and fiction in the Northwest. Harpooning these instructors as a collection of "posers, parasites, and pismires" unable to "castrate calves," Stevens and Davis demanded that the Pacific Northwest wake up, that it denounce these literary phonies and rediscover its true past, thus far camouflaged and distorted in the formula fiction of the region's "mental weaklings, numbskulls, and other victims of mental and moral affliction" claiming to be writers.[13]

Less bombastic, less inclined to undercut his precursors and opponents, H.G. Merriam, editor of the regional magazine *Frontier*, nonetheless traveled alongside Stevens and Davis in championing a redolent Northwest regionalism. In the Fall 1927 issue of *Frontier*, which approvingly mentioned *Status Rerum*, Merriam turned cheerleader for an expanded and expansive regional literature. Merriam's lead-off editorial, "Endlessly the Covered Wagon," urged northwesterners to stop turning east for cultural nourishment or accepting "uncourageous, unindigenous 'literary' expression of writers too spiritually imitative and too uninspired." Instead, a newly expanded and redirected *Frontier* would be a "pioneer endeavor to gather indigenous Northwest material." And the literature created from these regional materials must avoid stultifying stereotypes; rather, it must be "active," "spiritually alive," plunging into "ugliness" and "beauty . . . with equal energy."[14] Practicing what he preached, Merriam launched a new historical section in the journal to reprint the "stuff" of the region. He also carried an editorial by H.L. Davis in the Spring 1928 issue with the following challenge:

> If you, in the *Frontier*, can manage to turn up any young writers with any aristocracy of mind, any conception of what their duty is to their own people, and the courage and resolution to accomplish it unflinchingly, you will deserve to be canonized.[15]

The publication of *Status Rerum* and the expansion of *Frontier* into a notable literary magazine were not isolated cultural events springing up in a distant far corner. They were but one tributary to a rising current of regionalism that flooded over the United States in the 1920s and 1930s. In the South, Fugitive writers and Agrarians declared their cultural independence from what they considered an excessively urban, industrialized, and rationalistic North threatening to destroy a rural, agricultural South. In *I'll Take My Stand* (1930), some of these writers called for a return to an earlier South in danger of being destroyed by Yankeeism.[16]

Concurrently, western historians like Walter Prescott Webb and Bernard DeVoto warned against eastern influences plundering western provinces. Less defensive but nonetheless champions of increased recognition of western regionalism, editors of western journals like *Folk-Say*, *Southwest Review*, *Prairie Schooner*, and *Midland* urged writers and readers to turn inward, to examine their varied cultural traditions, and to produce a new crop of regional writing free from the noxious weeds of alien influences. The goals of these novelists, historians, and editors across the South and West were exactly those of the authors of *Status Rerum* and H.G. Merriam. This tocsin-sounding for regionalism and the works of such writers as H.L. Davis, Vardis Fisher, and a handful of others during the interwar years signaled a new stage in Pacific Northwest fiction: regionalists would now challenge earlier frontier writers as the major interpreters of the region's past. Although, as we shall see, the regionalists did not entirely derail the frontier perspective, they competed on more than even terms, and after World War II emerged as the leading fictional interpreters of the Northwest's heritage.

No writer better illustrates the purposes and achievements of the regionalists than does H.L. Davis. Son of a long line of pioneer farmers, fundamentalist ministers, and teachers, Davis grew up during a series of one- and two-year jumps across central and eastern Oregon as the family followed Davis's school-teacher father. A voracious reader but indifferent student, Davis worked variously as a crop hand, gandy dancer, sheepherder, surveyor, newspaper editor, and deputy sheriff. Like his father and brothers, Davis was a superb raconteur, especially drawn to the Local Color and frontier writings of Alfred Henry Lewis and Mark Twain. He also became a notable poet, winning the Levinson Prize in 1919 for a clutch of his poems published in Harriet Monroe's *Poetry* magazine. Then, in the late 1920s and early 1930s, spurred on by the encouragement and sponsorship of H.L. Mencken, Davis produced a series of vernacular, iconoclastic sketches and short stories for Mencken's immensely influential *American Mercury* and other magazines. Fleeing the Northwest on the strength of a Guggenheim grant to write a western poetic epic, Davis turned instead to fiction, and after a series of false starts, personal problems, and traumatic side turns finally finished his first novel *Honey in the Horn*, which won the Harper Prize in 1935 and the Pulitzer Prize the next year and which some still consider the most distinguished regional novel of the Pacific Northwest.[17]

From the beginning, Davis's intentions were historical. In the novel's introduction, he notes he "had originally hoped to include in the book a representative of every calling that existed in the State of Oregon during the homesteading period—1906-1908." But he discarded his dream when the already overly long novel threatened to turn into several volumes. Still, *Honey in the Horn* is a full-scale picture of selected parts of Oregon soon after 1900. Except for society in larger towns and southern Oregon, the novel brings to life a wonderfully provocative cross-section of men and women and occupations. For the most part, Davis is intrigued with ordinary citizens; his regional portraits are drawn primarily from homesteaders of all sorts, crop hands, Indian tribesmen, ranchers, sheepherders, and a variety of other wandering folk. So much fresh vintage is contained in the novel, in fact, that the old wineskins of a traditional plot are stretched to the breaking point.

Attempting to retrieve the historical landscape of a generation or two earlier, Davis cast his work in the picaresque form, allowing his hero (Clay) and heroine (Luce) to wander over the varied settings of Oregon. In a brief period, their odyssey allows them to confront a whole gamut of characters and experiences intended to illustrate Oregon's past as well as life there at the turn of the century. Indeed, the novel's form seems less amorphous if one notes Davis's conviction that Pacific Northwest history was so varied and recent that the regionalist must sample many of these variations if he were to achieve his purpose.

The tone of *Honey in the Horn*, however, raised the most controversy in the Northwest. Pungent and overflowing with hyperbole and humor, and despite Davis's claim that he had "no intention . . . of offering social criticism or suggesting social reform," the novel lampoons the Babbitry and boosterism Davis saw widely displayed among Oregon homesteaders. Roasting second- and third-generation Oregonians, he upset patriotic northwesterners and provided grist for newspaper critics throughout the region, one of whom dismissed the novel as, "a discredit to the true pioneers." For Davis, life in Oregon had been too easy; carefree, lazy newcomers lived off nature's generosity, and they were little interested in staying around to work out settled, unified communities. Too busy sticking their noses into the affairs of their neighbors, unwilling to stand up to the demands of pioneer life, and lacking the courage of tightly held convictions, Oregonians seemed satisfied to wander, to drift on to new settings and occupations. Not surprisingly, Davis won little affection and friendship among regional chauvinists. But, writing from California, Davis was not upset by what the "Portland fictionists" thought; he added caustically, "nobody cares anything about those flatheads outside of Woodlawn" cemetery.[18] He never returned for an extended stay in the Northwest, even though he utilized the region for such later novels as *Winds of Morning* (1952) and *The Distant Music* (1957). In his first novel, and in several later books and sketches, Davis provided a model of what premier regional fiction could be: a provocative combination of one's personal experience and knowledge of a region's past that avoided the straightjacketed formulas of the popular Western.

Although in many ways Vardis Fisher knew a Pacific Northwest much different from that of H.L. Davis, they also shared some reactions, ones that characterized a good deal of regional fiction in the three decades after 1920. In trying to understand the Idaho writer, one observer concluded that Fisher was born with a thistle in his diaper and spent most of his life trying to rid himself of the irritant or attempting to discover why he was not one of the elect. In his long, fruitful career, Fisher produced more than twenty novels tracing major trends in human history and examining important facets of the pioneer and early twentieth-century American Wests. Fisher dedicated himself to the fruitful union of history and literature to recapture the past and, if possible, cast additional light on traumatic questions complicating his life.[19]

Fisher's first historical fiction examined the close at hand. In such novels as *Toilers of the Hills* (1928), *Dark Bridwell* (1931), and *In Tragic Life* (1932), Fisher focused on Mormon and other pioneer families cockleburred into backcountry Idaho. Reflecting Fisher's own ambivalences about family and religious faith, these works dealt realistically with the enormously demanding life these settlers faced in trying to wrestle a living from the Antelope Hills country near Yellowstone Park. Fisher's love-hate reactions to his experiences, and his inordinate need for self-understanding, power these early realistic, regional works.

But answers derived from his own life, interior and exterior, seemed inadequate. Fisher then embarked on one of the most ambitious projects of historical fiction any American novelist has been courageous enough to attempt. For much of the next two decades, Fisher devoted his indefatigable energies to researching and writing the ten-volume Testament of Man series that traced human history from prehistoric to modern times. Here again, Fisher the historian-novelist shines through.[20]

Meanwhile, Fisher flung himself into another series of historical novels dealing with the nineteenth-century West. The best of these is *Children of God* (1939). Perhaps the premier novel about the Mormons, this work won the Harper Prize and wider critical attention for Fisher. It likewise reflects his increased ambivalence about the Latter-day Saints and his ties to their history. Much as he had in the earlier regional novels, Fisher praises the Mormons' hard work and the leadership of Brigham Young and yet questions the church's autocratic actions and what he considers strange doctrines. Interestingly, although the church at first roundly criticized the novel, many Mormon intellectuals now view it as a probing if not entirely satisfactory account of the Saints' heritage.[21] The popularity of *Children of God* and its good sales convinced Fisher that he should work a different lode of historical fiction once he finished the Testament series.

The best-known of these later western historical novels is *Mountain Man* (1965), although *Tale of Valor* (1958) also merits continued attention. Fisher's last major work, *Mountain Man* illustrates several of the techniques he used in his historical fiction. Based on wide examination of the best sources—primary and secondary—dealing with the fur trade, the novel is researched as if it were a doctoral dissertation (Fisher held a doctorate with high honors in English literature from the University of Chicago). Simultaneously, it bears the marks of an author profoundly ambivalent about the West he treats. Although Fisher celebrates the freedom, the spontaneity, and the perseverance of his trapper heroes, he also raises questions about their treatment of the environment and Indian traditions. Like H.L. Davis, Fisher was not an unquestioning celebrator of the regional Pacific Northwest. He too had many reservations about the bittersweet experiences of newcomers to the region.

Following a route much different from those of H.L. Davis and Vardis Fisher, Ernest Haycox became the best-known author of popular Westerns in the Pacific Northwest. His attitudes toward western history and his uses of the past were also at variance from those of his regionalist contemporaries. Yet even a snapshot view of his literary journey reveals notable transitions and changing literary perspectives.[22]

Haycox's boyhood, the circumstances of his teenage years, and other uncertainties of his adolescence combined to produce a cautious if ambitious writer. The son of divorced parents and a young man on his own in his early teens, Haycox early on exhibited a strong conservative bent—in his attitudes toward the past, toward his work, and toward writing fiction. Once he determined to become a novelist after flirting with journalism, Haycox embraced the Western because it offered an easily mastered format and the promise of ample remuneration. Although he began to publish his first short stories in the 1920s, during the highpoint of western regionalism, Haycox was rarely regionalistic—except in the closing years of his career.

Each stage of his career reflected Haycox's cautious temperament. First establishing a reputation as a solid producer of pulp fiction in the 1920s, he broke into *Collier's* in the 1930s when Zane Grey no longer contributed a steady stream of serials and short stories to that outlet. Within the next decade, Haycox became a nationally known writer of Westerns, hailed in his native Oregon as a "successful" writer because he sold steadily and because the eastern "editorial big boys" stopped off to see him during their annual swings through the West. By the 1940s, Haycox slipped into the lordly *Saturday Evening Post*, and in 1943, *annus mirabilis*, his serial Westerns ran simultaneously in the *Post* and *Collier's*. Finally, in the closing years of his career before his premature death in 1950, Haycox moved away from the formula Western in a series of well-made short stories and in the last novel he wrote, *The Earthbreakers* (1952).[23]

True to his cautiously innovative nature, Haycox experimented with historical fiction throughout his career, but particularly in the late 1930s and 1940s. Widely read in western American history since his days at the University of Oregon and the owner of a superb collection of research volumes on the Old West, Haycox began to churn out historical Westerns as early as *Trouble Shooter* (1937), a novel treating the building of the Union Pacific. The *Border Trumpet* (1939), focusing on the frontier military in the Southwest, *Trail Town* (1941), on a midwestern cattle town, and *Alder Gulch* (1942), on a Montana mining boomtown, all grafted historical backgrounds onto adventure stories. The best of the Haycox historical Westerns is *Bugles in the Afternoon* (1943), a stirring account of General George Custer and the Battle at the Little Big Horn. In these speedy narratives, Haycox uses history to authenticate his stories, as a platform on which to stage his western dramas.[24]

In *The Earthbreakers* Haycox abandoned many of his earlier patterns to produce a memorable historical novel about immigrants in their first year in the Oregon country. Utilizing three former mountain men and their adjustments—or lack of adjustments—to the nascent community being organized in the Willamette Valley, Haycox turns historian, interpreting the actions of the three men, as well as those of other pioneers in the settlement, in the light of their historical experiences. Like an apt disciple of Clio, Haycox focuses on important sociocultural shifts in early Oregon, emphasizing linkages between events and experiences and individuals' actions. These lines of influence were often missing in his earlier Westerns. Moreover, in demonstrating the shaping power of terrain, climate, and history on his characters, Haycox left the restrictive camp of formula fiction and moved in with the regionalists.[25]

If H.L. Davis, Vardis Fisher, and Ernest Haycox were the best-known Northwest novelists from the 1920s through World War II, A.B. Guthrie, Jr., quickly supplanted them in the next generation. Flashing on the scene in 1947 with the publication of *The Big Sky*, Guthrie garnered the Pulitzer Prize two years later for *The Way West* and occupied a conspicuous position among western novelists well into the 1980s. More impressively than any other western writer, Guthrie produced a full, penetrating fictional portrait of a century's history of the American West.[26]

Guthrie came late to his career as a historical novelist. A graduate of the University of Montana, where he was a student of H.G. Merriam, Guthrie turned to journalism and was a full-time newspaperman until the 1940s. Then a coveted Neiman Fellowship in 1944 at Harvard allowed him a full year of reading, research, and writing. From this rewarding year eventually came *The Big Sky*, Guthrie's mountain man novel, thoroughly grounded in major historical sources dealing with the 1830s and 1840s, particularly Englishman George Frederick Ruxton's *Life in the Far West*, on which Guthrie drew for trapper patois and semifictional characters.[27] The next two novels, *The Way West* (1949) and *These Thousand Hills* (1955), although less lively and engrossing than *The Big Sky*, nonetheless provide appealing accounts of the Oregon Trail and of Montana ranching. Then, *Arfive* (1970) and *The Last Valley* (1975) chronicle Montana towns during World War I and World War II. Finally, backtracking to fill in a previous gap, Guthrie wrote his remaining historical novel *Fair Land, Fair Land* (1982), covering the quarter century from 1845 to 1870. In all, his six novels depicted a full century of western history, from the mountain men to the dramatic impact of the Second World War.

But Guthrie's works are much more than novels merely chronicling the West's history. Indeed, few novelists of the Pacific Northwest have felt change over time as deeply as Guthrie. Each of his novels centers on a significant era of western history, its passing, and the traumatic reactions of several characters to these movements in time. In *The Big Sky*, for instance, protagonist Boone Caudill belatedly realizes that he and his raucous mountaineer companions have stripped the mountains of their beaver, killed more than they needed, and exploited what they encountered. Near the end, Boone senses that they have "spiled" the mountains, and he refuses to return. *Arfive* also focuses on a dramatic period of historical change. Residents of a small Montana town, especially those surviving earlier pioneer days, are forced to adapt to transformations flooding over the hamlet. Here Guthrie supplies a persuasive account of a notable era—the Pacific Northwest cantering from frontier to region.

The Last Valley displays Guthrie's talents as a historical novelist in still another way. Here he illustrates his absorbing interest in historical turning points, his preoccupation with change and progress, and his similarities to other novelists and historians. Resurrecting major characters from *Arfive*—Benton Collingswood and Mort Ewing—Guthrie makes them serve as bridges from past to present as well as commentators on a series of significant events throughout the interwar years. Their reactions and those of the other major figures function much as historiography does in illuminating multiple pasts: varying interpretations of a single event reflect the conflicting viewpoints of human interpreters. As it does for historians, this technique of employing several reactions to one event, idea, or person allows historical novelists like Guthrie to broaden the perspectives of their fiction and to demonstrate the complexity of the past.

Guthrie also uses *The Last Valley* to treat the shadowy boundaries between past, present, and future. By marrying past and present—sometimes jamming them together—the author discloses how much history is a continuous current rather than a series of separate, isolated eras. The dust jacket of the novel reinforces this theme. In the background, verdant mountains loom above the foreground setting, but the town and its streets, buildings, and smoking chimneys dominate the center of the painting. A single horseman rides away from the town, not in headlong flight, but he is nonetheless leaving. The book's cover, through the juxtaposed mountains, town, and horseman, dramatizes the same tensions that power the novel: conflicts between past and present, between nature and civilization. These symbols of tension and conflict, portrayed without and within *The Last Valley*, are central ideas in all of Guthrie's novels. In one speech, he summed up his ambiguous responses to history's inexorable movement: "I accept the fact that progress leaves us no retreat. We can only insist *no undue haste*. We can only try to guide it. We can't stay it. Neither should we."[28]

This sustained interest in accentuating the nineteenth- and twentieth-century Pacific Northwest in regional historical fiction follows a clear line from Eva Emery Dye to Davis, Fisher, and Guthrie, and on to Don Berry and Ivan Doig after 1960. Although many other recent writers, often influenced by the dramatic alterations that World War II and the 1960s triggered in the Pacific Northwest, moved in other directions, the historical fiction of Berry and Doig owed more to traditions of the past than to pathbreaking changes of the present.

In his three historical novels, Don Berry focuses on the Oregon coast, from the founding of Astoria into the 1850s. If *Trask* (1960) is a sensitive, moving fictional account of restless Elbridge Trask's march into the Tillamook country and *To Build a Ship* (1963) a seriocomic treatment of the same area a generation later, *Moontrap* (1962) plays up conflicts among former mountain men, farmers, missionaries, and town builders in the Oregon City area. As revealingly as any novelist in the region, and strikingly akin to Guthrie in his best work, Berry skillfully delineates the gear-grinding sociocultural changes that disrupted Oregon in the 1840s.[29]

One memorable scene in *Moontrap* illuminates Berry's imaginative uses of history. A former trapper, Webster P. Webb, arrives in Oregon City to renew his close friendship with Johnson Monday, also a refugee from the mountains. Immediately, Old Webb finds himself an outsider and estranged from Monday, who has married an Indian woman and is trying to farm. When the town-builders attempt to coerce Webb into subscribing to the nascent community's emerging social code, he dramatically demonstrates his yearning to retain his freedom and to throw off restraints by gut-shooting and scalping the preacher and fleeing to the nearby mountains. As a posse, including Monday, closes in on Webb, Berry has him act out a scene pregnant with meaning. Seeing the reflection of the moon in a mountain creek, Webb dams up the stream and tries to trap the moon's reflection. Even before he completes the dam, the moon has moved on, eluding Webb. Just as Webb has been unable to freeze history, to maintain his trapper tendencies in a new place undergoing traumatic change, so he fails to trap the moon. Here, in one of the most memorable symbolic scenes in Pacific Northwest fiction, Don Berry underscores the historian's sense of change over time and the searing impact of those transformations on a wide variety of participants.

Of the most recent Northwest historical novelists, Ivan Doig is the most notable. In two decades, he has produced several novels of extraordinary merit. Beginning with his autobiographical account of growing up in a series of three-saloon towns and sheepcamps, dumped along the eastern slope of the Rockies, *This House of Sky* (1978) and on through two other early works, *Winter Brothers* (1980) and *The Sea Runners* (1982), Doig exhibits a first-rank talent in yoking his journalistic training to his work in history. In addition to his first book, Doig is known especially for his trilogy of historical novels on twentieth-century Montana, *English Creek* (1984), *Dancing at the Rascal Fair* (1987), and *Ride with Me, Mariah Montana* (1990). In all these novels, Doig achieves the goal of a premier regional novelist: to show how physical terrain and sociocultural mixes shape peoples living in these areas, to illuminate a "sense of place."[30]

English Creek illustrates Doig's large achievements as a regional historical novelist. Part autobiography, part historical research, and an even larger part imagined characters and plot, this fact-drenched novel veraciously recreates rural Montana in the late 1930s. A coming-of-age story, Doig's smoothly written work adroitly combines provincial and national events, Montana settings, and careful descriptions of rural life to produce a notable historical novel. As historian William G. Robbins succinctly notes in this regard, "The historian's concern for accuracy; the writer's skill in shaping character and plot, and his mastery of description; and the storyteller's way with dialogue—these combine to forge good historical fiction." Less critical than a new crop of revisionistic western historians, Doig is just as willing as they to raise questions about westerners' treatment of the environment, their failures to learn from their mistakes, and the necessity of viewing Montana's history in the circumference of national and even international happenings. Doig is, fellow Montana author William Kittredge has asserted, like other recent western realists who, "are trying to rub their eyes clear of mythic and legendary cobwebs, and see straight to the actual."[31]

Even though one may trace clear lines of continuity from the work of historical novelists earlier in the twentieth century to the more recent writings of authors such as Don Berry, Ivan Doig, Dorothy Johnson, and Forrester Blake, and even though another tradition of the formula Western surfaced in the Westerns of B.M. Bower and continued through the careers of Robert O. Case, Norman A. Fox, Bill Gulick, and D.B. Newton, signs of discontinuity and change are equally clear. As we now see, World War II and the 1960s did more than any other events to jumble and reorient cultural and literary trends in the modern American West. These two eras of rapid transformation not only disrupted previous tendencies in the American literary West, they also ushered in new trends in western American literature during the next generation or two. Like historians and painters of the post-1945 period, novelists of the West began to see their region differently and to alter their fiction accordingly.

Granted, these metamorphoses were neither as dramatic nor as widespread in the Pacific Northwest as they were in California, the Southwest, and other western urban areas, but the Northwest nonetheless experienced the traumatic transitions too. Urban areas like Seattle and Portland boomed, and even interior cities such as Spokane, Boise, and Pocatello experienced exploding changes. These war-related shifts triggered parallel population changes throughout the Northwest. And New Deal programs that modulated the region during the 1930s and early 1940s continued to reshape regional life and culture in the next decade. A generation later the momentous disruptions that swept across the United States also flooded over the Pacific Northwest. During the 1960s and early 1970s, dissatisfactions with an unpopular war, a revolution in racial and ethnic consciousness, and dramatic new roles for women and families staggered northwesterners, as they did other Americans.[32] These upheavals encouraged not only revised visions of what Americans should be and should become; they also drove historians and novelists, writers of all kinds, to re-vision the past. In doing so, they revised the history of the Pacific Northwest as they experienced a tumultuous present. Frontier and regional themes remained in Northwest fiction, but new emphases on ethnicity, on innovative heroes and heroines, and on revisionistic views of the American West and Pacific Northwest signaled that a new postregionalism was emerging. This fresh spirit diversified and enriched the histories of the Pacific Northwest treated in a crop of novels published after 1950.

The winds of literary change that blew across the Pacific Northwest after Pearl Harbor brought about new voices, ideas, and forms in writing about the region. Notable among these shifts was the florescence of ethnic literature. Before World War II, no Indian, Hispanic, African American, or Asian American wrote a historical novel about the Pacific Northwest, but that would change, particularly after 1970 and especially among Native Americans.[33] Although such non-Indian authors as Don Berry, A.B. Guthrie, and Ken Kesey illustrated the increasingly sympathetic attitude toward Native American history and culture characterizing American fiction and historical writing after the 1950s, even more significant was the new crop of novels by Indians. At the same time that N. Scott Momaday and Leslie Marmon Silko were attracting attention elsewhere, D'Arcy McNickle, James Welch, Janet Campbell Hale, and Michael Dorris were publishing novels about Native Americans in the Pacific Northwest.

Of these novelists, James Welch (Blackfeet-Gros Ventre) is the most prolific. Drawing on his experiences growing up on the Blackfeet and Fort Belknap reservations in Montana, he has written four novels, *Winter in the Blood* (1974), *The Death of Jim Loney* (1979), *Fools Crow* (1986), and *The*

Indian Lawyer (1990). The best-known of Welch's novels, *Winter in the Blood* suggests an alternative way of viewing Northwest history, one that previous novelists overlooked. Through his nameless narrator, Welch depicts a full century of Native American history impinging on contemporary events. The "I" of the novel, a thirty-two-year-old Indian, is enmeshed in cycles of drunkenness, sterile sex, and severe depression. Only an Edenic boyhood and even more distant pasts seem havens from a bleak present, but even these heritages are flawed. Remembering the tragic death of his brother twenty years earlier, the loss of his father, and the passionlessness of his mother, the narrator wanders through a nightmarish present, without the nourishments of a stable, identifiable past.

But his journeying leads finally toward meaning—from the past into the present. He discovers that an aged, blind Indian living nearby, Yellow Calf, is his grandfather and in the distant past saved his grandmother from starvation, despite confronting tribal taboos in doing so. This shock of recognition seems to jolt the narrator, to rescue him from his depression. Returning home and discovering a cow caught in a slough, an animal he earlier dismissed as stupid and worthless, he risks his life to save her. That act, however small, suggests that not only has he found himself historically, he can now act, courageously and meaningfully.

Winter in the Blood steers a middle path between two recent extremes in dealing with the history of the West and Pacific Northwest. Avoiding the stereotypes of popular Westerns that so often depict Indians as opponents and barriers and rarely as humans with competing human strengths and limitations, Welch also avoids the opposite extreme of anti-Westerns like *Little Big Man* that, as we shall see, introduce counter western myths romantically treating Indians equally devoid of flesh and blood. Instead, in flat, direct prose Welch deploys strong images of Native Americans to stage a realistic drama illustrating the impingements of remote and contemporary history alike on a cluster of Montana Indians. In avoiding earlier and more recent extremes in western fiction, Welch supplies a moving account of subjects previously missing from most Pacific Northwest fiction.

Themes that power Welch's novel are also central to Janet Campbell Hale's *The Jailing of Cecelia Capture* (1985). At the same time, Hale links her treatment of Native American experiences to a clear feminist perspective and in doing so illustrates a second emphasis apparent in postregional fiction in the Pacific Northwest. More important than place in her novel are the stresses on ethnicity and gender. A member of the Coeur d'Alene tribe, Hale sets her novel in northern Idaho, western and central

Washington, and in Berkeley, California. Her protagonist, Cecelia Capture, now a thirty-year-old student at the University of California, is arrested for drunken driving and ends up in jail for a few days. During this time she recalls, through a series of flashbacks, her girlhood growing up in the Pacific Northwest. These historical vignettes supply other vistas of the region's heritage, especially difficulties facing mixed-race families. If Welch focuses on male dilemmas, Hale centers on pressures that bombard an unmarried, young Indian mother trying to find herself, make a satisfactory marriage, raise her children, and finish a law degree. Most of all, however, she drifts in a social sea without sufficient moorings to make her way in a white-dominated world.

Hale's novel follows a clear blueprint in utilizing historical snapshots to explain Cecelia's present actions. Depressingly aware of and insecure about her ethnic origins, Cecelia suffers at the hands of a termagant mother and an increasingly drunken father. Poverty, frequent moves, and faltering friendships further undermine the heroine's self-confidence. Insensitive welfare agents and a frigid husband impel Cecelia toward alcoholism and suicide. Hale suggests also that this troubled personal history leads directly to a traumatic present.

Although Hale's work is a particularly illuminating source on Native American experiences in the Pacific Northwest, it is ultimately a badly flawed novel. Not only are the historical flashbacks contrived and sometimes badly slanted, the central figure, as a tragic product of coercively destructive forces, is not believable. Cecelia rebounds from many hurts, graduates from college, and does well at law school, and yet she is pictured as otherwise victimized by a racist, uncaring society. If she has the strength and determination to succeed, then why not accept that she could be the agent of some of her own dilemmas? Hale seems unwilling to admit that Cecelia, as well as her milieu, brings about some of her difficulties.[34]

Marilynne Robinson's first novel *Housekeeping* is even more disturbingly provocative than Hale's fiction. Lyrically written, suffused with poetic prose, replete with carefully described eccentric characters, Robinson's novel, in the words of one reader, is characterized nonetheless by its "despairing nihilism."[35] Suicide, death, and meaninglessness invade each section of the work. A depressing tone and sense of interminable loss dominate *Housekeeping*.

The novel's narrator, Ruth Stone, exists, hangs on, and possibly wrings small meanings from the steady string of tragedies that define her life. Her grandfather lies in a watery grave in Fingerbone Lake, a victim of a railroad accident. Later, her mother commits suicide by driving her car into the same lake. Two spinster aunts try to set up "housekeeping" for Ruth and her younger sister Lucille, but their inflexible traditionalism destroys their good intentions. The most pronounced eccentric of the novel, Aunt Sylvie, then wanders into the girls' lives. Sleeping fully clothed, including her shoes, and keeping all her belongings in a box under her bed, Sylvie belongs in one of Charles Dickens's novels. Lucille soon discovers she wants peer acceptance more than she covets the company of her weird aunt and sister and moves out. In the closing section, Aunt Sylvie and Ruth burn down the house, march across the railroad bridge over the adjacent lake, and strike out on years of meandering.

Crossing the bridge, Sylvie and Ruth leave behind town, tradition, perhaps the traumas of trying to fit in, but they cannot slough off the past, memories that seem glued to Ruth's consciousness. Indeed, as one reviewer points out, "from Ruth's perspective, the boundaries between past and present, appearance and substance, dream and reality have permanently dissolved." Through a long line of women—no male character is more than a momentary shadow—Ruth tries to find a home to set up "house-keeping"; but instead she is forced to accept transience, flux, and near chaos. In the end, like Sylvie, Ruth never has "more than a tenuous grasp of the distinctions among dream, memory and present reality."[36] History continues to repeat itself, but seemingly in a self-destructive, near-despairing lack of security and trajectory.

Pacific Northwest novelists also participated in a third kind of postregional literature, a type often referred to as anti-Westerns or counter-classic Westerns. In the 1960s, a new crop of American writers not only questioned traditional views of the West as a free, open, and positive experience; they also wrote dozens of seriocomic novels satirizing this heroic and romantic myth. Robert Flynn, for example, undercut larger-than-life cattle drovers and the long drive in his humorous *North to Yesterday* (1967). Robert Day did much the same with modern cowboys in *The Last Cattle Drive* (1977). Even more ambitious—and satirical—was Thomas Berger's *Little Big Man* (1964). Perhaps the most damning novel of all, John Seelye's *The Kid* (1972), underscored the sexism, racism, and violence of the Old West. Together, these novels supplied a devastating critique of myths that magnified the West as Eden, Land of Promise, or Eldorado.[37] Like the more recent New Western historians, these novelists sometimes humorously, sometimes with murderous satire, depict a West leagues apart from the positive images rampant in the popular Westerns from Zane Grey to Louis L'Amour.

The most well-known of the counter-classic Northwest novels is Ken Kesey's *One Flew Over the Cuckoo's Nest* (1962). Utilizing the setting of an insane asylum for biting social criticism, Kesey describes his hero, Randle Patrick McMurphy, as part Christ figure and part energetic Lone Ranger. Living up to his initials (RPM), the protagonist re-energizes the inmates to do battle with the Combine, under the control of Big Nurse. Gradually they line up behind their new cowboy Christ and stir up a range war against Nurse Ratchet and the castrating bureaucracy she seems to symbolize. Most of all, the swaggering McMurphy raises the consciousness of Chief Bromden, who fled from cultural conflict and racism by voluntarily committing himself to a mind-numbing institution. Although the Combine and Big Nurse eventually lobotomize RPM, his energetic defiance transforms the Chief, who, in a pregnant symbolic gesture, hoists Big Nurse's control panel out the window and lights out for new territory, with a refurbished sense of his Indian identity. Obviously McMurphy is something of a sagebrush savior, and his disciple, resurrected and revived, sets out to embody the new message.

Kesey's second book, *Sometimes a Great Notion* (1964), is more often labeled a regional novel. Place and reactions to setting do play major roles; trees, rivers, logging, and the Oregon coast are central ingredients in this long novel. Moreover, Hank Stamper, the never-give-an-inch hero, seems cut from John Wayne cloth. Individualistic, a gyppo-logger par excellence, Hank attacks the nearby community, harpoons labor leaders, and seduces other men's wives, including his stepmother. Not surprisingly, his forbears can be traced to IWW loins. Obviously Hank subscribes, throughout the novel, to a heroic Code of the West.

Still, both of Kesey's novels, though set in the Pacific Northwest, deal as much or more with frontiers of new consciousness as with place. Even more than *Sometimes*, *Cuckoo's Nest* symbolizes a new kind of Western in which the Indian becomes the hero, much as he does in *Little Big Man*. Civilization is in crisis and under threat from the Combine; only the self-assertiveness that McMurphy preaches and Chief Bromden finally lives up to can save the West from numbing materialism and mental fog. Deeper and broader in its historiographical significance, *Sometimes a Great Notion* deals both with vertical (past upon present) and horizontal (multiple viewpoints) interpretations of the West. One critic is directly on target in his comparison: the earlier, "simplistic belief in historical discontinuity [in *Cuckoo's Nest*] has been replaced by a more realistic appraisal of the human situation [in *Sometimes a Great Notion*]. By changing his attitude toward history, Kesey addresses both the specifically American condition and the human condition in general." Together, the novels not only abandon the stereotypes of popular western fiction and the region as a Wild West; they also suggest "rich historical metaphors for a state of mind" in a more recent West and Pacific Northwest.[38]

Had one pages enough and time, several other tendencies in recent Pacific Northwest fiction merit extended comment. But at least two trends deserve brief mentions. As they did early in the century, outsiders continued to write about the Northwest after abbreviated, extended, or outlying stays. As one example, Bernard Malamud's *A New Life* is a comic but sad novel about an English professor, a Jew from New York, who comes to teach in a small western college. Obviously based on Malamud's professional experiences at Oregon State University, the book discloses how alienated and innocent he was about the sociocultural history and contemporary rhythms of the area. Much of the same distance is evident in the writings of Leslie Fiedler, another eastern Jew who spent nearly twenty years teaching at the University of Montana. In such books and essays as *The Last Jew in America* and "The Montana Face," Fiedler, like Malamud, betrayed his outsider status in the Pacific Northwest.[39]

On the other hand, although Wallace Stegner never lived in the Northwest for an extended period of time, his stays in the Canadian West, Great Falls, Montana, and Salt Lake City, Utah, and his treatment of those areas and the Pacific Northwest in such works as *Big Rock Candy Mountain*, *Wolf Willow*, *Angle of Repose*, and *Recapitulation* qualify him as something of an adopted son. Indeed, in *Angle of Repose*, a Pulitzer Prize winner and perhaps the best western novel of the last generation, Stegner provides a superb model for the western historical novel. Covering nearly a full century of frontier and modern western history, and basing his heroine on the western Local Color writer Mary Hallock Foote, he weaves a splendid tapestry of past and present, East and West, and man, woman, and family in the Far West. Most of all, Stegner proves that the skilled novelist, like a premier historian, will measure the shaping influences of history on present-day happenings even as he creates appealing vignettes of characters enmeshed in those events.[40] Of Pacific Northwest novelists, Guthrie, Berry, and Doig come closest to Stegner's premier performances as a western historical novelist.

Nor should one overlook the emergence of a notable "school" of Montana writers. Closely or loosely linked to the University of Montana in Missoula, as were earlier coteries surrounding H.G. Merriam and poet

Richard Hugo, the most recent group owes most to the encouragement and direction of William Kittredge, an English professor at Missoula. In his teaching, in his own fiction and essays, and in his sponsorship of numerous aspiring authors, Kittredge has helped spawn a gathering of writers throughout western Montana that rivals similar groups in Texas, New Mexico, and California as the most yeasty literary colonies in the contemporary American West. Kittredge and the Montana writers, although focusing primarily on the modern West, demonstrate an understanding of frontier and pioneer experiences and their influences on the present without loading up their fiction with the excessively dramatic settings, stylized characters, and rigid plots of too much popular fiction. In addition to Montana authors mentioned earlier, among the writers sometimes included in this school are Rick DeMarinis, Mary Clearman Blew, David Quammen, Richard Ford, and David Long.[41]

♦ ♦ ♦

After this dash through a century of the treatment of history in Pacific Northwest novels, one must raise a final question: in what ways have Northwest novelists replicated or diverged from trends in western American fiction? Do the region's fictionists illustrate how other westerners have treated the history of the American West, or have they broken from those traditions? The answers, of course, are complex.

In the first place, the frontier, regional, and postregional periods of the Pacific Northwest novel parallel trends in western American fiction. For example, the earliest Local Color, historical romance, and popular Western genres that the work of Frederic Homer Balch, Mary Hallock Foote, B.M. Bower, and Eva Emery Dye typified were also popular types in the fiction of Alfred Henry Lewis, Gertrude Atherton, Owen Wister, and Zane Grey in other subregions of the West. And the strong regionalist impulse in the novels of H.L. Davis and Vardis Fisher and in the editorial direction of H.G. Merriam in *Frontier* paralleled similar treatments of regional history and culture in the works of Willa Cather, Frederick Manfred, Harvey Fergusson, and John Steinbeck in the Great Plains, Southwest, and California. So too the ethnic, feminist, and counter-classic tendencies in postregional Pacific Northwest fiction echo similar emphases in the writings of such western novelists as N. Scott Momaday, Leslie Silko, Louise Erdrich, Joan Didion, Larry McMurtry, and Edward Abbey.

But one can make too much of these parallels. Northwest novelists were more than carbon copies of other fictionists of the larger West, more than unthinking followers taking their cues from alien literary Pied Pipers. As one might expect, Pacific Northwesterners have also broken from these predominant trends, have pioneered in their individualistic ways.

During the first two decades of the twentieth century, for instance, novelists of the Far Corner were reluctant Realists. No one in the Northwest produced a novel closely akin to the realistic fiction of Hamlin Garland, Frank Norris, or Jack London. At the same time, more women in the region seemed to be producing historical fiction than elsewhere in the West. In the nineteenth century, Margaret Jewett Bailey and Abigail Scott Duniway and early in the twentieth century Ella Higginson joined Foote, Bower, and Dye in producing historical novels about the Pacific Northwest. And some literary historians argue that the Northwest, more than any other section of the West, gains the dubious honor of producing the largest numbers of popular or formula Westerns in the first half of the twentieth century.

Later periods also exhibit differences. In the last two generations, fewer nationally influential feminist voices have spoken in the Pacific Northwest. No one in the region, as an example, has gained the notoriety of such western novelists as Joan Didion, Leslie Silko, and Louise Erdrich. Moreover, reflecting the less diverse ethnicity of the Pacific Northwest, not many historical novels about ethnic groups, aside from those about Native Americans, have appeared.[42] Nor have Northwesterners developed anything like the vitriolic anti-California and anti-Los Angeles myth that has emerged since the late 1930s. First, a group of detective writers, then John Steinbeck, and later novelists like Didion, Alison Lurie, and Ross Macdonald depicted southern California as an increasingly bizarre, overly civilized, and decadent place and society. Northwesterners have yet to lambast their region as such a blighted and decaying place. Finally, as noted above, the rise of the Montana school of writers in the last decade or so suggests that at least portions of the Northwest are literarily alive up to today.

For a full century, then, novelists of the Northwest have repeatedly turned to the history of their region for important ingredients in their fiction. Sometimes depicting the Northwest as an open, expanding frontier, as a developing region, or as a society and culture embodying postregional experiences, these novelists supply notable vistas for a fuller understanding of the Pacific Northwest and its shifting heritages. As such, they stand alongside historians, painters, and other representatives of regional culture as important sources for understanding our place and its peoples.

Notes

1. H.L. Davis and James Stevens, *Status Rerum: A Manifesto, Upon the Present Condition of Northwestern Literature, Containing Several Near-Libelous Utterances, Upon Persons in the Public Eye* (The Dalles, OR: n.p., 1927), n.p. For an excellent study of southern and western regionalism, see Robert L. Dorman, *Revolt of the Provinces: The Regionalist Movement in America, 1920-1945* (Chapel Hill: University of North Carolina Press, 1993).

2. The concepts of "frontier," "region," and "postregion," as used in this essay, receive extended treatment in Richard W. Etulain, *Re-imagining the Modern American West: A Century of Fiction, History, and Art* (Tucson: University of Arizona Press, 1996). The Pacific Northwest badly needs a thorough, well-researched literary history.

3. Frederic Homer Balch, *The Bridge of the Gods* (Chicago: A.C. McClurg, 1890). (After a first full citation in the notes, page citations to this novel and later works will appear in the text.) Unfortunately, the only book-length biographical study of Balch, although it contains much useful information, is excessively uncritical and unorganized: Leonard Wiley, *The Granite Boulder: A Biography of Frederic Homer Balch* (Portland, OR: n.p. 1970). Much more useful as a brief overview of Balch's life and literary career is Stephen L. Harris, "Frederic Homer Balch and the Romance of Oregon History," *Oregon Historical Quarterly* 97 (Winter 1996-97):390-427.

4. William Benson Helms to Alfred Powers, Authors Files, September 23, 1934, Film 11, Item 24, Oregon State Archives, Salem, Oregon; Frederic Homer Balch to Judge Matthew Deady, [?] 16, 1879, February 7, 1880, Deady Papers, Oregon Historical Society, Portland, Oregon.

5. This definition of "frontier" literature derives from Etulain, *Re-imagining the Modern American West*, 5-30; and Etulain, "Research Opportunities in Twentieth-Century Western Cultural History," in Gerald D. Nash and Richard W. Etulain, eds., *Researching Western History: Topics in the Twentieth Century* (Albuquerque: University of New Mexico Press, 1997), 148-49, 152-53.

6. The fullest secondary account of Foote's life and career is Lee Ann Johnson, *Mary Hallock Foote* (Boston: Twayne, 1980).

7. Foote tells her own story in *A Victorian Gentlewoman in the Far West: The Reminiscences of Mary Hallock Foote*, Rodman W. Paul, ed., (San Marino, CA: Huntington Library, 1972). The exact wording of her eastern-western comparison reads: "I love my West when I am in the East." Foote to Helena [de Kay Gilder], Letter 358, May 23, 1888, Mary Hallock Foote Letters, Huntington Library, San Marino, California.

8. Mary Hallock Foote, *The Desert and the Sown* (Boston: Houghton Mifflin, 1902), 53, 72, 260.

9. For two innovative studies that avoid dismissing B.M. Bower as an author of western subliterature, see Christine Bold, *Selling the Wild West: Popular Western Fiction, 1860-1960* (Bloomington: Indiana University Press, 1987); and Norris W. Yates, *Gender and Genre: An Introduction to Women Writers of Formula Westerns, 1900-1950* (Albuquerque: University of New Mexico Press, 1995).

10. B.M. Bower, *Chip, of the Flying U* (New York: G. W. Willingham, 1906). For the fullest account of Bower's life, consult Orrin A. Engen, *Writer of the Plains* (Culver City, CA: Pontine Press, 1973).

11. James H. Maguire provides a very useful overview of frontier and western novels in his "Fiction of the West," in Emory Elliott, ed., *The Columbia History of the American Novel* (New York: Columbia University Press, 1991), 437-64.

12. The most useful guide to important books and essays about regionalism is Michael Steiner and Clarence Mondale, *Region and Regionalism in the United States: A Source Book for the Humanities and Social Sciences* (New York: Garland, 1988). Richard Maxwell Brown

provides a superb overview of regionalism in his "The New Regionalism in America, 1970-1981," in William G. Robbins, et al., eds., *Regionalism and the Pacific Northwest* (Corvallis: Oregon State University Press, 1983), 37-96.

13. *Status Rerum* is conveniently reprinted in *H.L. Davis: Collected Essays and Short Stories* (Moscow: University of Idaho Press, n. d.), 359-66. H.L. Davis told one friend that *Status Rerum* was intended to "stir up a row," and that it had "scraped some hide off a number of the Eunuchs [sic] who resent being valued at any rate except their own." Davis to W. E. Kidd, November 5, 1927, Walter Evans Kidd Letters, University of Oregon Library, Special Collections, Eugene, Oregon.

14. H.G. Merriam, "Endlessly the Covered Wagon," *Frontier* 8 (November 1927):1.

15. H.L. Davis, "Status Rerum—Allegro Ma Non Troppo," *Frontier* 8 (March 1928):70.

16. Comparisons between western and southern regionalism are particularly extensive in Dorman, *Revolt of the Provinces*.

17. Paul T. Bryant, *H.L. Davis* (Boston: Twayne, 1978).

18. H.L. Davis, "Note," *Honey in the Horn* (New York: Harper and Brothers, 1935), n.p.; Giles French to R. W. Etulain, October 3, 1964; H.L. Davis to W. E. Kidd, September 19, 1935, Walter Evans Kidd Letters.

19. These paragraphs on Vardis Fisher and those later on A.B. Guthrie, Jr., and Wallace Stegner draw on Richard W. Etulain, "Western Fiction and History: A Reconsideration," in Jerome O. Steffen, ed., *The American West: New Perspectives, New Dimensions* (Norman: University of Oklahoma Press, 1979), 152-74.

20. George F. Day, *The Uses of History in the Novels of Vardis Fisher* (New York: Revisionist Press, 1976); Joseph M. Flora, *Vardis Fisher* (New York: Twayne, 1965).

21. Joseph M. Flora, "Vardis Fisher and the Mormons." *Dialogue* 4 (Autumn 1969):48-55; Leonard J. Arrington and Jon Haupt, "The Mormon Heritage of Vardis Fisher," *Brigham Young University Studies* 18 (Fall 1977):27-47.

22. Stephen L. Tanner, *Ernest Haycox* (New York: Twayne, 1996); Richard W. Etulain, *Ernest Haycox* (Boise, ID: Boise State University, 1988).

23. Richard W. Etulain, "Ernest Haycox: Popular Novelist of the Pacific Northwest," in Edwin R. Bingham and Glen A. Love, eds., *Northwest Perspectives: Essays on the Culture of the Pacific Northwest* (Seattle: University of Washington Press, 1979), 137-50.

24. John D. Nesbitt, "A New Look at Two Popular Western Classics," *South Dakota Review* 18 (Spring 1980):30-42; Richard W. Etulain, "Ernest Haycox: The Historical Western, 1937-43," *South Dakota Review* 5 (Spring 1967):35-54.

25. Robert L. Gale, "Ernest Haycox," in Fred Erisman and Richard W. Etulain, eds., *Fifty Western Writers* (Westport, CT: Greenwood Press, 1982), 183-93.

26. Thomas W. Ford, *A.B. Guthrie, Jr.* (Boston: Twayne, 1981).

27. Richard H. Cracroft, "*The Big Sky*: A.B. Guthrie's Use of Historical Sources," *Western American Literature* 6 (Fall 1971):163-76.

28. "Author Guthrie—'Going Toward the Sunset.'" *Exponent* [Montana State University], April 2, 1971. Guthrie deals with his interests in history in his "The Historical Novel: Tramp or Teacher," *Montana: The Magazine of Western History* 4 (Autumn 1954):1-8.

29. Glen A. Love, *Don Berry* (Boise, ID: Boise State University, 1978).

30. Elizabeth Simpson, *Earthlight, Wordfire: The Works of Ivan Doig* (Moscow: University of Idaho Press, 1992).

31. William G. Robbins, "The Historian as Literary Craftsman: The West of Ivan Doig," *Pacific Northwest Quarterly* 78 (October 1987):139; William Kittredge, "Voices and Spirits: Doors to Our House," *Northern Lights* 2 (January/February 1986):20, as quoted in Robbins, "The Historian as Literary Craftsman," 137.

32. For a helpful discussion of these dramatic changes in the Pacific Northwest during the 1930s and 1940s, see Carlos Schwantes, *The Pacific Northwest: An Interpretive History*, rev. and enl. ed. (Lincoln: University of Nebraska Press, 1996).

33. Some might point to D'Arcy McNickle's novel *The Surrounded* (New York: Dodd, Mead 1936) as an exception to this statement. Before they do so, they should read Dorothy R. Parker, *Singing an Indian Song: A Biography of D'Arcy McNickle* (Lincoln: University of Nebraska Press, 1992), for an illuminating account of the complexities of McNickle's ethnic identity.

34. Janet Campbell Hale, *The Jailing of Cecelia Captive* (New York: Random House, 1985).

35. Brina Caplan, review of Marilynne Robinson, *Housekeeping*, *Nation* 232 (February 7, 1981):154.

36. *Ibid.*; LeAnne Schreiber, "Pleasure and Loss," *New York Times Book Review*, February 8, 1981, 14. See also Robinson's illuminating comments on her backgrounds and methods of writing in "My Western Roots," in Barbara Howard Meldrum, ed., *Old West-New West: Centennial Essays* (Moscow: University of Idaho Press, 1993), 165-72.

37. Richard Maxwell Brown refers to these novels as counter-classics, "New Regionalism in America." Others have labeled them anti-Westerners or remythologized western stories. See Etulain, *Re-imagining the Modern American West*, 155, 158-59.

38. Bruce Carnes, *Ken Kesey* (Boise, ID: Boise State University, 1974), 20, 24.

39. Barnett Singer, "Outsider Versus Insider: Malamud's and Kesey's Pacific Northwest," *South Dakota Review* 13 (Winter 1975-76):127-44. Leslie Fiedler's "The Montana Face," which first appeared in *Partisan Review* (1949), is reprinted in William Kittredge and Annick Smith, eds., *The Last Best Place: A Montana Anthology* (Helena: Montana Historical Society, 1988), 744-52.

40. Wallace Stegner, *Angle of Repose* (Garden City, NY: Doubleday, 1971); Jackson J. Benson, *Wallace Stegner: His Life and Work* (New York: Viking, 1996); Charles E. Rankin, ed., *Wallace Stegner: Man and Writer* (Albuquerque: University of New Mexico Press, 1996).

41. For an appealing sampling of the work of the "Montana School," see Kittredge and Smith, *The Last Best Place;* William W. Bevis, *Ten Tough Trips: Montana Writers and the West* (Seattle: University of Washington Press, 1990).

42. I must note, however, that other commentators consider John Okada's *No-No Boy* (1957) a notable exception to my generalization here.

III
The Significance of Hanford in American History*

Patricia Nelson Limerick
(University of Colorado)

A NYONE WHO SETS OUT to find a reference to the Hanford Nuclear Reservation in the standard American history textbooks has embarked on a journey with no point of arrival. Look at the index where "Hanford" ought to be, and the closest entry you have is "Mark Hanna." The "H" section in textbooks thus reveals a curious measure of significance. Helping to elect William McKinley president gets one a permanent and prominent place in history, and being the site of the country's largest nuclear complex, and also the site of its worst contamination and waste problem, gets no attention at all.

Perhaps these priorities indicate a preference for the "up-beat," for accentuating the positive. After the election, Mark Hanna wired McKinley, "God's in his heaven, and all's right with the world." This is not a sentiment that has been heard much in connection with affairs at Hanford lately. But, beyond a preference for cheerfulness, the prominence of Hanna also represents a long-term problem with the center of gravity of American history. Hanna was eastern and Hanford is western, and thus, in the semiconscious thinking of most American historians, one is significant and the other is not.

In conventional textbook organization, the West usually makes two brief appearances, like a second-rank guest on the talk-show circuit. The West is there for a quick round on pre-Civil War expansion, and back for another brief interlude on post-Civil War development. Then the frontier ends on schedule in 1890; the Indians are removed; the buffalo killed; the minerals, discovered; the churches and schools, built; and there is no more West, outside a short paragraph or two on Gifford Pinchot, Hollywood, Indians, or Mexican-Americans in the twentieth century.

Who would expect anything more from the eastern intellectual establishment? What is more disheartening, however, is that western scholars have done no better, and may even have done worse.

Trying to find Hanford in a textbook on the history of the American West is just as futile as attempting to locate it in a general American history text. The accent in western surveys is so thoroughly on the nineteenth century and on the "frontier"—indeed these books usually end in the 1890s—that the entire twentieth century is lucky if it gets an epilogue. Traditional western history has, in other words, confirmed and encouraged the writers of mainstream textbooks in their worst habits of ignoring and discounting the significance of the West.

What possessed western historians? Why did they, for so long, deny the twentieth century, and refuse to pay attention to some of the most consequential factors in the region's history? The answer is, in part, loyalty to Frederick Jackson Turner, the enormously influential historian whose 1893 speech, "The Significance of the Frontier in American History," set the basic terms and propositions for Western American studies for decades to come. It is surely not Turner's weakness that he failed to anticipate the discovery and development of nuclear energy. But it was the shortcoming of his proteges and followers that they became priests to the prophet, enshrining Turner's thought in its 1893 form, and refusing opportunity after opportunity to give the continuing story of Western American its full dimension and power.

This, then, is the central paradox of Western American historiography: a forceful and courageous man gave a speech in 1893, when he was only 32 years old, and offered his best assessment of the meaning of western expansion, and then, for decades after, his followers preserved Turner's words and refused to imitate his example of courageous and forceful thought. This pattern is not, of course, unparalleled in human behavior. When my husband and I visited Frank Lloyd Wright's home in Wisconsin, we were struck by the remarkable deference of the Taliesin Fellowship to the memory of Wright. Inspired, we composed this piece of doggerel verse, a poem that applies as well to the followers of the Wisconsinite Turner as it does to the followers of the Wisconsinite Wright:

> The master informed us, "Find a new way,
> The styles of the past are dated and gray.
> Do not with tradition continue to stay,"
> And that is, of course, why we do things *his* way.

Hanford and Los Alamos and the Nevada Test Site and the Lawrence Livermore National Laboratory and Rocky Flats and hundreds of other significant places in Western America could not fit the Turner Thesis, and the Turner Thesis could not fit Hanford. Curiously enough, western historians have responded to this problem by retaining the Turner Thesis and paying little or no attention to Hanford.

Apart from the dated and inflexible terms of the 1893 thesis, there is another Turnerian legacy. In his essays, often with titles following the pattern "The Significance of X or Y in American History," Turner made many forceful statements, written in accessible prose rather than academic jargon. It is this Turnerian tradition that we can and should do our best to revive. It is time to put that formula to work on "The Significance of Hanford in American History."

Despite fine efforts from a number of journalists,[1] Hanford has not done much better at national public recognition than it has done at inclusion in American history textbooks. In 1989, just before I was scheduled to make a lecture trip to Whitman College in Walla Walla, I had an awful cold and my voice turned unworkable. I went to the doctor and told him how urgent it was that I get well. I simply could not miss the trip, because I had been promised a full day's tour of the Hanford Reservation after my speaking engagements.

The doctor said, "What's Hanford?"

This surprised me, but it is an experience I could have every day if I wanted to keep provoking it. "What's Hanford?" is a question many well educated people ask without apparent embarrassment. They would probably do a better job, one begins to suspect, at recognizing and identifying Mark Hanna.

In the last two or three years, I have campaigned for a model of Western American history with its roots in the reality of life in the Trans-Mississippi West, and not in the thinking of Frederick Jackson Turner in Wisconsin. In a round of recent press coverage, this model has picked up the name "The New Western History." Whatever the flaws or limits of the name, this fresh approach has plenty of room for Hanford.[2]

The tenets of the New Western History are simple:

1) There is no watershed between the nineteenth and twentieth centuries; in other words, neither the year 1890 nor any other year represents the "end of the frontier." Western expansion is a continuous and running story. Any number of classic events in western development—a great deal

of homesteading and countless booms in irrigation, timber, oil, coal, uranium, and the defense industries—occurred *after* 1890. Even the events of the nineteenth century that seemed to come to a halt—for instance, the Indian wars—produced long-term consequences and legacies that we live with today. Anyone who stands at the site of the Little Big Horn battle, and who thinks that the conflicts represented there were settled, ought to look at the record of Indian-initiated litigation in the last twenty years. Issues fought on battlefields are now fought in courtrooms. Those conflicts, and many others, make no sense unless we pay attention to the full, continuous account connecting the nineteenth and twentieth centuries.

2) The New Western History holds that we are best served by thinking of the American West as one of the great meeting grounds of the planet, the place where representatives from Indian America, Hispanic America, Anglo-America, Afro-America, and Asia all converged and jockeyed for position and power. This concept is quite a world apart from the old Turnerian "white wave" model, in which the dominant theme was one of white settlers rolling steadily westward into virgin and free land. The New Western History's model of convergence has a number of advantages over the earlier approach. Among its most appealing attributes is the ability to set historians free from the burdensome task of "choosing sides," of having to make white people the main characters and Indians the supporting actors, or of having to make Indians the main characters and whites the supporting actors. Resting on the acknowledgment and investigation of many points of view, the model of convergence virtually becomes aerobics of the mind; it requires the historian to move around, with vigor, in order to see the American West from various angles and judgements.

3) The New Western History drops the word "frontier," a term that has always been difficult to define clearly, and one encrusted with ethnocentric associations at that. Once we drop "frontier" and take up words like colonization or conquest, more accurate definitions come into focus. At the same time, with clear and down-to-earth terms, it becomes possible to compare the course of events in the American West to the process of colonization and conquest in other parts of the planet, from New Zealand to Argentina, from the Philippines to South Africa.

Under the New Western History, Hanford's historical fortunes have taken a turn for the better. Hanford has moved from the dismissible periphery under the Old Western History, to the center of the action in the fresh approach. Hanford's twentieth century status no longer disqualifies it from western history; it fits clearly in the whole attempt to master nature;

and it is an ideal place to exercise one's capacity to weigh conflicting testimony and to evaluate contradictory points of view.

At the end of the twentieth century, an understanding of the pride, and even affection, that some people have felt for the Hanford operations requires either concerted mental effort, or an encounter with the right person. In 1989, when I toured the reservation, our group met just the right person—a grandmotherly lady who was going to retire that very day. She had begun working at Hanford in 1951, the year I was born, the year that the Atomic Energy Commission began the construction of the Rocky Flats plant outside Denver. In 1951, when the AEC announced the building of Rocky Flats, the *Denver Post* ran the headline, "There's Good News Today," and the *Rocky Mountain News* reported that the Denver Chamber of Commerce was "elated." In one on-the-street interview, a clerk said: "I think it's wonderful . . . . These people who get frightened over such things give me a pain in the neck." A shoe repairman also gave his endorsement: "Son, a town as dull as this one could stand a few split atoms. I'm all for the new plant."[3]

Our grandmotherly acquaintance at Hanford had preserved this cheerful attitude into and throughout the 1980s, and she had loved her work from beginning to end. In the early years especially, she said, she hated missing a day; vacations were a trial and an annoyance. Having different attitudes toward vacations ourselves, we asked, "Why?" "Because we were pioneers," she said. "We were pushing back the frontiers of knowledge."[4]

Our group had not yet revealed that we were Western American historians; she chose her language out of her own convictions, and not to cater to our professional specialization. Even if western historians have not paid attention to Hanford, Hanford people have paid some attention to western history. Like the space program, the armaments and nuclear energy industries have adopted wholeheartedly the analogy of the frontier and of pioneers. "I never thought of Hanford in terms of being a factory," physicist John Wheeler said. "There was a sense of adventure about it. I associate it with pioneering."[5]

But when they compared their undertakings to western expansion, these nuclear innovators were, to their peril, dependent on the old model of western history. This concept appears in the introduction to the fifth edition of Ray Allen Billington and Martin Ridge's textbook, *Westward Expansion*: "The history of the American West is, almost by definition, a triumphal narrative for it traces a virtually unbroken chain of successes in national expansion."[6] If that was the product traditional western historians had available, no wonder the planners and workers of Hanford bought it wholesale.

But at least for an instant in 1876, George Armstrong Custer at the Little Big Horn had a different vision of western history. Leaving the media star Custer aside, western history is full of failures: abandoned towns, mines, and railroads; many, many people who invested their capital in enterprises that simply did not pay; and many, many others who rushed to the sites of boom economies, and got there in time for the bust.

Even some apparent successes turned out to be something other than pure. White Americans may have won the Indian wars, but they are still troubled by the problems of Indian unemployment, demoralization, and alcoholism on reservations. Public-spirited promoters built giant dams and reservoirs for hydroelectricity and water control, but they are still troubled by problems of silt filling up those reservoirs, and of different users competing for over-allocated rivers.

If the woman we met at Hanford had been better served by western historians, that phrase—"We were pioneers; we were pushing back the frontiers of knowledge"—might have carried an instructive set of lessons. It might have been a chance to reflect on success and failure, on impulsiveness and caution, on the many ways in which pioneers, literal or metaphorical, have a habit of acting in haste and repenting at leisure.

Our acquaintance at Hanford told us about her early laboratory jobs, standing behind a small wall of bricks, working on something radioactive, and guiding her actions by what she could see in a mirror placed behind and above the bricks. Even with these precautions, she could only be in the room for a few minutes at a time. Once, she said, she spilled a radioactive liquid on herself, but was redeemed by the peculiar customs of the 1950s: the fluid hit her hip, and she had the good fortune to be wearing one of those classic 1950s, industrial-strength latex girdles, a girdle that simply gave no ground to radioactivity, or any other dark force of the universe.[7] Even here, thoughts of the so-called Old West must come to mind. We have gone, it seems, from bullets miraculously intercepted by the vest pocket Bible, to radioactive particles miraculously intercepted by the latex girdle. This rather particular patter of continuity and change aside, plutonium is something new under the sun. The explosion of the first bomb near Alamogordo—with Hanford plutonium—did, in truth, inaugurate a whole new era in human history. And yet, in other ways, the story of Hanford makes a firm and close match with the basic configurations of western expansion.

First, Hanford fits in the pattern of cyclical displacements, by which one group's benefit meant another group's injury or removal. The anthropologist Edward Spicer used the phrase "Cycles of Conquest" to describe this concept, and it certainly applies here. The story of this particular spot along the Columbia River begins with Indian occupation, continues with the arrival of white settlers and the displacement of Indians, and then, in turn, takes up the removal of white settlers from their orchards by the forces of General Leslie Groves and his Manhattan Project. As elsewhere in western history, none of these displaced elements simply faded gracefully from the scene. Indian people still have their claim on the Hanford site, and there are still a number of white survivors available to mourn the disappearance of their homes in White Bluffs and Hanford.

One World War II veteran told of his feelings on returning to the area: unlike other ex-servicemen, he said, he had no home to go back to.[8] Another man told of his father's early struggle to develop a homestead by the Columbia, planting orchards and building a house and farm buildings. His parents' forced departure, the son remembered, broke their hearts.[9] "From the time I first remember," a Hanford resident recalled, "I loved those apple orchards."[10] When a nuclear reactor displaces an apple orchard, the symbolism becomes so heavy-handed that it seems like the invention of a clumsy novelist—except that it happens to be true.

It also happens to be true that irrigated agriculture (or horticulture), while it certainly looks more "natural" and adapted to its place than the construction of a nuclear reactor, is itself an exercise in the conquest and rearrangement of nature. We would, in other words, fall into sentimental error if we created the image of a pastoral Eden, a land of thriving and simple Jeffersonian farmers, driven out by Army Corps of Engineers bulldozers. But, innocent virtue on the part of former inhabitants or not, the development of Hanford certainly follows the general story of western history, a pattern summed up, a bit gracelessly but still accurately, by one of my students in a final exam: "The Indians felt impacted on,"—and, in this case, so did those who followed them.

Second, Hanford's history fits smoothly into the general Western American pattern of the dismissibility of deserts. When I was already at a fairly advance age, my brother-in-law told me that parts of eastern Washington and Oregon were really deserts. "Who would have guessed that!" I exclaimed like a bunch of other greenhorns before and since. "Washington and Oregon seem so green from everything I've seen and heard!" Despite my brother-in-law's pointed lesson, I joined up with a long-running tradition of Western American historians and left the desert part of the interior Northwest entirely out of my first book, and, by implication, out of western history, even though the study dealt with the attitude of Anglo-Americans toward arid places.[11] But Hanford would have made a fine fit in the book. To Manhattan Project planners, Hanford was a perfect site for their purposes. Beyond a few irrigated fields, it was desert; in their eyes, this land was already a waste and therefore would be improved by any use at all, an area already so unappealing that there was little to injure but sagebrush and jackrabbits.[12]

Since arid land was already, in the common phrase of the nineteenth century, a wasteland, what could be more appropriate than to put it to use as a place for containing real waste, a place simply to dig a trench, dump in contaminated water, and feel comforted in the belief that there was nothing much to injure anyway in land so tough and uncompliant? In other words, the Manhattan Project decision-makers had not awakened to the notion that the desert has its own delicately balanced and—on its own terms—abundant ecosystem. The selection of Hanford is thus a fine demonstration that the pattern of treating deserts as dismissible terrain continued in force into the twentieth century. The creation of the Nevada Test Site, as well as the Idaho Nuclear Engineering Laboratories, makes the same point: when it came to atomic enterprises, the American West's aridity gave it a considerable "advantage" in siting choices. Even Rocky Flats near Denver fell into that same capacious category of useless, arid land: it had supported some livestock grazing, the *Rocky Mountain News* reported, "otherwise, the area is barren."[13]

Third, Hanford fits into the pattern of the western boom/bust cycle. In mining, oil, timber, farming, and in cattle-raising, the story of western business has been that of a roller coaster. Hanford's economic history has also followed that rise-and-fall-and-rise-and-fall model. Hanford in wartime was like any number of other western locations; it experienced a wage bonanza, with rumors and recruiting ads pulling people in by the thousands. And, once they arrived, Hanford had all the classic problems of a western boom town; too many people, not enough comfortable housing, and too many temptations to drinking, gambling, prostitution, and fighting, with arrests for drunkenness and intoxication seeming to dominate the Hanford/DuPont plant protection staff's time.[14]

Like a number of other western booms, the Hanford development created a company town, Richland, with the federal government playing the role elsewhere filled by Kennecott Copper or Colorado Fuel and Iron.

And, in that central fact of dependence on the federal government, the growth of the Hanford Project fell squarely within the broader patterns of a western history, where federal money played a great role in Indian removal, land distribution, transportation development, and dam-building.

Fourth, just like other places that have ridden the boom/bust roller-coaster, Hanford is now full of ruins and relics of lost times. The reservation is a warehouse of signs and symbols of the rapid pace of change and of the uncertainty of human fortunes: artifacts of Indian settlements; the street layout and old high school in the displaced town of Hanford; the relics of the Hanford construction camp, built instantly, occupied for two years, and then abandoned; and now eight looming decommissioned nuclear reactors and a variety of dumpsites. And, true to the patterns of the western roller-coaster, these relics and ruins have been created in an astonishingly brief time, with reactors built at enormous expense and labor, dead in less than two decades, a pacing not unlike that of gold rushes and cattle booms.

Western American history proceeded at a gait we can only call fast-forward. As one of my students put it in a final exam, "After 1848, everything became frantic," and the only thing wrong with that statement is that it ignores a few occasions when things became frantic before 1848. The observation certainly holds true when it comes to characterizing the pace, the rapidity of the rise and fall, at Hanford. One by-product of the rapid change was a bumper crop of nostalgia, and this, too, is true to the patterns of western history. With events moving so fast, it was both natural and easy for participants to look back at the golden years, to see them as a period of giant achievements and full, free exercise of human powers, and to see the present, by contrast, as a time when everything bogged down, when life turned tedious and dull and regulated.

Fifth, Hanford history and general western history share common qualities in the disparity between what people said and what people did. Marcus and Narcissa Whitman came as missionaries to the Walla Walla area in the 1830s with a declared intention to help the Indians. Then the Whitmans introduced intrusive and disorienting religious and farming practices, and also diseases that devastated the Indians. Were the Whitmans hypocrites? Not at all. But how do we appraise the disparity between their high-minded intentions, and the outcome, in 1847, of the Cayuse Indians rising in quite understandable anger against their attempted helpers?

That same problem comes back over and over in western history because a powerful ideology, called Manifest Destiny or a variety of other names, powered the actions of Anglo-Americans. In the case of Hanford, as in other instances of western expansion, we do have a few clear examples of hypocrisy, or of direct cover-ups, of people doing one thing and saying another. But there are plenty of cases of people feeling that they were doing the right thing, believing that they were working in a good cause with their safety guarded and supervised by employers they could trust. Perhaps most important, to a large group of people, life at Hanford became so utterly routine that the need or urge to ask questions became vestigial. "We must improve our credibility," wrote Michael J. Lawrence, manager of the Department of Energy's Richland office, in the fall of 1985. "We will aggressively and professionally build confidence . . . in Hanford activities by opening our doors to the public."[15] In the 1987 annual report Lawrence said: "Hanford's future can be bright. As we seek this future, you have my personal commitment that Hanford remains unalterably committed to 'safety first.'"[16]

In between those two statements, in February of 1986, "the U.S. Department of Energy released 19,000 pages of environmental monitoring reports, letters, office memoranda, construction reports, and other documents which had been generated at Hanford from the earliest days of its selection as the United States' largest defense weapons production complex in 1943."[17] The revelations in that material made Manager Michael Lawrence's chosen task of improving credibility a lot tougher. "The most startling revelation," as Karen Dorn Steele has written, "was of a December 1949 experiment that deliberately contaminated eastern Washington." In the so-called "Green Run," without any public health warning, the plutonium processing facilities released "some 5,500 curies of iodine 131 and a still classified inventory of other fission products." The point of the experiment was evidently to "test how far, and in what concentrations, airborne fission products could be detected," in order to be able to monitor future Soviet tests and nuclear manufacturing plants.[18]

"Safety is virtually a religion at Hanford," the 1987 Hanford annual report announced. Religions sometimes do have a way of operating in the Hanford fashion, with principles chanted as justifications for actions which contradict those same principles, with piety reserved for public pronouncements and then dropped for expedient reasons.[19] In the case of the Green Run, as well as the returning of radiated cooling water to the Columbia River and the direct dumping of wastes into the soil (under the theory that a process of percolation would keep them out of the river), the Hanford record forces us to make some fundamental observations. In fact, these considerations lead western historians to pursue the most basic activity of their craft—the critical appraisal of assertions of the actors, keeping an eye on what they said and what they did, and recognizing that sometimes the relation is outright hypocrisy, sometimes self-deception, and sometimes the perfectly understandable breakdown of the human effort to live with consistency and principle.

The most valuable part of the whole exercise, in the study of Hanford and the American West, is that we can no longer take *anything* for granted; we must keep ourselves in a constant state of alertness. A few years ago, reporter Chris Bowman interviewed Bob Sheahan, whose family's mine was the closest occupied spot to the Nevada Test Site. The Sheahans had, for years, accepted the federal government's assurances that they were at no risk. After years of compliance, Bob Sheahan decided he had been misled and misguided, and he then changed courses. "I'm a good American," he said, "but what they've done to me and my family is bad"[20]

Western history has a full complement of people like Bob Sheahan, people who felt misled, tricked, betrayed, lulled into complacency by false promises, rendered vulnerable by their own hopes and expectations, and then caught in the gap between what spoken and written words promised them, and what reality actually delivered to them. Hanford has become, then, another western case study in the tensions and frictions along the hinge that connects expectations to outcomes, promises to deliveries.

Sixth and finally, it is in the waste, in the literal, non-negotiable, there-to-be-reckoned-with-for-the-ages waste, that Hanford's deepest connection to western history comes through. From the disruption of the landscape by hydraulic mining to the leaching of chemicals from abandoned deep-rock mines into the streams of the Rockies, from the erosion of the plowed-up plains to the distribution of pesticides in rivers and aquifers, we have all around us literal, concrete signs of the legacy of the conquest. History, this evidence announces, refuses to let us declare our independence from the past. The radioactive waste at Hanford hammers the point in; we simply must recognize and deal with the legacy of conquest that surrounds us.

I would like Western American historians to reappraise the significance of Hanford in American history along these lines. I would like the western public to move beyond the standard refrain, "What's Hanford?" and look at these issues. I would also like the writers of American history textbooks to rethink their standards of what is peripheral and what is central. In short, I want these authors to wrestle with the question: which is more peripheral to the main currents of American history, Mark Hanna or the Hanford Nuclear Reservation?

Once the textbook writers have figured out the answer to that question, I hope they will include in their books the obvious proposition that the American West has been the geographical center of gravity in nuclear affairs. Hanford, Los Alamos, Alamogordo, the Lawrence Livermore Laboratory, the plants at Rocky Flats and Pantex, the NORAD command facility, the unnumbered missile silos, the leading contestants for the national nuclear waste dump—put the whole complex together, and for all the significance of Savannah River and Fernald and Oak Ridge, the mass of American nuclear activities tilts westward. This array shows clearly that the American West is at the forefront of the most important national and international issues, and not a backwater of quaint frontier topics limited to the nineteenth century.

Finding national significance for Hanford and its western relatives is, then, no difficult matter. Take two of the more obvious implications. When World War II shifted into the Cold War at Hanford and at other nuclear sites, the culture of secrecy stayed in the saddle, with workers prohibited from discussing their work with their spouses, with penalties imposed on employees who asked questions. In daily life at Hanford, the historian can find the paradox of the Cold War embodied. The federal government undertook to suspend democracy and freedom *in practice*, in order to defend democracy and freedom in theory.

Or take the way in which Hanford and its waste tanks spotlight the central meaning of the West in the nation. The West was supposed to be the region where one could escape history, escape failure, escape the problems of Europe and the eastern United States. Instead, over time, the West proved to be the place where history accumulates most dramatically, where radioactive waste in leaking tanks reminds us that the past cannot simply be ignored, where the bills for previous successes abruptly come due.

In the most serious sense, the meaning of Hanford is a literary problem. The twentieth century has been rough on the West, but it has been a lot rougher on the English language, bombarding it with every kind of attack, and warping it into a variety of mutant forms we call jargon, or the language of expertise. It is hard to say which makes for drearier reading—the language of western water policy and history, or the language of western atomic policy and history. When we undertake to read or talk about these most crucial regional issues, with their acre-feet of water or curies of radiation, it is sometimes rather difficult to stay awake. This is only one of many ways in which the technologizing of language has worn away at democracy, sometimes even shut it down, as lay people are excluded from the discussion of complex, but crucial, issues.

Just as important, we are missing a chance to explore—and perhaps, in an odd way, celebrate—the power and depth of this whole study. When the unsettled and unsettling consequences of human action break into geological time, then this should be the occasion of great literature, as resonant with universal human meaning as the works of John Milton or of Emily Dickinson. Edward Gibbon contemplated the ruins of Rome, and felt driven to write *The Rise and Fall of the Roman Empire*. Hanford is still in search of its Gibbon.

While it is an extraordinary place to see and think about, Hanford is not easy to capture in writing. A view of the inactive reactors along the Columbia River is genuinely haunting; they are giant, windowless, blocky hulks, surrounded by empty parking lots, bulwarks of radioactivity far into geological time, dead after a lifespan of two decades or less, machines with no function left to fulfill, simply awaiting someone's discovery of the proper mode of burial. It is difficult to look at this landscape, or to reflect on it, without confronting one's failures as a writer.[21]

During and after my tour of the site, the only words that made even a start at capturing the place came from William Blake, who was, of course, writing of nineteenth-century English textile mills:

> And did the Countenance Divine
> Shine forth upon our clouded hills?
> And was Jerusalem builded here
> Among the dark Satanic Mills?[22]

The reference to Jerusalem addresses the yearning for better lives, the hope for a better world, that drove many Hanford people who took genuine pride in their contribution to a key national enterprise. Calling the reactors and separation plants "dark Satanic Mills" is not the same as calling the workforce that built them Satanic.

When we toured Hanford, we had an extremely likable guide, who was not only helpful, but crusty and charming. After the tour, I sent him a copy of my book, *The Legacy of Conquest*, in which I had briefly discussed the ways in which nuclear enterprise fits into a general pattern of western history, in which optimism and impulse are followed by a complicated mess. Our Hanford guide wrote back, thanked me for the book, and then said that he had had a memorable time reading the nuclear section, after his anti-emetic took effect. Now if the mild-mannered pages in *Legacy of Conquest* sent this man in search of his anti-emetic, just imagine what high-powered nausea-suppressor he would be driven to by anyone calling decommissioned reactors "dark Satanic Mills." The problems posed by millions of gallons of radioactive waste, of leaks and releases over the years since 1943, of eight dead reactors, and of many retired processing facilities are perfectly dreadful. And yet I very much liked our guide at Hanford, as I did the woman, of the latex girdle story, who had so enjoyed her nuclear work.

This personal dilemma of emotions in conflict is the main difficulty that confronts us in the whole business of appraising the significance of Hanford, and of all of Western American history. In the welter of confusion and disputed evidence, there are two salient facts about Hanford. First, the World War II exercise of beginning from scratch, with no models or precedents to draw from, with no guarantees of success or failure, and, in two years, completing a plutonium production reactor and a bunch of other facilities, is nothing short of astonishing, as human achievements go. If the people who had a part in the initial building of Hanford took great pride in their work, then surely, in the aerobic exercise for the mind that is the New Western History, we can share their point of view long enough to understand why they felt such satisfaction.

But then there is the second indisputable fact. This achievement rested on the taking of any number of shortcuts, placing high-level wastes in tanks that were supposed to be temporary, dumping other wastes directly into cribs and trenches in the soil. In spite of those shortcuts, the people in charge of Hanford continued to make pious declarations of their devotion to safety, and their constant carefulness in working with the dangerous force of radioactivity. "Safety is virtually a religion at Hanford," the Hanford annual report told us in 1987. "All design was governed by three rules," General Leslie Groves, head of the Manhattan Project wrote in his memoirs, and the first of those rules was "safety first against both known and unknown hazards." And yet the documents released, beginning in February 1986, tell another story entirely. It is everyone's challenge today, given equally to reporters, historians, and general citizens, to figure out the relationship between declared good intentions and troubling practices, to put together a picture of western history in which we see, simultaneously and fairly, the bad news and the good news, the occasions for admiration and for regret.[23]

As a child, I showed an early aversion to conventional myths and legends of Western America by becoming distressed during cowboy movies.

What troubled me about the cowboy sagas was this: inevitably, the boys made a mess, shooting up the saloon, smashing bottles, breaking windows, shattering the mirror over the bar; and then, at the peak of the chaos, they mounted their horses and rode away. Normal moviegoers could imaginatively ride away with them, but I stayed back in town, back at the saloon, looking at the clutter, and wondering, "Who on earth is going to get stuck cleaning this up?" In no western films of my acquaintance do the cowboys go a certain distance out of town, come to a sudden halt, and say to each other: "Good heavens, boys, do you realize what a mess we've left behind? We really ought to go back there and pick up all that broken glass."

And that is why the 1990s seem to me potentially the greatest, and most heroic, decade in the American West. Now the moment that never came in western movies is occurring all over the region. We are, in various ways and places, recognizing that we have both inherited and made problems that we can no longer ride away from; we are realizing that we must address ourselves to cleaning those messes up. The widespread acceptance of that conclusion is what makes me, in fact, an optimist, in spite of the fact that the media has labeled the New Western History glum.

Not only am I encouraged by the honest recognition of messes, I am loyal enough to certain western myths and symbols to be a great fan of the Sons of the Pioneers. When they sang, "Whoopee ti yi yo, Get along little dogies, It's your misfortune, And none of my own," they put the spotlight on the central political, economic, social, and moral problem of Western American history. "It's your misfortune, and none of my own" has been a guiding principle in western expansion, from the displacing of the Indians, to the habits of hydraulic miners freely washing silt and rocks into the fields of farmers downstream.[24] True to the patterns of continuity in Western American history, we have applied the "your misfortune, and none of my own" philosophy to the issues raised by nuclear enterprise, letting Hanford's neighbors, including small children and infants, carry the burdens of atomic risk. But the scale of the radioactive waste problem has finally broken down this attempt to quarantine misfortune. The costs involved in cleaning up—estimated as high as $200 billion—alone tie us together; nothing short of secession can release any individual or section of this nation from our collective burden.

The failure to reckon with nuclear waste is a national shortcoming, even an international one. Nuclear waste is everyone's misfortune, and while that is a burden and a trial, it is also our common ground. Writing his Manhattan Project memoirs, General Groves took an odd turn in the chapters on Hanford, dropped the subjects of engineering and science, and devoted several pages to the experience of women in the war years at the plutonium plant. Life at Hanford meant "isolation, security restrictions, spartan living conditions, monotony," Groves said, which was certainly true. And then he took an unexpected jump to a standing cliché of western history: "It was perhaps hardest, in many ways, on the women."[25] It is odd, but not altogether surprising, to see this tired old notion at work again in the reconstruction of a latter-day frontier. It was a standing stereotype of traditional frontier studies, the idea that western experience demonstrated, over and over again, the physical and mental frailty of women.

General Groves then dwelt on the hardships of women: for instance, their disillusionment on arriving at an isolated, dusty town, and then facing a long bus ride to the distant camp barracks. Curiously enough, the hardships and disappointments that Groves handed over to the women seem to have afflicted men equally. True, there were a few gender-specific problems, such as an absence of women's clothing stores and the existence of only one inadequate beauty parlor. The degree to which Leslie Groves chose to assign the tribulations posed by Hanford to a group of inconvenienced women is, nonetheless, striking. What one wants to say now to Grove's gender-assignment of hardship is this: the nuclear record encapsulated in Hanford's history has been hard on everyone, on men, on women, on patriots, on social critics, on workers far down on the employment hierarchy, and even hard on General Groves and others of his rank. "It's your misfortune, and none of my own" simply no longer applies.

Our fortunes, as well as our misfortunes, are intertwined; the western past and the western present are tied together; the nation at large must learn to take the history of the American West as seriously as it has taken the history of the Northeast and the South. Tracing the significance of Hanford in the American past is one route to the writing of what western American historian Donald Worster has called "a deeper history than any of us has yet imagined."[26] This version of western history will make a compelling case for the region's central significance in our times, and, in the textbooks, Mark Hanna will quietly yield ground to Hanford.

Notes

*This essay previously appeared under the same title in the Pettyjohn book *Washington Comes of Age: The State in the National Experience* (WSU Press, 1992).

1. Karen Dorn Steele, "Hanford: America's Nuclear Graveyard," *Bulletin of the Atomic Scientists* 45 (October 1989):15-23, and "Making Warheads: Hanford's Bitter Legacy," *ibid.*, 44 (January/February 1988):17-23; S.L. Sanger with Robert W. Mull, *Hanford and the Bomb: An Oral History of World War II* (Seattle: Living History Press, 1989); Paul Loeb, *Nuclear Culture: Living and Working in the World's Largest Atomic Complex* (New York: Coward, McCann, and Geoghegan, 1982). The Hanford Education and Action League, in Spokane, Washington, has been active in the study of Hanford; I am grateful, especially to Jim Thomas, for his suggestions.

2. On the New Western History, see Patricia Nelson Limerick, Michael P. Malone, Gerald Thompson, and Elliot West, "Western History: Why the Past May Be Changing," *Montana: The Magazine of Western History* 3 (Summer 1990):60-76. Among historians, the most active investigator of Hanford has been Michele Stenehjem. See, for example, her "Pathways of Radioactive Contamination: Examining the History of the Hanford Nuclear Reservation," *Environmental Review* 13 (Fall 1989):95-112, and "Historical Access to the Hanford Record: Problems in Investigating the Past," *Columbia: The Magazine of Northwest History* 3 (Winter 1989/1990):29-35. Also see, Wanda Briggs, "Historian's Search Details Hanford's First Chapters," *Tri-City Herald*, June 12, 1989, and "Thyroid Studies to Start in Spring," *ibid.*, October 3, 1989.

3. "There's Good News Today: U.S. to Build $45 Million A-Plant Near Denver," *Denver Post*, March 23, 1951; "Denver Gets 45-Million-Dollar Atomic Plant," *Rocky Mountain News*, March 24, 1951; "Atomic Plant Fine for Denver, Most Agree: 'Town as Dull as This Could Stand a Few Split Atoms,'" *ibid.*

4. Tour, February 27, 1989, Hanford Nuclear Reservation.

5. John Wheeler, in Sanger, *Hanford and the Bomb*, xiv.

6. Ray Allen Billington and Martin Ridge, *Westward Expansion: A History of the American Frontier*, 5th ed. (New York: MacMillan, 1982), viii.

7. Tour, February 27, 1989, Hanford Nuclear Reservation.

8. Interview in *Something to Win the War: A Videotape on Hanford's History.*

9. *Ibid.*

10. Annette Heriford, in Sanger, *Hanford and the Bomb*, 7.

11. Patricia Nelson Limerick, *Desert Passages: Encounters with the American Deserts* (Albuquerque: University of New Mexico Press, 1985).

12. One can see this attitude at work in Leslie Groves, *Now It Can Be Told: The Story of the Manhattan Project* (New York: Harper, 1962); and Arthur Compton, *Atomic Quest: A Personal Narrative* (New York: Oxford University Press, 1986).

13. "Denver Gets 45-Million-Dollar Atomic Plant," *Rocky Mountain News*, March 24, 1951.

14. Robert E. Bubenzer, in Sanger, *Hanford and the Bomb*, 69-73.

15. Michael J. Lawrence, in U.S. Department of Energy, Richland Operations Office, *Hanford Quarterly* 1, no. 1 (October-December 1985).

16. *Hanford Annual Report*, 1987.

17. Stenehjem, "Historical Access to the Hanford Record," 29.

18. Steele, "Hanford's Bitter Legacy," 19; Stenehjem, "Pathways to Radioactive Contamination," 102-03. No official statement of purpose for the Green Run has been made to date.

19. *Hanford Annual Report*, 1987.

20. Bob Sheahan, quoted in Chris Bowman, "Lifetime Spent under a Cloud: Nuke-Test Neighbors Blame US," *Sacramento Bee*, May 31, 1987.

21. Fortunately, landscape photographer Peter Goin's book, *Nuclear Landscapes* (Baltimore: Johns Hopkins University Press, 1991), has pictures of Hanford powerful enough to communicate much of this landscape.

22. Preface to *Milton*, in Geoffrey Keynes, ed., *Blake: Complete Writings* (London: Oxford University Press, 1972), 481.

23. *Hanford Annual Report*, 1987; Groves, *Now It Can Be Told*, 83.

24. Richard White's textbook on Western American history pays tribute to the theme with the title *"It's Your Misfortune and None of My Own": A History of the American West* (Norman: University of Oklahoma Press, 1991).

25. Groves, *Now It Can Be Told*, 90.

26. Donald Worster, "Summing Up: Grounds for Identity," plenary address at the symposium, "Centennial West: Celebrations of the Northern Tier States's Heritage," Billings, Montana, June 24, 1989.

IV
Two Faces West:
The Development Myth in
Canada and the United States

Donald Worster
(University of Kansas)

A LOCOMOTIVE WHISTLES SHRILLY as it approaches a small town on the North American prairie. Along the tracks ahead stands a grain elevator on one side, a wooden station and a brick hotel on the other, behind them a checkerboard of streets marking off a community's life. On the outskirts of the town a woman peers from her farmhouse window, watching the train approach against a background of snow-crusted mountains. A man plowing a field, preparing to plant wheat, stops to watch and listen too. All these images have been popular in the Canadian and American West for more than a century. They are signs of what the two nations have in common—a landscape, a technology, a set of hopes, a story of development.

These two nations share other signs and memories as powerful as that prairie scene, including the sound of a beaver slapping its tail on a lake; the sight of bison streaming over a wide plain, and of their carcasses lying in the grass; of cattle bawling and shoving in, taking the bison's place; of oil wells pumping wealth from the ground, smelly and viscous; of gold dust glinting in the bottom of a miner's pan, mixed with gravel and snow melt. Both nations have displaced proud Indian peoples who once occupied the land and are now living on the margins, expected to turn to farming or manufacturing to survive. Both nations have witnessed a diverse immigration of Chinese railroad workers, Russian peasant farmers, French or Spanish missionaries in black robes, and millions of English-speaking poor people.

Despite all these commonalities, however, interesting differences have separated the Canadian from the American West. There have been differences, for example, in the Indian policies followed on either side of the border and in the degree of violence that has occurred between native inhabitants and white Europeans. Historians have compared the "Wild West" of America to the "Mild West" of Canada.[1] Rather than treading down that familiar path, I want to suggest another comparison between our two countries, and between the two Wests within them, by focusing on a seemingly more innocuous subject, the idea of development. Despite its prosaic if not trite sound, that idea offers a fresh, provocative basis for exploring our differences.

Canadian historians, like their American counterparts, have frequently told the story of the West as a story of development, writing extensively on the development of railroads, industry, agriculture, towns and cities, culture, religion, and universities. That fact may not seem very noteworthy, but I want to argue that it is highly significant. Ubiquity, familiarity, and habit have all made us indifferent toward what we have been saying or about how we have imagined the past. There has been too little critical inquiry on either side of the Canadian-U.S. border into what the word development has meant, into its darker implications, including the costs of development both for people and nature, or into the question of how well the development idea accounts for our distinctive national and regional characteristics.

Both Canadians and Americans have given one fundamental meaning to development from which all other meanings derive: development refers to exploiting the land to get the wealth out of it. "Undeveloped" land is land that lacks roads, buildings, or mines; it is land that produces little or no profit. There is very little difference between the two nations in this regard. When the two Wests were at an early stage in that exploitation, they both saw themselves as economically underdeveloped, or put more positively, as economically developing—the advancing edge of the world's first new nations. Today, on the other hand, both Wests see themselves as having mature, well-financed, and well-developed economies, though both also describe themselves as still developing in the sense that all regions and nations see themselves as tirelessly driving to turn nature into wealth, with no end in sight.

Even on this basic level of economics, however, the word development has had a complicated set of meanings. Development first came into common use in the nineteenth century, an era that was awestruck by advances in biological science that had begun to show how organisms mature and evolve, not only growing in size but changing in form, passing from youth to maturity or from the one-celled amoeba to the multi-celled plant or animal. By analogy, human social development was supposed to follow a similar progression of stages, as natural as the passage from the embryo to the adult, starting with the savage life and ending up with the English gentleman. This idea of development as the progressive law of nature inspired not only the Victorians, but also such social philosophers as Karl Marx and Friedrich Engels, for whom history was an inexorable advance from primitive society to industrial capitalism and on to a socialist future, all stages in the technological domination of nature. According to Gustavo Esteva, "development became the central category of Marx's work: revealed as a historical process that unfolds with the same necessary character of natural laws."[2]

In the nineteenth century, development also became a transitive verb, with humans as the subject, nature as the object. That is, it became man's proper role on earth to "develop nature," meaning to make nature over into useful, marketable commodities. Undomesticated nature, civilized people believed, was incomplete and embryonic, a possibility waiting to be achieved. The special role of humankind was to release nature from its slumber, awaken its potentialities, and enable it to reach its grand destiny, which was nothing less than service to our own species' comfort and well-being. This second use of the word as a transitive verb first became popular in the outposts of the British Empire, particularly Australia and Canada, and later in the United States. The Australian scholar H.W. Arndt, who has written an interesting history of the word, quotes an 1846 article in the *Canadian Economist:* "Canada is now thrown upon her own resources, and if she wishes to prosper, these resources must be developed."[3] Challenged to achieve a measure of independence, Canadians understood that they must become an active agency in nature, no longer content to buy many of their necessities from England.

Development thus became a compelling international myth about the growth of nation-states. By myth I mean simply that it told a popular story about origins and destiny, one progressing from primitive life to civilization, from the simple to the complex, from an inferior colonial dependency to nation-state maturity—a heroic story that both capitalists and communists could share because it expressed their common ideals. The myth was part of the justification of European imperialism—helping other peoples achieve their own state-based identities and secure places in the global economy. It told what all people's attitudes and behavior toward the rest of nature ought to be, especially among those backward areas far from the centers of civilization. By the time of World War II the myth of development had spread everywhere, replacing older traditions of stasis and equilibrium, and wherever it went it offered a similar formula for improving the life of the nation and its people, one measured in higher per capita income and, so the promise goes, greater happiness and moral enlightenment.[4]

Because the United States and Canada emerged as nations during the very era when development was becoming the dominant political myth, their national histories were both conceived in terms of the myth. However, not one but two stories emerged to describe North American national development. Historians have analyzed them in isolation from one another, but I want to consider them together as different versions of the same myth. Both predict the final success of industrial capitalism, but then they veer off into different emphases and implications; and those differences reveal a great deal about each nation, especially how each has envisioned its place in history and how each has conceived of its relation with nature in the New World. We should not exaggerate the differences, for there are common elements, nor should we minimize their continuing power and persistence in the writing of history.

The first of those two stories may be summed up in these famous words: "The existence of an area of free land, its continuous recession, and the advance of American settlement westward, explain American development."[5] They come, of course, from Frederick Jackson Turner, whose frontier thesis, first presented in 1893, spawned an influential American school of development thinking. Turner was mainly interested in the origins of liberal democracy, which was an American invention in his view, and he saw it deriving from the extraordinary potential of the American land—its untapped abundance. True to his age, Turner portrayed nature as undeveloped raw material inviting a series of resource exploiters, beginning with traders and trappers, followed by ranchers, miners, and farmers, a succession of single individuals who gave way eventually to a more impersonal set of exploiting *institutions* in the form of cities, factories, corporations, and the nation-state. Turner accepted this growing exploitation of nature, even celebrated it, although ironically at the same time he celebrated the American love affair with a glorious pristine wilderness.

The most distinctive theme in Turner's story is the notion that development in America is always starting over, like an organism that returns repeatedly to its embryonic state. "All peoples show development," Turner acknowledged, but only in America did development become not a single linear process but a whole series of new beginnings, a process of birth and rebirth. "American social development," he pointed out, "has been continually beginning over again on the frontier."[6] Each new frontier offered an exhilarating moment of what we might call "un-development," when complex European civilization reverted to a more archaic life. From that moment came a sense of freedom from distant centers of power, a freedom that spawned democracy, egalitarianism, and individualism. Regrettably, Turner wrote, the rebirthing opportunities eventually must end, and development must become a fixed linear progression here as in Europe, leading to a single common destiny. Turner found that outcome disturbing because increasingly the American scene would become unfriendly to the freedom and democracy that had come out of the primitive wilderness. He could only hope that what had been so often born and reborn would not quickly fade away.[7]

North of the Great Lakes we find quite another story of development appearing. Often referred to as metropolitanism, it was the creation of such famous Canadian historians as Harold Innis, Arthur Lower, and Donald Creighton, writing in the 1920s and 1930s, and more recently of Maurice Careless. All were as fascinated as Turner with the great interior of North America—its forests, grasslands, waterways, and wildlife—and with the dramatic changes in the natural environment following European settlement. However, the Canadians could find none of Turner's multiple new beginnings in the wilderness; instead, they saw development as a straightforward march, controlled and directed by metropolitan forces far removed from the interior. The march had begun in Europe, and it was Europe's urban centers that continued to set the pace, along with the rising Canadian centers of Toronto and Montreal. Cities defined what development meant, they made sure that development was secure and orderly, and they propelled the frontier through its various stages of progress, from gathering beaver pelts to planting wheat.[8]

Despite this strikingly different emphasis on continuity with Europe, Canada's historians seem to have been at times as nationalistic and exceptionalist as those in the United States. For them as for Turner, the natural environment played a major role in creating a national identity, giving Canada a peculiar place among the older nations of the world. Their wilderness condition forced Canadians to become harvesters of raw natural resources called staples. "The trade in staples," wrote Harold Innis, ". . . has been responsible for various peculiar [i.e., distinctive] tendencies in Canadian development." Beaver was one of the most important of those staple products, he argued, and beaver had made a unique nation to the north, while fish, lumber, and wheat would contribute to its further growth.[9] If Canada looked to England for its model of economic progress, it also depended on those staples taken from and determined by nature. To be sure, in Innis's view as in Turner's, European technology must eventually overcome environmental factors, bringing industrial development. "The geographic unity of Canada which resulted from the fur trade," he wrote, "became less noticeable with the introduction of capitalism and the railroads."[10] Their effect was to free the country, region by region, from a dependence on the local products of nature while increasing that on technology and distant markets. Nonetheless, Canada's special historical relation with nature in the New World would never altogether lose its significance. The primitive extraction of fur and pine would leave its trace on Canadian identity.

Another leader of the metropolitan school, Donald Creighton, echoed this ambiguity about Canada's relation to the Old World. Following the standard terms of European development, he argued that Canada had emerged as a vibrant "commercial empire" by exploiting the vast Saint Lawrence river system.[11] The phrase "commercial empire" indicated that the country was not traditional in its relation with nature; it was modern and capitalistic, with businessmen rather than armies at its center. Yet those businessmen, Creighton suggested, even while following the established European model, had their lives shaped in subtle ways by the power of nature; the very form of the Saint Lawrence waterway, for instance, gave shape to their enterprise.

Like Turner's frontier story, this metropolitan story has had its own rich mythic potential. Canadians have liked to describe themselves as gathering staples from a vast northern country while becoming spiritually part of what they exploit. A nation pursuing capitalistic gain with great fervor, all the while remaining faithful to an ancient cultural heritage. A nation bringing law and order to the continent while obeying the laws of nature. A nation of traditionalists, unlike the Americans, yet like the Americans creating a distinctive civilization from the Europeans. While Turner hoped his countrymen would always remember their wilderness past as they made more and more money, the Canadians hoped that they would remain true to their European heritage while doing the same. Although both myths ended up in exactly the same place—in a powerful industrial-capitalist economy ransacking the land for raw materials—they arrived there with different memories of where they had been, of what nature had allowed them to do, and of what their relation to the Old World had been.

For reasons that Canada's historians understand better than anyone else, Turner's frontierism never quite caught on north of the border, although it has had a few advocates.[12] On the other hand, the metropolitan school of Canadian history has recently begun to creep south and influence a few American scholars. A leading example is William Cronon's recent book *Nature's Metropolis: Chicago and the Great West*, published in 1991, which is clearly indebted to the staples history of Innis, the commercial empire history of Creighton, the forest history of Lower, and the urban history of Maurice Careless.[13] Like his Canadian teachers, Cronon shifts the development focus from the frontier to the city, repudiating Turner's legacy.[14] He puts ambitious capitalists at the center of the story, men who set out to remake the face of the land, becoming developers on a continental scale, building railroads from Chicago into the prairies while using the Great Lakes as a supplementary mode of transportation. They transform the broad countryside into a mechanized, commercial system of agriculture and forestry, and they bring the land's products into the city for mass consumption.

Cronon's book is an important work not only in the new frontier and western history but also in the field of environmental history, which deals with human relations with nature. Among other things, he is concerned with the impact that urban people have had on nature, with the ecological consequences of their consumption. In keeping with the conventions of development thinking, however, Cronon portrays nature through most of the book as passive before the onslaught of boosters, businessmen, and consumers. Nature provides a flow of commodities, but in that role it is responsive to whatever demands men make, never becoming an active or disruptive obstacle in their way or forcing them to adapt. Nature does not wreak any vengeance, despite the many ravages committed by capital. The urban consumers, for all their ignorance and indifference toward the land that supports them, apparently suffer no disruption when they deplete the land. In the face of capitalism's overwhelming power, nature rapidly disappears from the scene, becoming transformed into what Cronon calls "second nature," an artificial world designed according to "the logic of capital."[15] Like the nineteenth-century's natural law of development, Cronon's logic of capital moves across the landscape like an iron horse of destiny, and so the book suggests, it is irrational and futile to oppose its progress.

Yet despite his fascination with the transforming logic of capital, Cronon also describes, with all the ambivalence of the Canadian metropolitan historians, a permanent legacy of nature for American cultural life. That legacy is a new region we now call the Midwest. The "logic of nature" turns out to be as important as the logic of capital to the making of that region. Corn and hogs coming into the metropolis from Iowa farmlands are the products of ancient prairie soils, while the beef cattle coming in from the grasslands to the west and southwest are the products of lands that are too dry to become a corn belt. The wood that furnishes housing for Chicago's immigrant multitudes is the product of the white pine forests of Michigan and Wisconsin, which have their own value and reason for existing. Depleting or destroying any of these environmental support systems must have a profound impact on the fate of the Midwest. Nature is, therefore, not truly passive before the onslaught of economic development; capital says to nature, here is what we intend to do in this place, and nature replies, here is what you *may* do. So a reader of the book may find in its narrative more than one conclusion. As in the writing of so many of Canada's great metropolitan historians, an ambivalence between admiring the invading, unstoppable power of the metropolis and admiring the absorbing, shaping power of nature lies at the heart of Cronon's book.

Both of these influential schools of North American history, frontierism and metropolitanism, focus on the process of economic and social development. Both define development as man's inexorable conquest over nature, of ever greater levels of wealth accumulation, of an increasing degree of technological control. Both see the process leading to the triumph of industrial capitalism on a global scale, and both hint of a withering away of national and regional distinctions. Then, unexpectedly, both schools of history reveal in culture and in nature, working together, an alternative to international homogeneity. In contrast to the classical development myth, both testify that people have not wanted exactly the same thing, that Canadians and Americans have wanted different things— different relationships with the wilderness, different relations with Old World culture, different relations with capital. They also suggest that nature does not always give people what they want, that nature has a continuing power over our lives, a power the development myth never allowed for. Thus, according to our historians, environmental differences (soil, climate, vegetation, the flow of waters) as well as cultural differences separate our two nations from each other, as they separate us from the European centers of civilization; and such differences also show up *within* the two nations, creating many distinctive regions, like the prairie West, out of a single continental whole.

Let us now turn to the westernmost part of North America to see how the same international mythology of development has come into this country too but, here as elsewhere, has had surprising, unpredictable outcomes. Again, the story takes an unanticipated turn or two, despite the spread of those homogenizing railroads and grain elevators and oil wells. By the western regions I mean the Canada that lies beyond the Shield, beginning with Manitoba and going on to British Columbia; and I mean the United States that lies west of the Mississippi Valley, beginning with the Great Plains and stretching on to the Pacific Coast.[16] Neither has developed into a form that any European thinker, or for that matter any early historian from Ontario or Wisconsin, ever quite anticipated.

If we take the coming of transcontinental railroads as signaling the beginning of full-fledged capitalist development in these two regions, then we have on the American side of the border the critical date of 1869, the year of the golden spike, and on the Canadian side the year 1885, the year of the plain iron spike—a mere sixteen-year gap. Before those dates there had been a great deal of exploring, trapping, mining, even some farming; but the railroads were to be the magical key that would release the land from its bondage.[17] In 1862 the Americans passed the Homestead Act, and ten years later the Canadians passed the Dominion Lands Act, both of which aimed to give land to family homesteaders. In each country the official plan of development required the enticement of immigrants out of Europe to resettle on New World soil, raising crops to sell to people in eastern cities, and buying finished goods from those cities. Thus, wheat was as critical as railroads. As a further part of the plan, each nation set up protective tariffs for their eastern manufacturers to secure an advantage in selling finished goods to western farmers.

Canadians call this triad of policies—a transcontinental railroad, an immigration and homesteading program, and a protective tariff for manufacturers—the "National Policy" and they credit Prime Minister John A. Macdonald with implementing it, though graciously acknowledging that he borrowed most of it from the United States.[18] It was not truly an American invention any more than it was Canadian; in its broad outlines the plan followed the international logic of capitalist development.[19]

If we look closely at the two development plans, we can detect small but intriguing differences. Canada, for example, was more accommodating to collective settlement, so that closely knit ethnic groups like the

Doukhobors could settle here easily.[20] Canada also was more friendly to rancher-capitalists than the United States government initially was. As David Breen has argued, Alberta set up a generous policy of leasing land on a large scale to cattlemen, though within a few decades, as more farmers arrived in the province and as ranchers in the United States got more recognition, the differences became harder to spot.[21] The railroad picture is more complicated in the United States where many private corporations competed against each other and where no government-owned railroad was ever attempted.[22] With such exceptions, the two nations did set off on similar paths to make the western part of the continent over into a land of open opportunity.

Here is how nature thwarted their grand designs. In the western part of the United States, the land proved far too arid to suit the original plans of railroad executives or government officials. Their logic of national development met a rugged desert and its semi-arid fringe, and it began to run off the tracks. Even Turner, with his vision of a continually rejuvenating life in the wilderness, ran off the tracks. Early on, he had written that it would be useful to know how environment played a part in "determining our lines of development," words that would later come back to haunt him.[23] Three years after his essay on the significance of the frontier, Turner discovered the writings of the explorer John Wesley Powell, who described a West that was more arid than anything Turner had ever experienced.[24] Powell was not only the first American to make a comprehensive analysis of those arid conditions in the West (published in 1878), he was also one of the first to envision America as a land of diverse regions shaped by natural conditions. Turner himself, after reading Powell, began looking into the ways in which his abstract "wilderness" was a complicated mosaic of natural environments, with diverse implications for development, though he could never quite figure out how to talk about that unfamiliar country beyond the hundredth meridian.

Other Americans did learn how, but doing so required a major revision in their thinking about development. The most serious weakness lay in the Homestead Act and its ambitious promise of an agricultural empire, a dream coming out of places like Illinois, Ohio, and Virginia, and drawing on older European models. Capital and labor together could not find a way to make that dream real in places like Idaho and Arizona. Both interests were forced to turn to the federal government as the chief organizer and bankroller of agricultural development in the West if they were to go forward. Beginning in 1902 the U.S. government undertook to reclaim arid lands through large irrigation projects. To a degree unprecedented in the East, the West henceforth became the protégé of the federal government, the beneficiary of what now, at modern prices, amounts to several hundred billion dollars' worth of infrastructure investment.

That unanticipated outcome was ironic in the extreme. Compared to Canadians, Americans were not accustomed to looking favorably on a strong, centralized state. Admitting their dependence on that state meant contradicting their self-image of frontier individualism and freedom of enterprise, but the environmental conditions of the West forced them to do just that—to adopt radical new policies, to look eastward for water. Consequently, the real American West, the West of fact rather than romance, became the domain of the Bureau of Reclamation and the Bureau of Land Management more than of Wyatt Earp or Billy the Kid.

One might call this outcome a triumph for metropolitanism, since it was the federal capital that henceforth began to lead and control western development. No more than the western frontiersman or the Chicago capitalist, however, was the federal bureaucracy prepared to cope with the western environment. It is still not prepared to do so today. After nearly a century of federally funded water projects, the American West remains highly vulnerable to aridity: on the Great Plains, where another dust bowl disaster is never far off; in the southwestern deserts, which are still deserts the last time anyone looked; and indeed around every western city except those located in the narrow, humid coastal strip of Oregon and Washington. The dream of developing the West into an empire inhabited by millions of agricultural producers has not come true on anything like the scale the dreamers hoped, and even where agriculture has succeeded, as it has in California's Central Valley, it remains extremely vulnerable to the limits of nature and to its own excesses: dams are silting up, soil salinity is increasing, the heavy pesticide use associated with irrigation is meeting public resistance, and there are fiercely competing claims on the limited supply of water. As other countries have discovered, water development is a far more uncertain, destructive, and expensive undertaking than we once thought— any of us, but the metropolitan elites most of all.[25]

Canada too has built a number of dams, like the Peace River and Bow-Saskatchewan projects, but there is no equivalent of the Bureau of Reclamation in that country, nor anything like the hydraulic civilization that has appeared south of the border along the Colorado, Missouri, or Columbia rivers. There has not been much of an aridity problem there either. Aside from the little patch known as Palliser's Triangle, which is not truly arid, Canada's West has not required so profound an adjustment to the problem of dryness.

Nonetheless, nature has played a powerful role in the pace and success of development in western Canada just as it has in the western United States. Up there, the great obstacle to an agricultural empire has come more from a high latitude and a short growing season rather than a lack of moisture, but the obstacle has been intensely real all the same.[26] With the annexation of Rupert's Land in 1870, an immense country seemed suddenly available for rural development. Toronto elites imagined a future West that would be the home of a hundred million people, that would surpass the country to the south in size, stability, enlightenment, and prosperity, that would become the world center of an invigorated British Empire. As Doug Owram has shown, that unbounded optimism began to disintegrate by the mid-1880s, as it came under attack by disillusioned westerners themselves. In Owram's words, "the great partnership which was supposed to develop between the metropolitan center and the hinterland was rejected by the hinterland even before it had been fully formed."[27] Ever since that first moment of reassessment, western Canadians have doubted that the eastern provinces really understand their situation—the hard, physical reality of creating a life on the prairies and in the mountains—or sympathize as much as they should. Subsequently, the Canadian West went on to seek a separate identity, more local control over its resources, and a closer fit to the land. To be sure, much settlement occurred after those dark days of the 1880s and 1890s; so-called "improved land" in Manitoba, Saskatchewan, and Alberta increased from less than 300 thousand acres in 1881 to nearly 60 million acres in 1931.[28] However, as impressive an achievement as this expansion was, it never represented a great imperial power base.

Still another way in which development had to be radically rethought came from land ownership in the West. The original idea in the United States was that development involved turning all the land into fee-simple private property, bounded by sturdy fences, from the East Coast all the way to West Coast. That plan broke down; it did not get over the Rocky Mountains intact. Thirty years after President Abraham Lincoln signed the Homestead Act, a monument to the private property ideal, another Congress gave another President the authority to withdraw lands from entry to safeguard vulnerable watersheds and secure a timber supply.[29] That act, which Marion Clawson and Burnell Held have called "one of the most important land administration measures ever undertaken in the United

States," eventually led to a national forest system covering nearly 200 million acres.[30] In the 1930s virtually all homesteading, and thus all further settlement of the public domain, came to an end, leaving much of the West in the hands of the federal government. Today, the federal government owns approximately one-third of the entire nation, making it the country's biggest landowner by far and the dominant power over national as well as western development. In some western states as much as fifty or even eighty percent of the land is public domain.[31]

Again, the impetus behind this change of course came partly from nature. The same environmental conditions that made federal water projects necessary, if agriculture was to succeed, required the preserving of watersheds from deforestation by private timber companies. Lands that could not be irrigated could not be homesteaded; therefore, they could not become fee-simple rural estates. Most of the public domain lies where nature has made the land too dry or too cold for agricultural settlement. What is more important is that these extraordinary changes in American land policy came about because of dramatic changes in peoples' attitudes toward private land ownership, and indeed toward the whole capitalist logic of development. By the 1890s many citizens had begun to worry about where that logic was leading—to a landscape depleted and degraded, they feared, by frontier exploiters and metropolitan businessmen.

We call this reaction the conservation movement and note that it grew out of outrage over the decline of American forests and wildlife. Organizations like the Audubon Society and the Sierra Club appeared in those years that produced the first land withdrawals, and they supported a permanent federal responsibility for controlling the effects of unbridled development. No one contemplating the West in 1869, when the first trains began running triumphantly across the continent, foresaw any of this change in public mood, any more than they understood the limits of the western land itself. They could not have imagined the intense reaction against privatization and exploitation of land that would begin to flare up within a few decades; nor foresee a future West perpetually under the management of federal resource agencies. The idea of federal subsidies to railroad construction was a familiar idea, but not a vast federal ownership and management of the land in perpetuity.

The Canadian government took a strikingly different course in land ownership, one that I believe has never received sufficient attention by historians in either country. Ottawa did not remain the major landowner in the Canadian West; in the North, it did, but not in the West. In 1930 the federal government turned over all its lands, except a few parks, to the western provinces. For the previous sixty years those lands had been federal property, the so-called "Crown lands," acquired from the Hudson's Bay Company in 1870. British Columbia was an exception to that pattern; its Crown lands became the provincial government's responsibility immediately upon joining the Confederation.[32] As other provinces formed, they too wanted the same local control over resources that British Columbia exercised, but for a long time their pleas were ignored. The "National Policy" of development, directed from far-away Ottawa, allowed the prairie provinces little say about railroad grants, agricultural settlement, or timber and mineral extraction. In 1930 that situation abruptly shifted. Ottawa proclaimed that it had fulfilled its major development goals in the West and handed over its huge estate to Winnipeg, Regina, and Edmonton.[33]

Exactly the same case could have been made in the American West, and around 1930 it was indeed being made, impatiently and stridently, by western state governors. They could claim the same kind of precedent as their counterparts to the north, for the states to the East, as well as the state of Texas among their own number, had not become or remained federal property for very long. But despite strenuous arguments, no handover occurred. The American public would not let it occur, then or at any time thereafter. They wanted to leave the federal government in charge of those acres simply because they trusted it more than they trusted the western states, with their open-door attitudes toward mining and timber companies. New attitudes had emerged that encouraged American public leaders to break a very old precedent, disappointing many westerners, and to assume a permanent resource stewardship in the West.

Why did such a federal responsibility emerge in the United States but not in Canada? Were the provinces such good resource stewards that the question of who to trust was never an issue? I doubt that such was the case.[34] One has only to look at the controversial record of British Columbia, where conservationists have severely criticized the cozy relation between the Ministry of Forestry and private timber companies, to see that there was reason enough to worry. The issue of conservation, however, does not seem to have even come up in Canada in 1930. The most plausible reason for that silence is that conservation was a less potent political movement in that country than in the United States, for reasons of culture and politics that invite further research. Quite tellingly, there were at the time almost no popular conservation organizations north of the 49th parallel—nothing like America's Sierra Club and the rest—to stir up debate over issues of land and conservation. In contrast, such a debate had been going on in the United States since the 1890s, and it explains why a strong federal responsibility over land emerged and why it continues down to this very day. Even as angry Sagebrush Rebels demand cession of the public domain to the states and its privatization, environmental groups like the Wilderness Society and Earth First! still fight for federal ownership.

Obviously, the federal land managers in the United States have not lived up to all of those early rosy expectations. These days they are the target of as much criticism as timber or mining companies, and for many Americans the government no longer seems to be the safe guardian of the public lands it once was. Moreover, conservation expectations themselves have changed from the late nineteenth century to the present, and changed unpredictably. A few decades back the Forest Service could not have foreseen the degree to which its historic sense of mission would be criticized by a post World War II environmental movement. Instead of aiming merely for a sustainable harvest, they now must learn to apply ecological science to land-use decisions. They must protect old-growth forests, endangered species, and millions of acres of wilderness, which was not part of their original responsibility. Nor, for that matter, do any of these conservation demands of today fit easily into the traditional logic of capitalism. Where then did they originate? From a rising affluence, which is to say from the very success of capitalism? Or do they stem from deeper cultural shifts—from fears and anxieties about the course of development and progress—that have produced a powerful challenge to capitalism? We do not really know the answer.

It is time to sum up the argument I have been making. Traditionally, both American and Canadian historians agreed that modern capitalism was where social evolution was taking us, yet both professed to find in the North American environment a powerful counterforce that gave each nation a distinctive identity in the world. Then the historians, along with government and business leaders, ran up against environmental challenges in the movement west, challenges that forced the course of development into deviations that became regions. Changing cultural attitudes toward development itself, toward capitalism and toward conservation, also forced deviations from the norm. The outcome of all those unanticipated events is a continent of diversities. The North America we see today is not the outcome of a simple linear process. Its history reveals natural obstacles that no amount of logic or technology could fully overcome and cultural turns that we cannot easily explain.

According to the classical idea of development, nature can be transformed into almost anything the human mind desires. Deserts and mountains should mean nothing. Since capital is the same universalizing force everywhere, it should be nonsensical to talk about the need to adapt to nature. Moreover, a distinctive regional West in either Canada or the United States should make no sense. The world over should become nothing but an abstract, logical hierarchy of urban centers ruling over their producing hinterlands or peripheries—a series of neat concentric circles drawn by the hand of money. The historical picture of North America, however, along with that of other parts of the earth, has been far more complicated, far more interesting, than that.

Despite the homogenizing hand of capital, regions have taken shape, just as national differences have appeared and persisted. Thus, the Canadian West has not only become different from the Canadian East, in ways that none of the metropolitan historians ever fully understood, but also has become, although often in subtle ways, different from the American West.[35] The differences stem in part from different cultural legacies brought into these two regions, but they also come from the inescapable truth that nature differs from place to place; it is not one unbroken thing, a single grand enemy to be defeated. Nature differs from east to west, and it differs from north to south. Those differences are most obvious around the Great Lakes: the Precambrian Shield lies to the north, creating a Canada of thin soil, rich forests, and mineral wealth, while on the American side a fertile savannah has given way to the corn belt, a landscape of incomparable agricultural productivity. Differences exist in the West too, and indeed they can be found from sea to shining sea.

According to the German writer Wolfgang Sachs, the idea of development "stands today like a ruin in an intellectual landscape, an outdated monument to an immodest era."[36] Whatever coherence it once had, it no longer enjoys, unless one defines it merely as increasing the gross domestic product. Once development suggested that there was, or there must be, a single cultural standard by which all people could be measured—essentially, a standard of living defined by nations like the United States, Canada, or England, and by the metropolises within those nations. No longer is that so, as people everywhere have begun to reject the notion of a single standard, for to accept such a notion would be to denigrate their history, their achievement, their cultural uniqueness. Even as a merely economic norm the idea of development is becoming more unacceptable, for it teaches an outmoded ethos of unlimited materialism and accumulation, claiming that such an ethos is a universal need or drive found among all people. Those who have questioned the universality of that ethos are, by the logic of development, irrational. Now, however, the doubters are increasing, and they have on their side all the generations who lived before the invention of development, all those who still live outside the development myth today, along with many of the great philosophers and moral teachers in history. Today the critics charge that the myth of development perpetuates exploitative attitudes toward nature, attitudes that are responsible for the global environmental crisis we find ourselves in. They say that the myth has brought problems as well as benefits, and that what it calls its benefits have often been temporary, fragile, and extremely costly in ecological terms.

Historians must agree with development's critics at least to this extent: as an idea organizing our study of the past it has not been very reliable. It has not given us a clear picture of the losses as well as gains, the failures as well as successes, the surprises that we have experienced over time. It has not accounted for the emergence of important national *and* regional differences that defy simple models or theories about a linear course of progress. Nature, we can see more clearly today than a few years back, has been a powerful, volatile force in our lives, complex beyond our understanding, never fully conquered despite all the capital, expertise, and technology we have deployed. Culture also has been an unfathomable, unpredictable force, capable of abrupt shifts in mood and value. The complicated history of nature interacting with culture in North America has made a shambles of development as a myth, as an ideology, as a program of action, and as a story to tell our children.

Notes

1. A provocative discussion of these themes appears in William G. Robbins, *Colony and Empire: The Capitalist Transformation of the American West* (Lawrence: University Press of Kansas, 1994), chapter 3. Robbins tends to see Canada as less aggressive toward its native peoples than the United States, a view some observers might dispute.

2. Gustavo Esteva, "Development," in *The Development Dictionary: A Guide to Knowledge and Power*, Wolfgang Sachs, ed., (London: Zed Books, 1992), 9.

3. H.W. Arndt, "Economic Development: A Semantic History," *Economic Development and Social Change* 29 (April 1981):461.

4. By the late nineteenth century the U.S. saw itself, and was so seen by many others, as the quintessential developed nation, essentially capitalistic but blending elements of socialism and populism. A stimulating account of this era of emergence is Martin J. Sklar, *The United States as a Developing Country: Studies in U.S. History in the Progressive Era and the 1920s* (New York: Cambridge University Press, 1992).

5. Frederick Jackson Turner, "The Significance of the Frontier in American History" [1893], *Frontier and Section: Selected Essays of Frederick Jackson Turner*, Ray Allen Billington, ed., (Englewood Cliffs, NJ: Prentice-Hall, 1961), 37.

6. Turner, "Significance of the Frontier," 38.

7. "Today," Turner wrote, "we are looking with shock upon a changed world." The best he could offer were hollow, half-hearted words: "Let us hold to our attitude of faith and courage. Let us dream as our fathers dreamt and let us make our dreams come true." In "The West and American Ideals" [1914], *Frontier and Section*, 106.

8. Among the sources I have drawn on here are J.M.S. Careless, "Frontierism, Metropolitanism, and Canadian History," *Canadian Historical Review* 35 (March 1954):1-21; Ramsay Cook, "Frontier and Metropolis: The Canadian Experience," in *The Maple Leaf Forever: Essays on Nationalism and Politics in Canada* (Toronto: Macmillan, 1971), 166-75; Carl Berger, *The Writing of Canadian History: Aspects of English-Canadian Historical Writing since 1900*, 2nd ed., (Toronto: University of Toronto Press, 1986), esp. 174-78; W.L. Morton, "Clio in Canada: The Interpretation of Canadian History," *University of Toronto Quarterly* 15 (April 1946):227-34; Carl Berger, "William Morton: The Delicate Balance of Region and Nation," in *The West and the Nation: Essays in Honor of W.L. Morton*, Carl Berger and Ramsay Cook, eds., (Toronto: McClelland and Stewart, 1976), 9-32. The continuing appeal of the metropolitan school of thought is demonstrated by the various essays in *Heartland and Hinterland: A Geography of Canada*, 2nd ed., L.D. McCann, ed. (Scarborough, Ont.: Prentice-Hall Canada, 1987).

9. On the forest staple, see A.R.M. Lower, *The North American Assault on the Canadian Forest: A History of the Lumber Trade between Canada and the United States* (Toronto: Ryerson Press, 1938); and *Great Britain's Woodyard: British American and the Timber Trade, 1763-1867* (Montreal: McGill-Queens University, 1973).

10. Harold A. Innis, *The Fur Trade in Canada* (orig. pub. 1930; New Haven, CT: Yale University Press, 1962), 401-02. See also Abraham Rotstein, "Innis: The Alchemy of Fur and Wheat," *Journal of Canadian Studies* 12 (Winter 1977):6-31; and William Christian, "The Inquisition of Nationalism," *ibid.*, 52-72. The similarity of Innis's work to modern dependency theory is the theme of Mel Watkins's "The Staple Theory Revisited," *ibid.*, 83-95.

11. See D.G. Creighton, *The Commercial Empire of the St. Lawrence, 1760-1850* (Toronto: Ryerson Press, 1939). Creighton's "environmentalism" consisted of a great river system inspiring economic development, giving as it were nature's approval to commerce. In the midst of a panegyric to the Saint Lawrence he wrote: "From the river there rose, like an exhalation, the dream of western commercial empire."

12. The reaction to Turner's thesis is summarized in Michael S. Cross, ed., *The Frontier Thesis and the Canadas: The Debate on the Impact of the Canadian Environment* (Toronto: Copp Clark, 1970). Most authorities seem to concur that the staple school (or Laurentian, or metropolitan—the names seem to be interchangeable) was influenced by Turner, but not in terms of explaining the origins of democracy. See also George F.G. Stanley, "Western Canada and the Frontier Thesis," *Canadian Historical Association Report* (Toronto: University of Toronto Press, 1940), 105-14; Paul F. Sharp, "Three Frontiers: Some Comparative Studies of Canadian, American, and Australian Settlement," *Pacific Historical Review* 24 (November 1955): 369-77; Robin Fisher, "Duff and George Go West: A Tale of Two Frontiers," *Canadian Historical Review* 68 (December 1987):501-28; and Robin W. Winks, *The Relevance of Canadian History: U.S. and Imperial Perspectives* (Toronto: Macmillan, 1979), 14, 21.

13. Much of Cronon's book seems to be an application of ideas first laid out by J.M.S. Careless in "Metropolis and Region: The Interplay between City and Region in Canadian History before 1914," *Urban History Review* (1978):99-118. "Behind the rise of frontier, hinterland or region in Canada," writes Careless, "lay the power of the metropolis, which ultimately disposed of their resource harvest, strongly fostered their expansion, and widely controlled their very existence."

14. William J. Cronon, *Nature's Metropolis: Chicago and the Great West* (New York: W. W. Norton, 1991), 46-54.

15. *Ibid.*, 85.

16. These two Wests include, of course, many diversities, as Jean Barman has argued in "The West Beyond the West: The Demography of Settlement in British Columbia," *Journal of Canadian Studies* 25 (Fall 1990):5-18.

17. The best guide to this subject is John A. Eagle, *The Canadian Pacific Railway and the Development of Western Canada, 1896-1914* (Kingston, Ont.: McGill-Queen's University Press, 1989). A splendid visual guide is Bill McKee and Georgeen Klassen, *Trail of Iron: The CPR and the Birth of the West, 1880-1930* (Vancouver, BC: Douglas and McIntyre, 1983).

18. Kenneth H. Norrie, "The National Policy and the Rate of Prairie Settlement," *Journal of Canadian Studies* 14 (Fall 1979):63-76.

19. This is not to deny that there were many ways in which Canada looked south for a model, if only out of self-defense; see, Richard Preston, ed., *The Influence of the United States on Canadian Development: Eleven Case Studies* (Durham, NC: Duke University Press, 1972).

20. C. J. Tracie, "Ethnicity and the Prairie Environment: Patterns of Old Colony Mennonite and Doukhobor Settlement," in *Man and Nature on the Prairies*, Richard Allen, ed., Canadian Plains Studies 6 (Regina, Sask.: Canadian Plains Research Center, 1976), 46-65.

21. David H. Breen, *The Canadian Prairie West and the Ranching Frontier, 1874-1924* (Toronto: University of Toronto Press, 1983), 125-27; and the same author's "The Turner Thesis and the Canadian West: A Closer Look at the Ranching Frontier," in *Essays on Western History*, Lewis H. Thomas, ed., (Edmonton: University of Alberta Press, 1976), 147-58.

22. That a conservative like Robert Borden would support nationalization of railroads would be unthinkable in the United States. See John A. Eagle, "Sir Robert Borden, Union Government and Railway Nationalization," *Journal of Canadian Studies* 10 (November 1975):59-66.

23. Turner, "Problems in American History" [1892], *Frontier and Section*, 30.

24. Ray Allen Billington, *Frederick Jackson Turner: Historian, Scholar, Teacher* (New York: Oxford University Press, 213-14. Turner read Powell's 1896 essay, "Physiographic

Regions of the United States," and thereafter began working on a "sectional" interpretation of American history, though it never achieved quite the impact that his frontier thesis had.

25. The literature on western water development is growing rapidly. For a recent overview of the environmental problems it has created, see Marc Reisner, *Cadillac Desert: The American West and Its Disappearing Water* (New York: Viking, 1986); and for historical perspectives, see Norris Hundley, Jr., *The Great Thirst: Californians and Water, 1770s-1990s* (Berkeley and Los Angeles: University of California Press, 1992); Donald Pisani, *To Reclaim a Divided West: Water, Law, and Public Policy, 1848-1902* (Albuquerque: University of New Mexico Press, 1992); and my own *Rivers of Empire: Water, Aridity, and the Growth of the American West* (New York: Oxford University Press, 1995), and "Water as a Tool of Empire," in *An Unsettled Country: Changing Landscapes of the American West* (Albuquerque: University of New Mexico Press, 1994), 31-54.

26. A fine study of Alberta settlement, with a shrewd discussion of the interactive role of the metropolis, the frontier, and the environment, is Paul Voisey, *Vulcan: The Making of a Prairie Community* (Toronto: University of Toronto Press, 1988). See also Max Gerhart Geier, "A Comparative History of Rural Community on the Northwest Plains: Lincoln County, Washington, and the Wheatland Region, Alberta, 1880-1930," Ph.D. thesis, Washington State University, 1990.

27. Doug Owram, *Promise of Eden: The Canadian Expansionist Movement and the Idea of the West, 1856-1900* (Toronto: University of Toronto Press, 1980), 220. Also, on the rise of a western identity see R. Douglas Francis, "From Wasteland to Utopia: Changing Images of the Canadian West in the Nineteenth Century," *Great Plains Quarterly* 7 (Summer 1987): 178-94; and "In Search of a Prairie Myth: A Survey of the Intellectual and Cultural Historiography of Prairie Canada," *Journal of Canadian Studies* 24 (Fall 1989):44-69.

28. R.W. Murchie, assisted by William Allen and J.F. Booth, *Agricultural Progress on the Prairie Frontier*, vol. 5, Canadian Frontiers of Settlement series (Toronto: Macmillan, 1936), 8.

29. On March 3, 1891, Congress passed the Forest Reserve Act, authorizing the President to reserve forested lands from the public domain. An earlier reservation of land took place in 1872, with the creation of Yellowstone National Park as "a public park or pleasuring ground for the benefit and enjoyment of the people."

30. Marion Clawson and Burnell Held, *The Federal Lands: Their Use and Management* (Lincoln: University of Nebraska Press, 1957), 28. The Americans had, in effect, to reinvent an institution of public ownership that was never discarded in Canada. See H.V. Nelles, *The Politics of Development: Forests, Mines, and Hydro-Electric Power in Ontario, 1849-1941* (Hamden, CT: Archon Books, 1974), 2-9.

31. The most recent figures appear in U.S. Department of Interior, Bureau of Land Management, *Public Land Statistics 1990*, vol. 175 (Washington: Government Printing Office, 1991).

32. See Robert E. Cail, *Land, Man, and the Law: The Disposal of Crown Lands in British Columbia, 1871-1913* (Vancouver: University of British Columbia Press, 1974), which is mainly about the wise leadership of Governor James Douglas in forming a provincial land policy.

33. An old but still valuable discussion of this issue is Chester Martin, *"Dominion Lands" Policy*, which comprises the second half of the second volume of the Canadian Frontiers of Settlement series, edited by W.A. Mackintosh and W.L.G. Joerg (Toronto: Macmillan, 1938). See especially chapter 12, which deals with the transfer of 1930. Martin was a strong provinces-rights advocate, particularly for Manitoba. For a general review

of federal policy, see Kirk N. Lambrecht, *The Administration of Dominion Lands, 1810-1930* (Regina, Sask.: Canadian Plains Research Center, 1991).

34. According to John Herd Thompson and Allen Seager, "the attitude of the federal government, Liberal or Conservative, to resource development did not differ significantly from that of the provinces." In *Canada, 1922-1939: Decades of Discord* (Toronto: McClelland and Stewart, 1985), 84.

35. This is also the argument of Gerald Friesen in "The Prairie West since 1945: A Historical Survey," in *The Making of the Modern West: Western Canada since 1945*, A.W. Rasporich, ed., (Calgary: University of Calgary Press, 1984), 1-10; and in Friesen, *The Canadian Prairies: A History* (Lincoln: University of Nebraska Press, 1984), 466. Friesen, however, places more emphasis on local economic control than on environmental adaptation. Maurice Careless has also noted the growth and persistence of regional identities in Canada, but he tends to emphasize racial and ethnic identities over environmentally-based ones, which may reflect his Ontario-Quebec background. See his "'Limited Identities' in Canada," *Canadian Historical Review* 50 (March 1969):1-10. Finally, William Westfall writes on the growing interest in regional studies in "On the Concept of Region in Canadian History and Literature," *Journal of Canadian Studies* 15 (Summer 1980):3-15, though he too dismisses environmental factors in history as irrelevant. It is unclear to me why stressing cultural factors only should be considered less reductive or simplistic.

36. Wolfgang Sachs, "On the Archaeology of the Development Idea," *The Ecologist* 20 (March/April 1990):42. See also his "Global Ecology and the Shadow of 'Development,'" in *Global Ecology: A New Arena of Political Conflict*, Sachs, ed., (London: Zed Books, 1993), 3-21.

V

From 54° 40' to Free Trade: Relations between the American Northwest and Western Canada[1]

Gerald Friesen
(University of Manitoba)

CANADA'S 1988 FEDERAL ELECTION, which was called just after my visit to Washington State University, and the Free Trade Agreement between Canada and the United States, which was due to be implemented on January 1, 1989, established the context in which this lecture was delivered. During my conversations and lectures at Washington State, I suggested that the adoption of the Canadian-American trade treaty, which was extended to include Mexico in the North American Free Trade Agreement (NAFTA, 1993), would change the relations between the two countries. The following brief survey of trans-border regional history illustrated my belief that the new circumstances would require patience and understanding from citizens on both sides of the boundary.

When the lecture was delivered, Canadians were anticipating a heated debate in the general election campaign over whether to approve the Free Trade Agreement. I had just heard from a friend in the advertising industry about a rumoured script being prepared for a national party television advertisement. According to this report, the camera would approach two well-dressed men seated across from each other at a table littered with paper, including one neatly-stacked pile about a foot high (the actual trade agreement); they are clearly at the end of a difficult but successful negotiation. One says to the other, in an unmistakable American accent, that there was only one further line he wanted to change and the deal could be wrapped up; his counterpart replies that that could certainly be accommodated—one line would pose no problem. The camera then zooms in on the paper between the two men to reveal a map of North America, where the American is erasing the boundary line between Canada and the United States. A version of the advertisement did, indeed, figure in the election campaign.

Whether for or against the trade deal, Canadians genuinely believed that their nation was at a crossroads in 1988. True, no political leader has ever entered a campaign declaring that the election about to be contested is irrelevant. But there was something different about the atmosphere in the autumn of that year. I thought then that historical understanding should also be a part of the public debate. This is why it seemed appropriate to ask what light might be cast on contemporary affairs by the history of the Northwest.

An American reader might be interested in a few words of explanation about why a mere tariff reduction measure should seem so important to a modern nation of thirty million people. I suggest that, buried in the Canadian psyche along with Mountie uniforms and hockey, are two fears about North America's structure and destiny. The first is that continental economic forces are well-nigh irresistible and that the continent must eventually be shaped into a single, regionally specialized, productive unit. The second, slightly different in approach, is that the dominant communications media of a given era might permit the survival of only one political entity north of Mexico.

An article published in the *Times* of London in 1866 and reprinted some months later in Northwest Canada illustrates the fear of economic integration. The article advocated the sale of Canada's Northwest to the United States, just as Alaska was about to be sold, because the newly re-united American federation was prepared to offer the then proprietor, the Hudson's Bay Company, a higher price than could the Canadian government. The business column in the *Times* went on:

> patriotism, like philanthropy, in business is rarely anything more than a pretence, and is nearly always a mistake. If the Americans can turn the territory to better account than our own people for the great use of mankind, it is desirable that they should be permitted to do so; and in any case, it is certain that all political attempts to prevent the country from being settled by those who are best adapted for the work must, by rendering perpetual irritation, prove worse than futile.

Naturally, Canadians resented this argument but the declaration, along with the Canadian reaction, neatly captures one Canadian perspective on the future of northern North America: economic forces override political decisions, willy nilly, and there is nothing that anyone can do to sidetrack businessmen determined to follow this inexorable logic. As a famous Canadian tract of the 1960s, George Grant's *Lament for a Nation*, declared, "No small country can depend for its existence on the loyalty of its capitalists."

The second Canadian fear is also based partly on perceptions of the geography of the continent, but its emphasis rests on the perception that communications technology may subvert historic cultural and political loyalties. It is evident that adjoining regions of Canada and the United States are remarkably similar; by referring to physical maps of the continent, one might conclude that, but for historical accident, this vast land mass should be divided quite differently or, indeed, should belong to a single country. This observation periodically raises doubts in Canadian hearts, doubts expressed most bluntly and forcefully by a transplanted British scholar then living in Toronto, Goldwin Smith, in his famous book, now almost 100 years old, *Canada and the Canadian Question*. The first sentence warned readers that, if they wanted "to know what Canada is," they should begin by turning from the political to the physical map. The political map displays a large united land; the physical map displays "four separate projections of the cultivable and habitable part of the Continent into arctic waste." The four parts were the Maritimes, Old [Central] Canada, the Northwest [Prairies], and British Columbia. Each was divided from the others "by great barriers of nature, wide and irreclaimable wildernesses or manifold chains of mountains" and each was "closely connected by nature, physically and economically" with the adjoining American region. Thus, Smith concluded,

> Whether the four blocks of territory constituting the Dominion can forever be kept by political agencies united among themselves and separate from their Continent of which geographically, economically, and with the exception of Quebec, ethnologically, they are parts, is the Canadian question.

Smith had expressed a second fundamental Canadian worry: that is, that there is not only an economic reason for continental unity but a logic, a "natural" destiny, rooted in geography and communications.

Assumptions about geography, communications, and economics went to the heart of the free trade debate in 1988. Supporters of the trade deal argued that business must be free to respond to global economic changes and that, anyway, Canada is a natural partner of the United States because the two nations "share a continent." Opponents consistently raised the same arguments but perceived them as threats: continental economic unity would destroy a distinctive nation and require North American political and cultural unity in all but name. The free trade discussion of 1988 was not a minor episode in Canadian life. Citizens took the election seriously because they believed their decision went to the very heart of national existence.

If one turns to a cartographical collection to survey cross-border regional history, one discovers not only that knowledge about this district changed during recent centuries, but that *location itself is relative*. We understand where we are situated (note Northrop Frye's suggestion that the appropriate Canadian question is "where is here?"), by reference to *other* places, and thus to the *relations* between sites. Changes in resource use, trade patterns, communications technology, diplomatic and military alignments, even in national will, can alter our *location* as they change our perceptions of geography. About 150 years ago, American and British mapmakers disagreed on the hue of northwest North America; as recently as the 1920s, Canadian military strategists planned that Canadian troops should lay siege to Seattle and thereby defend Canada from its only perceived external threat. These present boundaries, these places that we think of as permanent, are not fixed and immutable.

In any cartographical survey of the American Northwest and Canadian West, four patterns or configurations seem to crystallize. The first reflects an era of Aboriginal dominance. This pattern is evident long after Europeans had settled and "claimed" the continent. The second pattern expresses the impact of European trading empires which became evident in the seventeenth century and imposed itself upon the territory during the closing decades of the eighteenth and early decades of the nineteenth century. One product of the French-British-Spanish contest was the emergence of a new power, the United States. A third pattern reflects the development of European and American industrial capitalism, and stretches from the middle of the nineteenth to the mid-twentieth century. In this era the lines that we recognize as familiar were drawn on maps, including the national and state boundaries, rail networks, local road systems, and land surveys. A fourth pattern illustrates the global reorientation of military and cultural power that commenced during World War II, when not only the international balance of power began to shift, but so did the *types of lines* that defined our places on the map, whether microwaves, pipelines, satellite transmissions of television signals, or football team loyalties.

Lying behind this categorization of the region's cartography is a caricature of modern history. Rough and ready though it is, this model asserts, first, the primacy in regional history of European contact with North America's Aboriginal people; second, the influence of European capitalism and literacy on the course of world history; third, the central place of nations during the nineteenth and twentieth centuries; and, fourth, that the events of the last four or five decades have created a world sufficiently different in kind to warrant a distinctive pattern in regional cartography.

The distance between Aboriginal and European cultures in northwest America was wide in some respects, narrow in others. The technology that enabled the Europeans to contemplate a global empire—especially the technology of communications—was indeed outside the experience of the Aboriginal people. However, within the North American continent, Europeans relied on Aboriginal knowledge of the terrain and Aboriginal technological adaptations. Europeans did not challenge Aboriginal sovereignty in the northwestern districts of North America during the seventeenth and eighteenth centuries.

The two cultures, Aboriginal and European, defined the political territory, as opposed to its cultural dimensions, in comparable fashion. The 1801 "ak ki mo ki map" was built around the Great Divide in the Rocky Mountains: two worlds shared this part of the continent, one focused on the Columbia and looking coastward, one focused on the Missouri and looking toward the plains. European maps of the same era introduced another demarcation, one that separated the northern from the southern plains. Thus, in addition to the distinction between the Great Plains and the Pacific coast, they also divided the Saskatchewan-Churchill river system draining into Hudson Bay from the Missouri-Mississippi system flowing to the Gulf.

Neither of the two regional maps—one European, one Aboriginal—is superior to the other. As the Canadian economist, Harold Innis, recognized, both relied heavily on the river systems as routes of communication. Innis added that the river systems, in conjunction with the dominant staple export goods, eventually established the boundaries of distinct national communities: "The northern half of North America remained British," he wrote, "because of the importance of fur as a staple product." Surely this, written in 1930, was an early and effective answer to Goldwin Smith's observations on the natural destiny created by the north-south currents in the geography and economy of North America. It was also a declaration of the continuing autonomy of a Northwest region within the international trading system. Global trade in the seventeenth and eighteenth centuries had not dislocated the native cultures of Northwest America. The two civilizations, Aboriginal and European, lived in juxtaposition. Neither controlled or dictated the nature and pace of change of the other. But, as Innis noted, the experience with fur as an export staple influenced the historical trajectory of actors living north of the forty-ninth parallel.

Was there a type of regional unity within the northwestern segment of America? Surely the answer is no. The native political and trade map featured numerous divisions, especially the line of the Rocky Mountains that distinguished groups east and west. The European map was divided between corporate empires and, of course, after 1818 and 1846, by political ambitions associated with government policy in the United States, Mexico, and Great Britain as well as British North America.

A third pattern developed during the nineteenth and first half of the twentieth century. It was shaped by the industrial capitalist economic system which spread from England to Europe and America and then around the globe. This trading and financial system imposed new pressures on the relatively empty fertile zones of the world. By displacing native peoples, European immigrants could, in turn, establish settler capitalist economies to satisfy their homelands' demand for food and raw materials. The struggle for control of these so-called empty lands—in Australia, South America, southern Africa, and western North America—produced comparable episodes in every zone: conflict with native people, struggles for control of the terms of trade, the emergence of railway corporations as central instruments of development, and, in certain districts, border problems. In North America, control of the boundary became a political issue. Today's residents of Washington state will be familiar with the 1844 presidential campaign slogan of "54° 40' or fight"—the American claim that the boundary with the British colonies should be located in what is now central British Columbia. Americans may not be as familiar with the fact that this contest did not end in the 1840s. Nor was it truly settled when the newly united Canada (the British North America Act linked Ontario, Quebec, Nova Scotia, and New Brunswick in 1867) negotiated the admission of the western interior (1870) and British Columbia (1871) to the federation. Indeed, Canadians continued to worry about the fate of "their" West, and their alternative to the American national dream, to the end of the nineteenth century.

The Alaska boundary dispute, which erupted at the turn of the century, illustrated this deep anxiety among Canadians. It was believed in Canada that the United States would always attempt to ride roughshod over its northern neighbour and that the British government, when put to the test, preferred to mollify the Americans, even if, as in the case of the Alaskan panhandle, Canada's interests must be sacrificed.

Trade interests dominated these battles. Canadian leaders believed that, if American manufacturing companies dominated the economy of the northwest interior, and shipped via American routes in American conveyors, Canadian national sovereignty over these districts would soon be lost. Only the Canadian "National Policy" protective tariff of 1879, the extraordinary effort to build the Canadian Pacific transcontinental rail line in the 1880s, and the efforts to settle the prairies under Canadian supervision in the next three decades ensured that Canada retained its western empire, according to this view. As late as the 1890s, when American mine and rail promoters tried to exploit several mineral discoveries in the Kootenay region for their own advantage, the battle still raged. In response, the Canadian government underwrote an expensive rail project (the Crow's Nest Pass line), in order to ensure that the British Columbia mining towns traded with and shipped to Canadian rather than American businesses.

Many of the institutions established during the last half of the nineteenth century remain with us today. Indeed, in our daily lives, we still assume the fixity of the institutions that date from that era, including the international boundary. We assume that the two economies are relatively separate and distinct. We assume that, despite their friendship, the two countries march to different drummers, as they did during the two world wars. (Americans do not always understand the different Canadian perception of twentieth century military history, in which the Canadian response was to join the British Empire/Commonwealth forces in August 1914 and September 1939, rather than entering the fray when the Americans did in April 1917 and December 7, 1941.)

While accepting these turn-of-the-century assumptions, residents of the continental Northwest have learned in recent years that economic forces have substantially changed the political environment. The oft-heard cliches about the heightened profile of the Pacific Rim emphasize the extraordinary shift in economic power in the last four decades. The steady trend to Western European unity, the collapse of the Soviet Union, and the growing economies of China and India are further evidence that the economic assumptions of the pre-1940 decades are gone forever.

Global economic reorientation has travelled on the wings of new technologies. World-wide communications systems and transportation networks have created not just shifts in national power, but strides toward a global marketplace and even a global market-oriented culture. It should be no surprise that the "entertainment sector"—movies, music, television, and publishing—has become the second-largest export sector in the United States. Even the habits of consumerism are now standardized and exported. The very idea of a bumper sticker reading "Born to Shop" would have been outlandish in 1900, but the practice of "recreational shopping" exists today not just in Seattle but in Hong Kong and New Delhi; the so-called "malling of America" has not stopped on the shores of this continent, but now circles the earth; and tourism—which of course is directly linked to these trends—has become a leading industry in many nations and is said to create one in nine jobs worldwide. More and more human activities are now allocated to the marketplace. Child care, weight loss, fitness, leisure, health: name the niche, advertise it, and soon it can be bought and sold, or refined into various levels of excellence and exclusivity.

The nature of employment is different today. At the turn of the century, two of every three prairie Canadians lived in rural areas and over half the prairie work force worked in agriculture. In 1940, this proportion was still over 60 percent rural, and 40 percent of the work force lived in farm households. Today, fewer than 20 percent of prairie Canadians live on farms or in small towns and a smaller fraction—under 10 percent—actually farms for a living. In that most rural of regions—according to our image of it— as in the rest of North America and western Europe, two of every three jobs are now in the service (tertiary) sector. Health and education, government-sponsored social services, construction and transportation, retail and wholesale trade, food and lodging, real estate and finance, insurance and law, entertainment and consulting, computers and communications now constitute the job descriptions of a majority.

Changes in communications, work, and culture during the twentieth century suggest why we should regard the last fifty years as a distinct era in national and international history. The relations among the various regions of the globe have taken on a new aspect; the very means and types of self and community expression are different.

Global forces demand regional adaptations. As a consequence of the changed communications systems, the differences in the work force, and the new circumstances in Asia, the very relations between the Canadian and American parts of the continental Northwest have altered. Most Canadians, especially in western Canada, are not aware of the magnitude of this departure. And yet, as the free trade debate intensified during the 1980s and 1990s, they heard repeatedly that 70-80 percent of Canadian exports go to the United States and that about 70 percent of Canadian imports come from the United States.

Surely this cannot be true for the West, they reply. Perhaps the central Canadian provinces of Ontario and Quebec are trading more with Americans? Perhaps it is Ontarians and Quebeckers who drive up the tourism deficit? Surely western Canadian export patterns have altered little in this century?

Such notions are wrong. Indeed, the United States has become far and away western Canada's largest export market—nearly twice as important as any other region of the world. The proportions are striking: the U.S. takes over half of the region's exports, Asia about one-fourth, and Western Europe 8 percent. This marks an extraordinary change from the situation that prevailed as late as 1950.

The fundamental cause of this interdependence is the American quest for "safe" or "secure" energy supplies. The discovery of large quantities of crude oil and natural gas in Alberta (and, to a lesser degree, in Saskatchewan and British Columbia), combined with the exploitation of Canada's greatest natural resource, water (one-seventh of the world's supply of fresh water and substantial production of hydroelectric power), has resulted in the shipment south of over $10 billion of oil, gas, and hydropower annually. Mining products, ranging from copper to uranium to potash, account for another $3-4 billion each year. Forestry is an equally large export industry and over $4 billion in forest products, notably softwood lumber and woodpulp, travelled south in the late 1980s. A number of smaller Canadian export industries also rely heavily on the American market, including fisheries, cattle and hogs (live, slaughtered, or processed), petrochemicals, steel products, distillery products, and clothing. In sum, Western Canada is dependent on the United States as an export market. This circumstance developed during the 1970s and 1980s, but Western Canadian recognition of the interdependence dawned only slowly.

The relations between the two regions offer another lesson in international trade. This lesson concerns American shipments to Canada. Washington and Idaho potatoes, California vegetables and fruits, Washington apples, western poultry and poultry products, northwest forest products and minerals are part of a longer list of "natural" products that, in the popular mind, constitute the bulk of trans-border transactions. To this catalogue one might add western Canadian purchases of southern textiles and clothing, midwest steel, petrochemicals and vehicles (including farm implements), and western computers, music, films, and airplanes. Western Canada buys handsome volumes of all these goods.

One additional area of this exchange, services, merits attention. When one considers that the service sector is the fastest-growing sector of the economy, it is surprising that one hears so little about the *exchange* of services. The Canadian government has predicted that almost all future job growth in the Canadian and American economies will be in the service sector. Moreover, the United States is the largest service producer and exporter in the world.

The United States provides $24 billion in services to Canadians; the reverse flow is about $11 billion (1988 estimates). The $35 billion total represents over 20 percent of the total cross-border trade. Parts of this trade account are the normal consequences of such a gigantic bi-national exchange. For example, Canadian tourists run up a half-billion dollar deficit annually. The services category also includes freight and shipping, investment income, and dividends. None of these categories would cause one to pause. But another important subdivision within the services sector is business services—$5 billion in Canadian imports of American know-how, including the largest purchases of American television, publishing, and movies outside the United States itself.

By focusing on the exchange in the continental northwest, this brief commentary has not done justice to the cross-border traffic in eastern North America. The same pattern, an increasingly regionalized Canadian-American exchange, has developed there. Plants in Ontario ship goods across the border into New York, Ohio, and Michigan; Quebec sends products to New York and Massachusetts; the Atlantic provinces to New England. The northward flow is similarly regionalized. This is a very different continent from the one displayed on maps a century ago. The flow of trade and communications, in particular, is much closer to Goldwin Smith's "Canadian question" than one might have imagined. The changes in the global economy have had profound effects on regional life. The North American regions are aligned differently than they were even forty years ago.

What of nation and continent? How will the new technology and communications, and the addition of the FTA and NAFTA, affect northwestern American relations with western Canada? I believe that they will have a dramatic impact and that, to appreciate the point, one must refer to the history of Canada.

The desire for a separate nation in North America took root in the second half of the nineteenth century. It originated in the profound distinctiveness of French Catholic agrarian culture and, to a lesser degree, in the "loyalty" of those who rejected the American Revolution and then emigrated to Canada. It had its roots, too, in a separate economy which grew up within the Second British Empire (ca. 1784-1846), and in distinct business networks in fur, shipping, timber, and grain that perceived their interests to be different from those of American entrepreneurs. This cultural and economic foundation was reinforced when successive Canadian national governments implemented "national policies" between 1870 and 1930. Such policies have assumed mythical proportions in Canada partly because they were said to counteract an American challenge to Canadian sovereignty. Moreover, Canadian citizens' self-perception had more obvious European connections, especially French and English ties, than did the American, and its institutions of law and government (including the monarchy itself), all referred to the "Old Country" more fervently than was the case in the United States. By the turn of the twentieth century, Canadian separateness on the North American continent was a fact, confirmed dramatically in two national elections fought over free trade with the United States, in 1891 and 1911, when the dangers of the American tie were assessed and the "British connection" was affirmed.

While Canadians have inherited a nineteenth century sense of separate nationhood—of a Canadian patriotism—the twentieth century has added to that separateness a difference in the Canadian and American perceptions of the role of the market or "free enterprise" in the shaping of public decisions and private lives. Even casual students of Canadian life are aware of the greater role of the state in the Canadian economy. The Canadian Pacific Railway was a joint achievement of government and a private corporation. Later, its two competitors were brought under government ownership as the Canadian National Railways. Until 1988, the national air carrier, Air Canada, was a publicly owned company. Many of the major utilities that provide Canadians with electricity and telephone service are, or once were, "crown-owned" corporations. The Canadian Broadcasting Corporation is similarly government-owned, and so are almost all hospitals and educational institutions. Medical insurance is pre-paid, universal, compulsory, and state-supported from coast to coast, and so are seniors' pensions, child allowances, and unemployment insurance. These differences grew in importance in the decades after World War II and were brought into sharp relief for Canadians by the rhetoric and policies of the Reagan era. Despite apparent Canadian-American agreement on public policy, especially as voiced by Prime Minister Mulroney between 1984 and

1993, and by the Chretien administrations (1993-97, 1997-), these contrasts remain important. For example, while the unionized proportion of the American work force dropped below 18 percent in the 1980s, the comparable Canadian proportion was about twice as high, around 35-38 percent. In short, Canada has been much affected in recent decades by European currents of state capitalism, trade unionism, and social democracy. Canada's partial rejection of the iron law of the marketplace contrasts with American practice and American ideology. In the generation after 1945, Canada articulated a distinctive North American version of the just society.

To the nineteenth century inheritance of patriotic independence and the more recent strain of social justice I would like to add a third factor that resists the apparent transnational trend to homogeneity: culture. The term itself poses problems because we immediately translate it into the entertainment industry, on the one hand, or the arts, on the other. I mean it to include both but to mean neither: following Raymond Williams' definition, I propose that culture should be understood as the signifying practices—the signifying system—through which a social order or community meaning is communicated, reproduced, experienced, and explored. The process by which a community establishes its "signs" or hallmarks is always contested terrain. Corporate leaders in the United States have been particularly effective in this endeavour in the twentieth century as they have shipped around the globe an integrated vision of ideal government, "free" trade, and military superiority by means of "Rambo" and "Leave It To Beaver" and *Time* magazine. Most affected by the spillover from this, the single most powerful community signifying system in the world, was America's northern neighbour, Canada.

All expectations to the contrary, these cultural forces did not produce a uniform result or direction in Canada. Just as there are many Americans who do not subscribe entirely to the values of the dominant system, and criticize it from right or left, from religious or environmental or other assumptions, so there are many Canadians who dissent from one or another aspect of that American ideal. Canadians have found effective means of articulating these differences and asserting alternative visions of the community. Canadian "news" programmes, fiction, short films, and scholarly writing have been especially influential expressions of this dissent. Taken together with the social democratic tradition and the nineteenth century patriotic determination to be "not American," this cultural resistance to continental and global centripetal forces can be labelled in derogatory fashion as merely Canadian nationalism, cultural elitism, or socialism. However, it is an important force in Canadian public life and in the expectations of Canadian citizens. Indeed, it shaped one of the most important political and cultural debates in the history of Canada, the 1988 election campaign on the free trade agreement.

This debate did not address an apolitical ideal, "free trade," but rather concerned a particular treaty draft and a substantial alteration of the fundamental relationship between what once were relatively distinct economies. The debate was made more complicated by the very global and regional forces of the last generation that have knit regions such as the two Northwests more closely together. The FTA and NAFTA address access to Canadian resources, especially energy and water, but also wood and minerals, which will be pivotal for both Canada and the United States in the twenty-first century. Not only the exchange of manufactured goods, but also, and even more important, despite all the protestations to the contrary, cultural products and services are affected by the treaty clauses. At bottom, the trade deal encourages Canadians to entrench "free-market forces," as Americans would define that phrase, in more aspects of their community life.

The fact that Canadians have been divided over whether the trade deal is a good or a bad idea is a rough measure of the state of Canadian culture. The popular vote in the 1988 general election was just slightly greater for parties opposed to the deal than for those in favour, though Canada's "first-past-the-post" electoral system based on geographical constituencies allocated the greatest number of seats to the free trade proponents. The global forces that have facilitated international capital flows, greater commodity trade, and broader cultural exchanges have pushed Canadians to accept more extensive use of the marketplace. The threat of economic unions elsewhere, notably in Europe but also in Asia, and of international trade wars, makes the North American harbour seem safe. Moreover, the interchange without restriction of certain commodities—petroleum, natural gas, fruits and vegetables, minerals, many manufactured goods—seems merely to build on the foundation of regional integration that grew increasingly important over the course of the twentieth century.

There is popular concern about these trends. The exchange of services across the international boundary opens the door to American-style, profit-driven private hospitals, personal care homes, and daycare facilities; how will they affect the corresponding Canadian systems? The exchange of manufactures puts enormous pressure on unions, as the Mexican "free-trade corridor" has demonstrated; how will NAFTA affect Canadian labour-management relations and the role of the state in such matters as the automatic check-off of union dues, the closed shop, and the minimum wage laws? Talk of trade in fresh water raises environmental concerns about the mixing of organisms from different drainage basins. The contentious clauses on cultural trade, which leave the door open to American penalties against Canadian "subsidies," may enshrine the American definition of culture and cultural goods in international law, thereby permitting the United States "entertainment industry" to establish what is meant by freedom of trade and what is a permissible restriction. Between the 1960s and the 1990s, Canada has relied on a battery of state measures to counteract the American cultural juggernaut, including the state-owned CBC and National Film Board, but also broadcast regulations, postal rate assistance to serial publications, grants in aid of book publication, national preferences in taxes on advertising expenditures, and a variety of others. These rules interfere with the free flow of "commodities" and, thus, are subject to appeal, penalty, and eventual dismantling.

Canadians, like citizens of every country, are engaged in a continuous debate about the nature of the society in which they wish to live. At the close of the twentieth century, they are finding that the country's constituent regions—and the continent's constituent regions—are being knit together in new ways by changing trade and communications patterns as well as by different economic activities and cultural forces. Changing regional relationships and a different global context require a *rethinking* of political arrangements.

When Canadians raise the spectre of "becoming American," as they often do in contemporary debates, they are saying that economics and communications are forcing them to reconsider the role of market forces and social legislation in their environment. They are saying that American needs, priorities, and collective choices are weighing ever more heavily in Canadians' own calculations. It is not that the lines and colours on the map are changing, necessarily, but that some of the circumstances which originally necessitated such diagrams no longer exist. It may be harder to map "Batman" and "Oprah" and *USA Today*, or to understand the lines that accompany private hospitals and non-union shops, but in a so-called global economy where the service sector provides most of the new jobs, such vehicles are pivotal instruments of cultural and political education.

The challenges raised by the London *Times* in 1866 and by Goldwin Smith in 1893 are once again requiring a Canadian response.

The greatest achievements in Canadian-American relations in the last 100 years have been a mutual reliance on the rule of law, and a willingness on the part of each partner to debate freely with the other. Now, as in the past, Americans are called upon to contend with, to study, and to assimilate a wide range of Canadian topics because many of the fields I have mentioned will become negotiating issues in continuing trade debates. The interregional relationship within the Northwest has changed forever. Just as global forces created new circumstances in the early seventeenth century, at the end of the eighteenth century, in the closing decades of the nineteenth century, so we are now living through a fourth decisive era of change in regional history. The Pacific Northwest and the Canadian West are at another turning point; but, this time, because global and regional changes have intersected, they force Canadians to reconsider their national loyalties and political ideals as well.

Note

1. This is a slightly revised version of the Pettyjohn lecture I delivered in 1988. I would like to thank professors David Stratton and Margaret Andrews and the faculty and students at Washington State University for their gracious hospitality during my visit. I also wish to thank professors Jacqueline Peterson and William Swagerty, who did so much to make the visit possible and memorable.

Sources

Canada West Foundation, *The Effects of U.S. Protectionism on Western Canada* (Calgary, 1988).

_____, *Export Opportunities: Analysis for the Western Canadian Economy* (Calgary, 1988).

Department of Energy, Mines and Resources [Canada], *Free Trade and Energy* (Ottawa, 1988).

Economic Council of Canada, *Venturing Forth: An Assessment of the Canada-U.S. Trade Agreement* (Ottawa, 1988).

_____, *Western Transition* (Ottawa, 1984).

William H. Goetzmann, *Looking at the Land of Promise: Pioneer Images of the Pacific Northwest* (Pullman, WA, 1988).

Governments of British Columbia, Alberta, Saskatchewan and Manitoba, *An Evaluation of the Impact of the Tokyo Round of the Multilateral Trade Negotiations on Western Canada* (n.p., 1979).

George Grant, *Lament for a Nation: The Defeat of Canadian Nationalism* (Toronto, 1965).

Richard Gwyn, *The 49th Paradox: Canada in North America* (Toronto, 1985, 1986).

Michael D. Henderson, ed., *The Future on the Table: Canada and the Free Trade Issue* (North York, 1987).

Mary Javorski, *The Canadian West Discovered: An Exhibition of Printed Maps from the 16th to Early 20th Centuries* (Calgary, 1983).

Katie Macmillan and Canada West Foundation, *Putting the Cards on the Table: Free Trade and Western Canadian Industries* (Calgary, 1986).

Paul A. Phillips, "Easternizing Manitoba: The Changing Economy of the New West," unpublished manuscript, University of Manitoba, 1987.

Murray G. Smith and Frank Stone, eds., *Assessing the Canada-U.S. Free Trade Agreement* (Toronto, 1987).

Denis Stairs and Gilbert R. Winham, eds., *The Politics of Canada's Economic Relationship with the United States* (Royal Commission on the Economic Union and Development Prospects for Canada, Research Studies, vol. 29, Toronto, 1985).

Raymond Williams, *Culture* (Glasgow, 1981).

VI

A Matter of Context:
The Pacific Northwest in
World History

Kenneth S. Coates
(University of New Brunswick)

THE ACCOUNT IS A FAMILIAR ONE: a frustrated gold miner, unsure of local prospects, in contemplation turns his eye toward the future. Then, as though manna from heaven, news arrives:

> Everyone seemed to be Klondike mad with excitement, and the newspapers were looked for eagerly to get the latest news from the field and the number of tons of gold already produced and the number of boats that been sent down the Yukon from Dawson City laden with gold and also the latest gulches found and the number of tons of gold taken from the Discovery Claim. I amongst the rest was getting a bit excited, and it only wanted a few more good reports to start me going, the excitement was just about up to fever heat . . . I was Klondike mad sure enough.[1]

What makes the case of William Sharman Crawford Nicholl stand out a bit from the crowd of Klondike stampeders who responded to the call of northern gold in 1897 is his point of departure. Nicholl was living near Waihi, at the southern end of New Zealand's Cormandel Peninsula. Although that mining camp showed signs of promise, the lurid tales of Klondike fortunes proved overwhelming, and Nicholl set off in New Zealand's spring of 1897 (October) for Vancouver, British Columbia, and the Yukon gold fields. Only a few months after news of the Klondike discovery shocked and amazed North America, miners thousands of miles to the south were setting their course for the Yukon River valley.

Gold rushes are unique events, unusually dramatic, and stimulating those most base of human emotions: greed and the search for adventure. Perhaps Nicholl's situation, and that of the Klondike Gold Rush generally, is best considered a special case, and not a useful starting point for a consideration of a vital element in the history of the Pacific Northwest. However, to overlook the implications of the excitement in Waihi—a beautiful coastal community tucked between the verdant forests of the North Island of New Zealand and the sandy beaches of the Pacific Ocean—about developments in the sub-Arctic wilderness, thousands of miles, many degrees of latitude, and many degrees of temperature removed from New Zealand is to miss one of the more important elements in the evolution of the Pacific Northwest.

Consider a second example, that of Kang Youwei, a Chinese migrant to the west coast of North America. Kang arrived via Japan from Hong Kong, where he had fled in 1898 after Empress Dowager Cixi dramatically ended attempts to reform the monarchy in China. Numerous reformers were ordered arrested, and executed; Kang Youwei escaped before these fates befell him. Having reached British Columbia, he passed on to the United States, moved on to England, and then returned to Victoria, British Columbia. Once back in the Pacific Northwest, he founded Bao Hunang Hui (the Save the Emperor Society or the Chinese Empire Reform Association), which soon emerged as the first mass political party in China. The reform association, while focusing on political structures in China, was strongly influenced by British Columbian developments. The experience of the Guangdong merchants in Canada, where they learned the importance of cultural self-defense and used their exclusion from local and national government to create institutions that gave them control over their destiny, influenced the Bao Hunang Hui and therefore had a significant impact on the evolution of Chinese politics.[2] While the little-known connection between British Columbia and Chinese political development was not of profound impact within the Pacific Northwest, it provides a second, and very different, example of the importance of understanding local developments within an international and global context.[3]

Oregon's Hood River Valley is an unlikely place to consider the social and economic impacts of the Meiji era in Japan, but the life and career of Matsuo Yasui provides an important window on the connections between the internal dynamics of Japan, and ethnic and business development in the Pacific Northwest. Yasui's father was raised in the midst of the Meiji transformation of Japan, when the country abandoned its isolationist policies and embraced international trade and cultural connections. His father, struggling with high land taxes in Japan, was attracted to the United States of America, as were many Japanese at that time. Matsuo Yasui, who remained behind with his mother until he was older, discovered that Japan offered few opportunities for social mobility; the United States, in contrast, appeared to provide limitless options. The Japanese government, anxious to protect its citizens from the racism and hostility experienced by Chinese migrants, screened Matsuo Yasui and thousands of others for literacy, character, and suitability.[4] Yasui passed the test, migrated to the Pacific Northwest, and worked variously on the railway, in an Astoria salmon cannery, and in Portland, before moving to the Hood River valley where he set up a store to serve the Issei in the area.[5] Matsuo Yasui's story is not particularly bold or dramatic, but it is a single example, drawn from thousands, of the relationship between transformations and crises in Japan and patterns of migration, work, and settlement in the Pacific Northwest.[6]

However much the Pacific Northwest exists as a region, it sits as well as an integral part of a complex and ever-changing global web of economic, social, political, cultural, and environmental relations. It is not a singular pattern. In some instances, as in the case of the Klondike Gold Rush, regional developments take on international significance. In others, as with Chinese migration, social and economic trends in far distant lands end up having a direct impact on the Pacific Northwest. In still others, broad intellectual currents washed across North America or the Pacific and affected public and political thinking in the region.[7] And more often than one might suspect, the Pacific Northwest has seen its ideas picked up and sometimes transformed in the process of spreading to distant corners of the globe.

The call for context in the writing of regional history is not new. W.L. Morton, a leading historian of the Canadian West, long held that regional historians had to pursue a "delicate balance" between region and nation. Although himself a passionate western Canadian, Morton did not support or practice the parochialism, chauvinism, and boosterism that often crept into the writing of regional history. The perception of regional bias made it far too easy for "national" historians to by-pass regional scholarship and to relegate it to the background of the historical profession.[8] British Columbian labor historian Mark Leier repeated a long-standing criticism of regional history when he recently argued, "regional history is only useful and exciting when it treats the region as a case study, as a field of investigation in which theory can be applied, tested and criticized." Leier goes too far, suggesting that regional history has limited merit on its own and finds purpose and substance only when it addresses questions of broader significance. But there is a germ of truth in his observation: "By focusing on the region rather than on the larger issues, we risk turning our gaze inward and becoming less interesting, less creative, and more inclined to find out more and more about less and less."[9]

The growing awareness of global developments seems, on the surface, to run counter to the development of historical scholarship on the Pacific Northwest. The Pacific Northwest has, for many years, struggled to find a historiographical identity. Numerous borders—national, state, provincial, territorial, and cultural—have stood in the way of developing a strong and logical sense of the evolution of regional society and of the interconnections between the various political jurisdictions that make up the area.[10] The region's many historians work largely within the confines of national, state, and provincial boundaries. Increasingly, thematic connections between labor, encounter, women's, and economic historians have created some cross-border historians who have helped to clarify the influence of the national boundary on regional developments. These scholars have begun to identify the nature and structure of a trans-boundary regional order. The loosening of national blinders in recent years, through a series of borderlands projects, increased academic interchange between Canada and the United States, and a growing sense of common cause in the contemporary era has prodded scholars, particularly those relatively new to the field, to examine developments that transcend national boundaries, historiographies, and conceptual structures.[11]

The search for global patterns and characteristics that sits at the heart of the emerging field of world history seemingly calls on historians to eschew the local and the regional, and to recognize the intense interdependency and interplay of the world's many connected cultures. The lively discussions among world historians cover the broad themes of history—modernization, cultural encounters, economic integration, and market relationships—and local developments appear as little more than footnoted examples. World history is historical inquiry on the widest possible scale—rather more like painting a house with an industrial paint-sprayer than the intricate landscapes of the regional scholar. The two—world history and regional history—appear to be polar opposites, the former an implicit commentary on the irrelevance of the latter. World history seems, at first blush, to be the antithesis of regional scholarship, a rejection of the idea that there are unique characteristics that set regions such as the Pacific Northwest off from world events.

Few world historians would be comfortable with such a view of their work, for the emerging sub-discipline sees its contribution as resting with the ability to provide context and perspective to historical work that otherwise might fall short of its potential. For the writing of world history is not about knowing the whole world—and even the most arrogant scholar would shy away from such a robust claim—but rather about being alert to the global influences that impinge upon regional developments and to the potential international implications of experiences within a confined setting. As Jeremy Bentley suggested:

> During the past two or three decades, though, historians have become increasingly aware of some inherent limitations in historical writing focused on national communities. At the same time, they have recognized the challenge and promise of a historical perspective that transcends national frontiers. Many powerful historical forces simply do not respect national or even cultural boundary lines, but work their effects instead on a regional, continental or global scale. To name but a few, these forces include population movements, economic fluctuations, climatic changes, transfers of technology, the spread of infectious and contagious diseases, imperial expansion, long-distance trade, and the spread of religious faiths, ideas, and ideals. In their efforts to analyze and understand these forces, scholars have generated a body of literature increasingly recognized as world history—historical analysis undertaken not from the viewpoint of national states, but rather from that of the global community.[12]

Regional historiography, particularly of the Pacific Northwestern variety, has started to overcome the national preoccupations of the broader Canadian and American professions. The balance of region and nation that Morton sought has, in the hands of many fine Pacific Northwest historians, been achieved. Margaret Ormsby, the author of *British Columbia: A History*[13] and a strong promoter of regional history, saw herself as a national historian who occasionally worked on regional projects. Her studies of British Columbia were rich in their understanding of national influences. Work by many recent historians of the Pacific Northwest has integrated national developments with regional realities and has illustrated the vital interplay between internal and external factors. As Brian Dippie asserted, regional histories "are predicated on the assumption that there are meaningful differences between local and national developments."[14] Stephen Ceron makes a similar case: "It (this essay) contends that the recent history of the western states still makes more sense when it is prefaced by the history of conquest, colonization, and capitalist consolidation of the continent, which under the republic moved basically from east to west."[15]

Regional history is not in crisis; the abundant scholarship on the writing of Western and Pacific Northwest history and the expanded output of first-rate historical essays and books provide convincing evidence of the strength and growing complexity of Pacific Northwest historical writing.[16] And it would be wrong, in the extreme, to accuse the region's historians of parochialism. Much recent work is strongly founded in national contexts and rooted in contemporary theoretical and conceptual developments. Sarah Deutsch has captured the complexity and energy of the new western history:

> The West is a messy place. The experience of both majority and minority groups occurred in the context of multiracial and multicultural dynamics. Any larger historical narrative of the region must partake of an interactive multifaceted model. It must allow the constant interaction and diversity within and between groups itself to become the story. In doing so, it builds a framework within which we can understand the continual tensions created by forces that simultaneously erode boundaries and re-create them.[17]

Twenty years ago, however, regional history did tend toward antiquarian and narrowly descriptive work, making it easier for national historians to ignore such literature. While the Pacific Northwest does not yet sit at the center of national historiographies in either Canada or the United States—and while British Columbia sits largely separated from the historical writing focusing on the prairies that attracts more national attention, and the Northwest American states seem only weakly connected to the ongoing debates about the "new" western history—regional scholars are acknowledged for their many and significant contributions to North American history.[18] Studies of indigenous history and indigenous-newcomer relations focusing on the Pacific Northwest, for example, have illustrated indigenous resistance to government policies, their creative responses to economic transitions and immigrations, and the devastating impact of European diseases on local populations. Likewise, growing understanding of the nature of working class life and of the social and economic roots of labour radicalism in the Pacific Northwest—a region noted for the extremism and ideological intensity of its trade union movements—has done much to help historians understand the complexity of working class culture and political activism. This work also illustrates the connections that stretched across the border and that connected workers in the Pacific Northwest to the broader world; as one unionist argued: "There is no 49th parallel of latitude in Unionism. The Canadian and American workingmen have joined hands across the Boundary line for a common cause against a common enemy."[19]

Efforts to understand Pacific Northwest history have rarely taken into account a global perspective, although individual historians of the Pacific Northwest have successfully set their studies of local events within broader national social, economic, political, and cultural contexts. But regional history teeters between the nuts and bolts of historical analysis—abundant sources, the nuances of personality, and fluid social conditions—and the search for an appropriate context or framework for understanding. Placing regional developments within the sweeping setting of world history, and searching for interconnections with distant lands and peoples, seems like an ambitious, even unreasonable challenge for scholars who seek to explain unique elements of regional character and root developments within a specific local context. But placing the Pacific Northwest within world history presents new opportunities for regional historians to understand the significance of local developments, to assess the significance of well-known international and global developments, and to begin the process of recognizing the impact of the Pacific Northwest on other regions and nations.

The early history of the Pacific Northwest provides several key illustrations of the region's global connections. The initial occupation of the area, still hotly debated by scholars attempting to explain the origins and timing of the arrival of the first peoples, is in itself an element in the world's most important migration.[20] The indigenous peoples of Asia, drawn by population pressures behind them and opportunities lying in front, moved across to North America and quickly populated an entire continent. Although the backward cultural connections have become substantially obscured by time, the process of settling the region is, appropriately, the first example of the connections between the Pacific Northwest and distant lands. Ironically, in the years following European exploration, the indigenous peoples faced the depredations of hitherto unknown diseases. The biological colonization of the Pacific Northwest—the introduction of alien microbes, plants, and animals—connected the region to Europe, Asia, and other parts of North America.[21] In the process, indigenous societies faced significant depopulation through the smallpox epidemics of the late eighteenth and nineteenth centuries and from dozens of smaller outbreaks—although the scale is still the subject of much debate—and found their natural world substantially transformed. Biologically speaking, the world became a much more interconnected place as a consequence of European expansion, and the Pacific Northwest found itself incorporated into a global ecological order.[22]

The assertion of European sovereignty—ranging from the initial explorations of the coastal and inland regions and the subsequent division of the area between Britain, Spain, Russia, America, and Canada—offers another illustration of the global influences on the history of the Pacific Northwest. The first explorations along the Northwest coast were extensions of Spanish, British, and Russian attempts to extend colonial empires, a general European endeavor to comprehend a world beyond their knowledge, and an international market-driven search for a passage between the Orient and Europe.[23] The boundaries that have long influenced, bedeviled, and shaped development in the region were not determined by the geographic features or settlement history of the region itself. The establishment of the 141st meridian as the principal boundary between Russian America and British North America in 1825 followed the classic colonial model of European diplomats drawing straight lines that bore little relationship to local conditions; their reliance on less precise geographic demarcations along the Alaska Panhandle created much subsequent confusion and provided the foundation for Canada's intense but ill-founded claims for access to the sea during the Alaska boundary debates of the late nineteenth century. No such confusions attended the straight-line establishment of the 49th parallel as the northern boundary of the United States.

The establishment of colonial boundaries underlay the process of bifurcating the region into its American and British/Canadian elements, and in so doing tied the respective areas to separate national systems. The expansion of the United States and, later, Canada into the Pacific Northwest seemed to sound the death-knell for the prospect of unity in the region and set the different areas onto divergent paths.[24] While the new national political order, coupled by the ascendant nationalism of the late nineteenth and early twentieth centuries, focused attention inward—a preoccupation that has been shared by most regional historians—it did not eliminate the global connections that had hitherto shaped regional development.

The resource industries upon which the Pacific Northwest has long built its enviable level of prosperity have, from the earliest time, been strongly influenced by international markets and investments. While regional and national business has supplemented, sustained, and enriched local entrepreneurs, companies and industries, prices and demand set on a global stage have often played a vital role in underpinning economic development in the Pacific Northwest. This has been the case from the early days of the coastal fur trade, when pelts were fed into a complex trading web that connected America, Britain, China, and Russia.[25] The dynamic and exploitative coastal fur trade rested as much on seemingly endless Chinese demand for the expensive pelts as on British and American rapaciousness. And this arrangement continues through the late twentieth century mining boom, when minerals from British Columbia, the Yukon, and Alaska feed industries in Germany, Japan, and other countries. The first export market for coastal salmon developed in Hawaii, in turn stimulating a small but notable migration of workers from the islands to the Pacific Northwest. Global trading connections underlay the development of the western railways in the late nineteenth and early twentieth centuries.

And so it has gone, with developments in other parts of the world creating opportunities or, at times, crises for the economy of the Pacific Northwest. The completion of the Canadian Pacific Railway sparked an expansion of trade with the Orient and the development of strong steamship and rail links designed to provide Canadian traders with access to the opening markets in Asia. Vancouver sought to capitalize on the opening of the Panama Canal and to position itself as a major export centre, a theme illustrated in the early history of the Vancouver Exhibition (precursor to the Pacific National Exhibition).[26] Seattle also tried, through such efforts as the Alaska-Yukon-Pacific Exposition in 1909 and the Century 21 World's Fair in 1962, to position itself as an international city of the future. The recent flurry of activity surrounding the APEC summits and the encouragement of greater trade with Japan, China, and the growing economies of South-East Asia is, therefore, not a new phenomenon but rather a continuation of an old approach to trade development. Few question the significance of the international economy in determining the prosperity of the contemporary Pacific Northwest, but far less attention has been paid to the historical origins and the ongoing importance of global trading networks (be they of the early fur traders or the Hong Kong Chinese), international trade (from the development of markets for Pacific coast salmon to marketing Boeing aircraft in Asia),[27] and global competition (for regional minerals in the late nineteenth century to the unsettling and expanding rivalries faced by regional fruit producers, wheat farmers, and forest products companies).

Historians have, it is important to note, been very good at identifying the global connections in the early western economy.[28] Keith Bryant's essay on the early western United States economy was, appropriately, titled "Entering the Global Economy." As Bryant observed, in a manner which attaches little value to the depth and sophistication of indigenous knowledge:

Europeans occupied "free land" in North and South America, Asia, Africa, and the South Pacific throughout the nineteenth century. A treasure trove of minerals spurred that process. The movement of peoples into the trans-Mississippi West introduced both material progress and concepts of liberty even as it destroyed those non-European indigenous cultures that resisted. Technologically superior Europeans simply overwhelmed less-sophisticated societies. Transportation and communication accelerated this expansion as peoples of low skill levels were pushed aside. These "frontiers" quickly joined a world-capitalistic core market centered in western Europe. Maturation beyond self-sufficiency brought rising levels of participation in the world economic order to peripheral areas like the American West. As the French historian Fernand Braudel has shown, capitalism is an identifying theme for studying the modern world, for it provides structure and organization for examining relationships within a society. Capitalism emerged as the prevailing force in world history by the nineteenth century and as an all-pervasive aspect of American life, especially in the West.[29]

The face of the Pacific Northwest—originally indigenous, then substantially European, later transformed by substantial Asian migration, and recently enriched by influxes of African Americans and Latin Americans—provides evidence of the global demographic and cultural tapestry that has been woven in this region. Japanese and Chinese migrants, drawn by the seemingly endless wealth of the West Coast (what the Chinese called Gold Mountain), flooded into the Pacific Northwest in the late nineteenth century. So many came and so many more wished to come that non-Asian residents protested openly and insisted on the restriction of immigration. As part of the British Empire, British Columbia was an attractive and seemingly automatic point of entry for the thousands of East Indians who sought access to North America. When the governments of the United Kingdom and Canada, anxious to stem xenophobic outbursts, passed restrictive measure to keep the "foreigners" out, the East Indians persisted, sending a ship, the *Komagata Maru,* to Vancouver in 1914. Authorities blocked the ship from landing, and Vancouverites gathered by the thousands to watch the stand-off in English Bay. The ship was forced to leave without letting off its passengers of would-be immigrants. And so it has continued, as new waves of migrants have entered the region—wealthy Asians fleeing unrest in Hong Kong, impoverished Vietnamese seeking to escape Cambodian refugee camps, Greeks, Italians, and Eastern Europeans alternately fleeing difficult conditions in their home country or drawn by the physical beauty and prosperity of the West Coast.

At the broadest level, the settlement of the Pacific Northwest is part of the process of establishing neo-Europes in the New World, a lengthy, remarkably successful process of transcendent global significance; it was also part of the outward migration of Asia, a pattern seen in its early decades as an irritant to the host countries but which has emerged in recent years as a potent economic force in its own right.[30] As Gail Nomura observed in calling for greater attention to context in the study of Asian American history:

> It is impossible to view Asian American history without understanding the "far Eastern" context. Asian American history connects the United States West to the global experience of the diaspora and interchange of people and ideas from the colonial to the post-colonial era, to transnational labor migration, to international assembly lines in Asia, and to multi-racial financial and corporate structures in the Pacific Rim . . . envisioning the United States West as a vital component of the Pacific Basin we challenge the Eurocentric focus of both western and national United States history.[31]

And Nomura is far from alone in recognizing the international connections that have influenced and shaped the history of the Pacific Northwest. The settlement history of the region is the sum of thousands of individual stories—heroic, tragic, frightening, ennobling—and is often best understood at the personal and family level. These stories begin not in the Pacific Northwest, but in the social, cultural, economic, and political ferment of home countries from Eastern Europe to Asia. Domestic turmoil, visions of North American riches, the dynamic pull of a gold rush, the experiences of other community members, as well as other influences pushed and forced tens of thousands into the heart-wrenching decision to migrate. For some, the journey to the Pacific Northwest brought hardship, pain, destitution, and a retreat to the home country; for most, however, it brought at least an acceptable measure of opportunity and prosperity, even if the reception from the English-speaking majority was often less than welcoming.

The cumulative impact of global settlement, and the waves of migrants from the east, south, and west, was to provide the Pacific Northwest with tangible evidence of the human connections that bind this region to the rest of the world. The personal networks created by individual migrants with families, communities, and business contacts in their homelands proved to be vital conduits for knowledge, commerce, subsequent migrations, and the maintenance of Old World cultural traditions. Italian migrants, many of them poor, unskilled workers drawn to the region to work in the hard rock mines, illustrate the connections that tied the Pacific Northwest to Europe and that bind the area together. Many of the Italian migrants came first to Canada and subsequently moved across the border. The Corsinis, a large Italian family, moved initially to Extension, British Columbia. While four of the children stayed in the area, one daughter moved to San Francisco with her husband and another two relocated to Seattle.

In Canada, the Italian immigrants of the early twentieth century maintained strong ties to their homeland, operating an Italian-language newspaper, *L'Italia nel Canada,* a network of social and cultural clubs, a mutual aid society (Società Mutuo Soccordso Figli d'Italia), and often living together in small residential enclaves.[32]

Over time, the multi-cultural population of the Pacific Northwest assumed a North American social character—with sufficient differences between the Canadian and United States sections to justify the rhetoric of both regional chauvinists and cultural nationalists. But as contemporary developments have made clear, the historic ties to the home countries provided migrants in their private diaspora with important cultural strength sufficient to over-ride decades of attempted cultural assimilation and to leave the Pacific Northwest's ethnic minorities with a strong sense of their unique history and a continuing connection to their country of origin.

Broad processes, such as international migration or global economic connections, provide strong evidence of the international influences that have shaped the history of the Pacific Northwest; specific events, like the Klondike Gold Rush of 1897-1900, likewise illustrate the region's place within world history. The Klondike appears, at first glance, to be a quintessential local and regional event. It started with the discovery of gold on Rabbit Creek and leapt into prominence by the reception granted to the prospectors when they arrived in Seattle and Portland in 1897. Most of the stampeders who headed to the Yukon came from the Pacific Northwest, raising Canadian fears that the "lawless" Americans would overwhelm the small Canadian presence in the area.

But while the American dominance of the Klondike Gold Rush will always be a key, even central, part of the story, the reality is more complex. The rush for gold rests itself in an ancient and persistent infatuation with the precious metal, one nurtured in many cultures around the world. The Klondike stampede was not a solitary event, but rather the culmination of a process that, in narrow North American terms, moved steadily across the continent, reaching California and turning northward through Oregon, Washington, and British Columbia before culminating in the rush to the Yukon. As David Goldman wrote of the California Gold Rush, "Given the tendency toward national aggrandizement, historians too often have ignored the larger imperial story which spawned those mining frontiers."[33] (The frontier continued on to Alaska, although the latter rushes failed to match the Yukon for drama and magnitude.) More broadly, the Klondike Gold Rush hit a special global nerve, generating tremendous interest in many corners of the world. Stampeders flocked to the region from England, Europe, Australia, New Zealand, and other countries, flushed with the prospect of instant riches and soon to be disappointed by the bitter discovery that the vast majority of the gold-bearing land had been claimed long before the would-be miners reached the district. And the Klondike lives on in world historical memory—perhaps the only event in Canadian history that is known around the world—a historical metaphor for the excitement, potential, and disappointment that was an integral part of the frontier and gold-mining experience.[34]

A less precise, but no less important, illustration of the global influences on the development of the Pacific Northwest rest within the world of ideas. Tracing international connections in this area may be more difficult than establishing the paths of miners in the gold fields, but there is little doubt about their importance. When Europeans first arrived in the region and established relations with the indigenous population, they saw these peoples through the filter of existing values and images. British experiences with Polynesians, Spanish understandings of societies on the southern Pacific coast, and Russian images of indigenous peoples in Siberia colored their impressions and expectations of the First Nations in the Pacific Northwest. Perhaps the best illustration of this was the tendency of newly arrived Europeans to assume the First Nations were cannibals. Expecting to see cannibals, they took a large number of indigenous acts and customs to be evidence of this "fact," when the actual cultural situation was much more complex than they assumed.[35]

Much the same was true of the reaction to Asian immigrants. Sweeping North American and European images of Asia and Asians shaped the local response to Chinese, Japanese, and East Indian immigrations into the region. European migrants carried established stereotypes and racist assumptions within them to the Pacific Northwest and judged the immigrants on these terms. The result, as Peter Ward wrote of the British

Columbian reaction to the Chinese, was a legacy of discrimination and race hatred:

> "John Chinaman" was what they usually called him, though sometimes they also dubbed him the "heathen Chinese" or "the almond-eyed son of the flowery kingdom." These were names nineteenth-century North Americans commonly gave the Chinese immigrant. They were part of the rhetoric of race of white America. Essentially the names were terms of derision, not as disparaging as the twentieth century's "Chink," but with heavy overtones of mockery and contempt. Together they revealed something of the animus with which both Canadians and Americans greeted the Oriental immigrant who touched the Pacific margin.[36]

The relationship between local intellectual influences and broader patterns of thought extends to a variety of other areas: the competing political traditions of American republicanism and British parliamentary democracy, the nineteenth-century development of nationalism, national identities, and belief in the efficacy of the border as a meaningful dividing line between the United States and Canada, and a variety of reform and protest movements (including women's and workers' rights, socialism, utopian sentiments, and the like) that can trace their origins to a variety of national and international intellectual influences. Events like the 1919 general strikes, while shaped by the actions and ideas of hundreds of local labor leaders, politicians, and business and community leaders, owed much to the intellectual currents of socialism and communism and the countercurrents of anti-communism sweeping the western industrialized world. Industrial workers were, in the early years of the twentieth century, caught up in the international rhetoric of class war; organizations such as the Industrial Workers of the World brought them together—and caused terror among government officials and business leaders.

The 1903 railway strike in Vancouver, which lasted for four months and resulted in more than 2,000 workers laying down their tools—with sympathy strikes and work-stoppages expanding beyond the United Brotherhood of Railway Employees—is a good case in point. Community leaders saw the strike as being the result of American-inspired intrigue, and blamed the difficulties on a "socialist" conspiracy.[37] The men who struck in 1903, like those who brought on the turmoil of 1919, were tied in with broader organizational and intellectual developments, and did see their local situation through lenses defined by the international class struggle. These were regional strikes—Canadian, American, or cross-border—but they reflected the force of ideas then sweeping the industrial world. It does not diminish the significance of developments in the Pacific Northwest to recognize the intellectual origins and connections—many of which have practical and personal ties, as well as conceptual links—of the ideas that shaped political and social change in the region.

While historians have well documented the spread of disease in the period of initial indigenous-newcomer contact, less attention is generally paid to the ongoing epidemiological relationship between regional populations and the world as a whole. While the AIDS epidemic of recent decades illustrates this pattern, so do key developments in earlier times. In 1918, on the heels of the military mayhem of World War I, a great influenza pandemic swept around the world.[38] The so-called Spanish Flu exacted an enormous toll and disrupted life throughout the Pacific Northwest:

> [N]one knew how best to combat the new scourge. Some people thought laundering money—literally—might help; others tried staying away from crowds. Thanksgiving festivities had to be canceled in some parts of the region because of bans on public gatherings. Various communities required people to wear gauze masks in public, deferred any type of public meetings, or closed theaters. The pandemic, which subsided in December and then made a brief comeback in early 1919, ultimately took a higher toll of life than the war itself: 500,000 to 700,000 Americans died of influenza, whereas the combat toll was 50,000. The influenza killed between 20 million and 40 million people worldwide.[39]

The military history of the twentieth century demonstrates, once again, the multifaceted connections that bound the Pacific Northwest to the broader world. In World War I, national and imperial decisions committed first the Canadian West and, three years later, the western American states into the largely European conflict. Thousands of soldiers headed for the Western Front; many more residents supported the war through war bond drives and, less voluntarily, through rationing programs and by suffering through war-induced shortages. While, particularly in British Columbia, western businesses did not share in the war-time industrial boom that accompanied World War I, a few corporations (the best known of which is Boeing) used military contracts as the basis for expansion and post-war profitability. Following the war news tied regional residents to European developments in new and immediate ways, and the widely shared experience of fear, grief, and loss cemented a regional (and largely separate national) sense of common cause and collective commitment.

World War II and the Cold War that followed had an even more profound impact on the Pacific Northwest. At the most obvious level, the prospect of a Japanese invasion convinced the American government to finance a series of defense projects designed to protect the far Northwest, and spurred Canadian and American officials to plan for the defense of the coastal regions. Although developments on the Pacific front soon rendered many of these preparations unnecessary, the highways, telephone lines, and other projects undertaken due to the war would have a lasting impact on settlement and development patterns in the Northwest. Similarly, American military spending in World War II had a much more pronounced western dimension, fueling the rapid industrialization of the Pacific Northwest and providing a foundation for an industrial and military economy in the post-war era.[40] (The economic impact north of the border was far less direct, as the federal government directed most military spending to established factories in central Canada; overall, the Canadian government paid much less attention to the Japanese threat than did the Americans.) Fear of Japanese attack generated other reactions, including an outpouring of hostility directed at Japanese-Canadians and Japanese-Americans and culminating in their incarceration in government-run internment camps away from the coast.[41] This sad chapter in the history of the Pacific Northwest, in turn, carried over into subsequent decades, perpetuating the debate about the meaning, intensity, and impact of North American racism.

The pattern continued into the Cold War era, as the region found itself deeply immersed in the military politics of Russian-American rivalry. Carlos Schwantes provided an excellent description of the regional fall-out from the Cold War rhetoric:

> In the late 1940s and 1950s, the Cold War haunted the imaginations of Pacific Northwesterners even as it took tangible shape in defense-related products such as atomic bombs and long-range aircraft and in the parade of troops shipping out from the docks of Seattle to fight a grim new hot war with Communism in Korea. Closer to home the media was filled with talk of Communist conspiracy. Schools ran atomic-bomb drills along with fire drills, and a Boy Scout "Family Be Prepared Plan" of 1951 admonished people to stockpile food and to keep doors and windows shut during an atomic attack, advice better suited to the dangers of World War II than to the realities of the 1950s.[42]

The impact was most noticeable in Alaska, which became something of a military dependency in this period, and around Puget Sound, which emerged as a major military site. In Canada, limited federal involvement with the Cold War largely limited the visible signs of post-war military activity to radar sites associated with the Mid-Canada, Pine-Tree, and

Distant Early Warning lines. There was, however, the development and expansion of military bases from the Queen Charlotte Islands (a high technology listening post targeted at the Soviet Union) to Victoria (a major West Coast naval base). And, reversing the pattern, the recent decline in military tensions between the United States and the former Soviet Union (combined with ongoing technological change that alternately provides new economic opportunity for regional business or renders regionally based military hardware obsolete) has resulted in substantial reductions in West Coast military spending, with substantial economic and social implications for the region.

The Pacific Northwest has, as well, played an important role in the development of a global social and environmental consciousness. First Nations groups in Washington, British Columbia, the Yukon, and Alaska have, for thirty years, been at the forefront of the indigenous rights movement. And while the sense of injustice and demands for the resolution of grievance have spread largely in the realm of ideas, there have been practical manifestations as well. Regional First Nations leaders, particularly George Manuel of British Columbia, were instrumental in establishing the World Council of Indigenous Peoples.[43] (The first meeting of the organization, held on Vancouver Island, brought home to First Nations the desperate condition and very serious political and military crises facing indigenous communities in other parts of the world.)

A similar pattern evolved with the environmental movement. While the roots of contemporary environmentalism are very deep and broad, the Pacific Northwest has long held pride of place in the field. It was one of the first regions to politically internalize the conservation ethic (at least in the southern, urban, and coastal areas of the Northwest; developments in the interior and to the North tend to follow a separate path). But the founding of Greenpeace, as a result of a Canadian protest over an American action, is perhaps the best illustration of the environmental movement's Pacific Northwest connection. As Greenpeace International, a large, famous, international organization, defines its origins:

> Greenpeace was conceived in 1971 when members of the Don't Make A Wave Committee in Vancouver, Canada, renamed their organization the better to proclaim their purpose: to create a green and peaceful world. Greenpeace today adheres to the same principle that led 12 people to sail a small boat into the US atomic test zone off Amchitka in Alaska in 1971: that determined individuals can alter the actions and purposes of even the most powerful by "bearing witness," that is, by drawing

attention to an abuse of the environment through their unwavering presence at the scene, whatever the risk.[44]

It was a fitting, Pacific Northwest beginning.

For decades now, the political struggles over old-growth forests, the establishment of national parks, attempts to set limits on resource development (the ongoing Alaska National Wildlife Refuge campaign being one of the best examples) have attracted regional, national, and international attention. It would be simplistic and inaccurate to assert that the Pacific Northwest created the indigenous rights or environmental movements. In both instances, regional politicians and organizers combined local conditions and concerns with global sentiments and ideas, generating tremendous interest and public concern in the process. British Columbia's seemingly endless battles between environmentalists and developments—over Clayoquot Sound, the Stein River valley, the Windy Craggy mine project, and the Kemano Completion project—have all been tied into international networks of supporters. Over the past five years, environmentalists have tried (and on occasion, succeeded) to organize European boycotts of British Columbian pulp and paper products and lumber as a means of protesting against clear-cut logging. At one point, British Columbia Premier Glen Clark referred to the environmental activists as "enemies" of British Columbia. These intensely regional battles over the use and protection of resources are generally seen in domestic terms. This, in turn, has obscured the degree to which their intellectual and political movements are connected to forces that extend far beyond the Pacific Northwest.

There is, perhaps, no better example of the interconnections between region and world than the re-conceptualization of "wilderness" and the related development of the tourism industry.[45] In the latter case, the connections are fairly obvious. The rapid expansion of the coastal cruise ship industry was given a sharp boost by terrorist activities in the Mediterranean more than a decade ago. Ironically, a similar process occurred during World War I, when the loss of travel opportunities in Europe convinced many to shift their holiday plans to the far Northwest, sparking a short-lived tourism boom in the Yukon River basin. The Pacific Northwest is known globally for its attractive natural setting, and for the comparatively limited despoliation of the physical environment.[46] Regional tourism promotion—much of which is handled collectively, is a good example of cross-border integration and cooperation—capitalizes on European and Asian fascination with the "wilderness." This concept (for, as Morgan Sherwood and others have demonstrated, wilderness is as much a concept as a place) has itself evolved dramatically over the past century. In the late twentieth century, the undeveloped regions of the Pacific Northwest were seen either as wasteland or potential industrial or resource areas, albeit with relatively little commercial potential. In the post-World War II era (although elements of the re-thinking of wilderness are evident before this time), the Pacific Northwest has been a major focus for the re-examination of the meaning of wilderness, the preservation of the wild, and the marketing of the outdoors to international tourists. This has, over the past thirty years, emerged as a vital element in regional economic planning, the foundation of thousands of jobs, and, just as important, the underpinning of the Pacific Northwest identity.

The Pacific Northwest's role in the contemporary world order is in little doubt, ranging from Vancouver's development as the North American outpost of Hong Kong[47] to Seattle's contribution to the global marketing of cappuccino/espresso. The region holds a prominent place in the technological revolution, as home to the global Microsoft empire, and, in the form of hundreds of small companies on both sides of the border, is a vital contributor to the evolution of computer and telecommunications capabilities. There are countless examples of the influences of the global economy—evident in consumers' shopping carts, the investment patterns of regional corporations, the international orientation of Pacific Northwest-based consultants and advisors, the continued presence of global competition for resource producers, and high-profile Asian investments in major regional assets, such as timber and minerals.[48]

The Pacific Northwest is now well-aware of the global nature of its economic relationships. Several examples help illustrate the point. There has been a vast expansion of trade with Asia in the last twenty years. The lumber industry is very strongly tied to the world's fastest growing economic zones; in 1988, 3.6 billion board feet of raw lumber was shipped from Oregon and Washington to Japan alone. Three quarters of regional production in 1988 was sold overseas (at prices 40 percent higher than domestic); the Weyerhaeuser corporation exported 40 percent of its product. In 1989, half of the wheat crop in the American Pacific Northwest was sold to China, Japan, Russia, Korea, and Egypt. In northern British Columbia, perhaps as much as one-quarter of the local economy is directly tied to Japan—ownership and joint ownership of sawmills, contracts for coal, sea products from the Prince Rupert area, pine mushrooms, and production from the world's largest chopstick factory in Fort Nelson. Seattle and Vancouver have, in particular, emerged as important global centers, linked by commerce, airlines, and technology to the fast-growing Asia-Pacific economy.[49]

The search for an understanding of regional history must take on a new, global dimension. The incorporation of the global and regional is in no way a repudiation of the fundamental importance of regional history. The Pacific Northwest has a very different society and culture than Minnesota and Manitoba, let alone the North Island of New Zealand, the Yangtze valley of China, or the Scottish Highlands. And historians will, and must, continue their efforts to identify that which is unique and transformative in the history of the region. But just as it is vital to know how and why a particular region stands out among other parts of the nation and the world, it is crucial to recognize the degree to which broad social, economic, political, and cultural influences have affected life in the Pacific Northwest. Recognizing the patterns—the global influences on the region and the region's influence on the world—is a critical building block in the attempt to fully understand the development and evolution of society in the Pacific Northwest.

The Pacific Northwest deserves to be better known, both inside and outside the region.[50] It is home to some of the world's richest, most prosperous, most innovative peoples; it is a land of unrivaled physical beauty and resource potential. It is the source, and recipient, of some of the most powerful influences in the modern age. Regional history, however, continues to suffer from a lingering identity crisis, the implicit charge that it is inherently antiquarian, descriptive, and inward-looking. While much remains to be done to explore the personalities, influences, and developments that shaped the Pacific Northwest, perhaps it is useful to begin with a consideration of the appropriate context for our investigations. The Klondike Gold Rush, as much as the emergence of the Microsoft empire, was a global phenomenon, one that can only be understood when explained as a regional development of world-wide significance and impact; the labor unrest of the early twentieth century was part and parcel of a global reconsideration of the values of industrialization; the ideas embodied in the anti-Oriental political movements reflected significant elements of the culture clash between west and east. When regional history is placed in its appropriate context, and when it is seen as a complex interplay of personality, region, nation, and world, it reaches its full potential. Just as the Pacific Northwest has clearly come of age in recent years, establishing itself globally as a region of international significance and importance, so too should regional historians not shy away from the opportunity to seek meaning, insight, and audience on the broadest possible scale.

There is a vital congruence between the development of world history and contemporary changes affecting the Pacific Northwest.[51] That the region is now part of an integrated globalizing economy and society is accepted as a given—at times, too uncritically. The struggle to come to terms with globalization has been a difficult one, and is typically presented as an issue with a complicated present and a unknown future, but without a significant past. As the region searches for an understanding of the present and future, it urgently requires the context and perspective offered by historians, including those who adopt a world history perspective in their studies. Consider the appeal by world historians Michael Geyer and Charles Bright:

> This conclusion underscores both the promise and the challenge of the twentieth century as an age of world historical transition—that, in forging a world in which "humanity" has become a pragmatic reality with a common destiny, we do not arrive at the end of history. World history has just begun.[52]

And so, too, has the historiographical effort to place the Pacific Northwest in the context of world history.

Notes

1. W.S.C. Nicholl, "The Thames Today and as It Opened 60 Years Ago," typescript, n.d. (1927), p. 9. Material kindly provided by Philip Hart, Department of History, University of Waikato, Hamilton, New Zealand.

2. T. Stanley, "Chinamen, Wherever We Go: Chinese Nationalism and Guandong Merchants in British Columbia, 1871-1911," *Canadian Historical Review* 77, no. 4 (1996):475-503.

3. For the broader context on the Chinese in British Columbia, see E. Wickberg, ed., *From China to Canada: A History of the Chinese Communities in Canada* (Toronto: McClelland and Stewart, 1982).

4. Mitziko Sawada, "Culprits and Gentlemen: Meiji Japan's Restrictions of Emigrants to the United States, 1891-1909," *Pacific Historical Review* 15 (1991):339-60.

5. Lauren Kessler, "Spacious Dreams: A Japanese American Family Comes to the Pacific Northwest," *Oregon Historical Quarterly* 94 (1993):141-66.

6. For an interesting Canadian example of the process from a woman's perspective, see Midge Ayukawa, "Good Wives and Wise Mothers: Japanese Picture Brides in Early Twentieth Century British Columbia," *BC Studies* 105/106 (1995):103-18.

7. One of the best studies of the spread of ideas throughout the region is Carlos Schwantes, *Radical Heritage: Labor, Socialism, and Reform in Washington and British Columbia, 1885-1917* (Seattle: University of Washington Press, 1979).

8. See Morton's essays in A. B. McKillop, ed., *Contexts of Canada's Past: Selected Essays of W.L. Morton* (Toronto: Macmillan, 1980).

9. Mark Leier, "W(h)ither Labour History: Regionalism, Class and the Writing of British Columbia History," *BC Studies* 111 (1996):61-75.

10. There is, as a starting point, no general consensus on what constitutes the Pacific Northwest. While Washington, Oregon, and British Columbia are almost automatically included in the tourist and public conception of the region, historians rarely venture across national boundaries. Adjoining areas—Idaho, the Yukon, and Alaska—are typically ignored, dismissed as too marginal, too distant, or too historiographically insignificant to be included. For the purposes of this paper, I have defined the Pacific Northwest in broad terms, encompassing the four American states in the Northwest—Washington, Oregon, Idaho, and Alaska—and including British Columbia and the Yukon in Canada. I would argue that the failure to fully understand the historical interconnections of this region has resulted in uncertainty about the definition of the region. As David Emmons discovered in his analysis of the "west": "More than a few of the respondents, however, excluded all or parts of California, Oregon, Washington, Hawaii and Alaska. These areas were, presumably, 'West of the West,' too new, too urban and sophisticated, too well-watered and too economically favoured. All of this suggests that the 'true' West must be rural, semi-primitive as well as semi-arid, and broke." David Emmons, "Constructed Province: History and the Making of the Last American West," *Western Historical Quarterly* 25, no. 4 (1994):437. See also, Edward Ayers, et al., *All Over the Map: Rethinking American Regions* (Baltimore: Johns Hopkins University Press, 1996).

11. It is important to note that comparative history, which has contributed substantially to the study of the American and Canadian wests, is a very different form of historical analysis. For an introduction to this approach, see Walter Nugent, "Comparing Wests and Frontiers," Clyde Milner II, et al., eds., *The Oxford History of the American West* (New York: Oxford, 1994), 803-33.

12. Jerry Bentley, "A New Forum for Global History," *Journal of World History* 1, no. 1 (1990):iii.

13. (Toronto: Macmillan, 1964).

14. Brian Dippie, "American Wests: Historiographical Perspectives," in Patricia Nelson Limerick, et al., eds., *Trails: Towards a New Western History* (Lawrence: University of Kansas Press, 1991), 122.

15. Stephen Ceron, "From Frontier to Region: Frederick Jackson Turner and the New Western History," *Pacific Historical Review* 64 (1995):479-502.

16. One useful study that takes a different approach sets the North Pacific as the region of analysis. See Walter McDougall, *Let the Sea Make a Noise: A History of the North Pacific from Magellan to MacArthur* (New York: Basic, 1993).

17. Sarah Deutsch, "Landscape of Enclaves: Race Relations in the West, 1865-1990," in William Cronin, et al., eds., *Under an Open Sky: Rethinking America's Western Past* (New York: W. W. Norton, 1992).

18. On the situation in British Columbia historiography, see Robin Fisher, "Matter for Reflection: BC Studies and British Columbia History," *BC Studies* 100 (1993-94):59-77. See also, Jean Barman, *The West Beyond the West: A History of British Columbia* (Toronto: University of Toronto Press, 1991).

19. Quoted in Bryan Palmer, *Working Class Experience: The Rise and Reconstitution of Canadian Labour, 1800-1980* (Toronto, 1983), 149.

20. Brian Fagan, *The Great Journey: The Peopling of Ancient America* (London: Thames and Hudson, 1987).

21. As this relates to the spread of European diseases, see Cole Harris, "Voices of Disaster: Smallpox around the Strait of Georgia in 1782," *Ethnohistory* 41 (1994):591-626; Robert Boyd, "Commentary on Early Contact-Era Smallpox in the Pacific Northwest," *Ethnohistory* 43, no. 2 (1996):307-32; and R. M. Galois, "Measles, 1847-1850: The First Modern Epidemic in British Columbia," *BC Studies* 109 (1996):31-43.

22. Alfred Crosby, *Ecological Imperialism: The Biological Expansion of Europe, 900 to 1900* (Cambridge: Cambridge University Press, 1986), provides an excellent introduction to this theme. On the cultural underpinnings of this transformation, see Richard Mackie, *The Wilderness Profound: Victorian Life on the Gulf of Georgia* (Victoria: Sono Nis Press, 1995).

23. Among the very large literature on exploration, some useful studies to consider include Carlos Schwantes, ed., *Encounters with a Distant Land: Exploration in the Great Northwest* (Moscow: University of Idaho Press, 1994); Robin Fisher and Hugh Johnston, eds., *From Maps to Metaphors: The Pacific World of George Vancouver* (Vancouver: University of British Columbia Press, 1993); James Rhonda, *Revealing America: Image and Imagination in the Exploration of North America* (Lexington: D. C. Heath, 1996); Barry Gough, *The Northwest Coast: British Navigation, Trade and Discoveries to 1812* (Vancouver: University of British Columbia Press, 1992); and H. Beals, ed., *Juan Pérez on the Northwest Coast: Six Documents of His Expedition in 1774* (Portland: Oregon Historical Society, 1990). See also, Graham MacDonald, "The Exploration of the Pacific," *Journal of Interdisciplinary History* 24, no. 3 (1994):509-16.

24. Ken Coates, "Boundaries and the Pacific Northwest: The Historical and Contemporary Significance of Borders in Western North America," in Lars-Folke Landgren and Maunu Häyrynen, eds., *The Dividing Line: Borders and National Peripheries* (Helsinki: Renvall Institute, 1997).

25. J.R. Gibson, *Otter Skins, Boston Ships, and China Goods: The Maritime Fur Trade on the Northwest Coast, 1785-1841* (Seattle: University of Washington Press, 1992).

26. David Breen and Ken Coates, *Vancouver's Fair: A Political and Administrative History of the Pacific National Exhibition* (Vancouver: University of British Columbia Press, 1982).

27. For a sweeping history of world trade, see Peter Hugill, *World Trade since 1431: Geography, Technology and Capitalism* (Baltimore: Johns Hopkins, 1993).

28. See, in particular, Bill Robbins, *Colony and Empire: The Capitalist Transformation of the American West* (Lawrence: University of Kansas Press, 1994).

29. Keith Bryant, Jr., "Entering the Global Economy," Clyde Milner III, et al., eds., *The Oxford History of the American West* (New York: Oxford, 1994), 196.

30. John Naisbitt, *Megatrends Asia* (New York: Simon and Schuster, 1996).

31. Gail Nomura, "Significant Lives: Asia and Asian Americans in the History of the U.S. West," *Western Historical Quarterly* 25, no. 1 (1994):69-88.

32. Patricia Wood, "Outside the Lines: Borders and Identities among Italian Immigrants in the Pacific Northwest, 1880-1938," in Ken Coates and John Findlay, eds., *On Brotherly Terms* (forthcoming).

33. David Goldman, *Gold Seeking: Victoria and California in the 1850s* (Stanford: Stanford University Press, 1994).

34. Douglas Fetherling, *Gold Crusades: A Social History of Gold Rushes, 1849-1929* (Toronto: Macmillan, 1988) is the best analysis of the global nature of the gold rushes. On a more limited scale, see James Drucker, "Gold Rushers North: A Census Study of the Yukon and Alaskan Gold Rushes, 1896-1900," in Steve Haycox and M. Childers Mangusso, eds., *An Alaska Anthology: Interpreting the Past* (Seattle: University of Washington Press, 1996), 219.

35. Robin Fisher, *Contact and Conflict: Indian-European Relations in British Columbia* (Vancouver: University of British Columbia Press, 1977).

36. Peter Ward, *White Canada Forever: Popular Attitudes and Public Policy Toward Orientals in British Columbia* (Montreal: McGill-Queen's University Press, 1978).

37. Patricia Roy, *Vancouver: An Illustrated History* (Toronto: Lorimer, 1980).

38. Alfred Crosby, *Epidemic and Peace, 1918* (Westport, CT: Greenwood Press, 1976).

39. Carlos Schwantes, *The Pacific Northwest: An Interpretative History* (Lincoln: University of Nebraska, 1996), 360.

40. For an overview of the Northwest defense projects, see Ken Coates and W. R. Morrison, *The Alaska Highway in World War II: The U.S. Army of Occupation in the Canadian Northwest* (Norman: University of Oklahoma Press, 1992). For a more U.S.-focused study, see Heath Twichell, *Northwest Epic: The Building of the Alaska Highway* (New York: St. Martin's Press, 1992). On the impact of World War II on the economy of the western United States—and the war had a tremendous impact—see Gerald Nash, *The American West Transformed: The Impact of the Second World War* (Bloomington: Indiana University Press, 1985).

41. For the Canadian side of this story, written from an interesting Japanese and Canadian perspective, see Pat Roy, et al., *Mutual Hostages: Canadians and Japanese during the Second World War* (Toronto: University of Toronto Press, 1990). On the American side, see Roger Daniels, Sandra Taylor, Harry Kitano, eds., *Japanese Americans: From Relocation to Redress,* rev. ed. (Seattle: University of Washington Press, 1991).

42. Schwantes, *The Pacific Northwest,* 425.

43. Peter MacFarlane, *Brotherhood to Nationhood: George Manuel and the Making of the Modern Indian Movement* (Toronto: Between the Lines, 1993). See also, Paul Tennant, *Aboriginal Peoples and Politics: The Indian Land Question in British Columbia, 1849-1989* (Vancouver: University of British Columbia Press, 1990).

44. The quote is taken from the historical overview on the Greenpeace World Wide Web site (http://www.greenpeace.org:80/gpi.html).

45. For a very interesting comparison of Canadian and American attitudes in the area of wilderness and environment, see Donald Worster, "Wild, Tame, and Free: Com-

paring Canadian and American Views of Nature," in John Findlay and Ken Coates, eds., *On Brotherly Terms: Canadian-American Relations West of the Rockies* (forthcoming). See also, William Cronin, ed., *Uncommon Ground: Toward Reinventing Nature* (New York: Norton, 1995).

46. The *Pacific Historical Review* devoted a special issue (vol. 65, no. 4, November 1996) to the study of tourism in the American West; see, M. Shaffer, "See America First: Re-Envisioning Nation and Region through Western Tourism," 559-83.

47. See, for example, Jim Simon, "Uncertain Canadians," *Pacific Magazine*, February 23, 1997, 10-15.

48. The information presented here on the Pacific Northwest came from Schwantes, *The Pacific Northwest*. The material on northern British Columbia is from Carin Holroyd, "The Japanese Presence in the Northern British Columbia Economy," *The Northern Review* (1997). On the global reach of the modern logging industry, see Patricia Marchak, *Logging the Globe* (Montreal: McGill-Queen's University Press, 1995), and her article, "From Whom the Tree Falls: Restructuring of the Global Forest Industry," *BC Studies* 90 (1991):3-24.

49. For an interesting analysis of why Seattle has emerged as an important global centre and why Portland has not done so, see Carol Abbott, "Regional City and Network City: Portland and Seattle in the Twentieth Century," *Western Historical Quarterly* 23, no. 3 (1992):293-322.

50. For a very interesting study of the broad conceptualization of the Asia-Pacific region, see Arif Dirlik, "The Asia-Pacific Idea: Reality and Representation in the Invention of a Regional Structure," *Journal of World History* 3, no. 1 (1992):55-80.

51. And other areas as well, it hardly needs to be said. See Walter LaFeber, "The World and the United States," *American Historical Review* 100 (1995):1015-33.

52. Michael Geyer and Charles Bright, "World History in a Global Age," *American Historical Review* 100 (1995):1034-60.

Section Two
Natives and Newcomers

VII

"The Heathen Are Far Different from What You Imagine": The Life of Narcissa Whitman

Julie Roy Jeffrey
(Goucher College)

ALTHOUGH THE AMERICAN MISSIONARY movement has often been considered irrelevant or embarrassing, recently historians and others have been reexamining the significance of missionary work both within and outside of the United States. New studies point out that the missionary impulse to do good and to refashion other peoples and cultures has been a central theme in American history since the seventeenth century. As missionary efforts expanded outside the continental United States in the early nineteenth century, missionaries became important agents of modernization. "If . . . the making of this modern world was as much a matter of culture as technological revolution," one scholar suggests, "then we have grossly underestimated the pervasive significance of Christ's foot soldiers, at home and abroad."[1]

Yet if missionaries can be considered successful proponents of modernization, what often strikes observers today is how many of their efforts at transformation failed. Perhaps contemporary uncertainties about the ability of the United States to deal with problems at home and abroad encourage an emphasis on the limits of American influence and a reconsideration of the appeal of American values and ideals.

This reassessment of the American missionary movement suggests the need to reexamine the Protestant missions established in the Oregon country during the 1830s and 1840s.[2] Their history reveals themes and issues that are central to understanding the American missionary enterprise and also provides useful insights into nineteenth century cultural atitudes and practices. New studies of Protestant evangelicalism, the position of women in antebellum America, and middle-class culture, as well as the work done in Indian history over the last two decades, contribute to an understanding of the complexity of cultural and religious encounters between the white missionaries and the Indians whom they hoped to convert. The lives of individual missionaries like Narcissa Whitman and her husband, Marcus, reveal the crucial role gender played in mediating and shaping the character of the encounters between two races and also helps to explain the different strategies male and female missionaries adopted to help them cope with the stresses of missionary work.

▲ ▲ ▲

Writing from the Waiilatpu mission in the Oregon country, Narcissa Whitman recalled some of the books that had influenced her when she was growing up in the village of Prattsburg in upstate New York. One book she remembered reading was the popular biography of Harriet Newell, an early nineteenth-century American missionary to India. The moving account, which included excerpts from Harriet's journal, letters, and a sermon preached after her death, highlighted Harriet's spiritual struggles with her "cold, stupid heart." As a young teenager, Harriet was already anguishing over her sinful nature, the time she wasted with "trifles," and her light and gay behavior. When she was eighteen, she met Mr. Newell who intended to go to the foreign missionary field. His proposal that she share his calling led to more soul-searching. Was she qualified for the work? Were her motives pure? Was she courageous and persevering enough to take on "the dangers, the crosses, and the manifold trials of such an important undertaking?"[3] In the end, of course, Harriet sailed for India. There she died of consumption within a year (1812)—never realizing her ambition to save the souls of those she believed were doomed to hell because they had not heard of her Christ.

The ironic contrast between Harriet Newell's long anguished preparation for a life of Christian work and her very brief missionary career was one her biography did not highlight. Rather the book provided an encouraging message for pious readers like Narcissa. Though short, Harriet's life surely had to be considered a success. Possibly "the millions of Asia, whose salvation she so ardently desired" might commemorate her name. But whether remembered in Asia or not, the "lovely saint['s]" death would inspire those at home to adopt her "glorious cause." Indeed, as the funeral sermon that concluded the book confidently asserted, Harriet Newell did not "pray, and weep, and die in vain. Other causes may miscarry; but that will certainly triumph."[4]

Prevented from reading novels which her mother considered "vain trash," Narcissa found excitement and inspiration in missionary biographies such as the *Memoirs of Mrs. Harriet Newell.* The depiction of heroic Christian women fueled her own dreams of converting the heathen in some exotic place far from Prattsburg. The likelihood of being able to follow in the footsteps of these women, however, was not great. While the expansion of the American foreign missionary movement in the early decades of the nineteenth century had made it possible for women to participate, the missionary board was reluctant to commission single women. But since wives offered "a protection among savages," and "men can not . . . make a tolerable home without them," a handful of American women gained missionary appointments, usually as their husbands' assistants.[5]

No matter how fervent Narcissa's desire was, no matter how much her family and church might encourage her commitment to the glorious cause, as a single woman, Narcissa could do little to shape her own future. She spent her early 20s awaiting "the leadings of Providence" as she put it; more specifically, she hoped for a marriage proposal from someone who, like Reverend Newell, had a missionary appointment and needed a wife "well selected in respect to health, education, and piety." When Marcus Whitman approached her in 1835, she was quick to accept his offer though she could scarcely have known him well. While middle-class Americans in the 1830s expected a courtship and marriage based on romantic love, would-be missionaries like Narcissa had other values and norms. As one contemporary novel entitled *The Wife for a Missionary* made clear, missionaries "do not *fall in love* . . . [or] let fancy run away with . . . better judgement."[6]

Like his future wife, Marcus Whitman had also thought about missionary work for many years, though it is less clear than in Narcissa's case what role reading played in fueling his ambitions. The usual course for young men like Marcus who hoped for missionary service was first preparation for the ministry and then an application for a missionary appointment from the American Board of Commissioners for Foreign Missions (ABCFM), the interdenominational organization directing Congregational and Presbyterian foreign missionary efforts. But, when at the age of eighteen, he broached the subject with his family, they opposed his scheme. They were too proud to have Marcus attend seminary as "a charity scholar."[7] After spending several years working in his stepfather's shoe and tannery shop, Marcus escaped from the family business and apprenticed to a local doctor. Eventually he secured his license and began to practice medicine.

Though by all reports Marcus succeeded as a country doctor, he found it impossible to forget his youthful ideals. At the age of twenty-eight, he gave up medicine and tried to prepare for the ministry by reading theology on his own. His course of study was ended ostensibly by ill health although his early "deficient" education and practical mind may well have contributed to the failure.[8] A few years after this frustrating effort, however, he began to think about the possibility of becoming a medical missionary. Another disappointment was in store, for the ABCFM board concluded that his health was not "such as to justify your going on a mission at all."[9]

Most men would have abandoned their efforts, but Marcus was as stubborn as the Reverend Samuel Parker who was recruiting in New York state for what he hoped would be a new ABCFM mission among the Oregon Indians. Parker was inspired by the widely published report that Flathead Indians had journeyed to St. Louis in 1831 supposedly seeking knowledge of Christianity. The ABCFM board was much less enthusiastic about a possible Oregon mission than was Parker and only approved his exploratory trip after he had raised much of the money for it from other sources.[10]

When Parker reached central New York to recruit members for the Oregon initiative, he talked to Marcus on several occasions. Reporting to the ABCFM board that the doctor was a "choice" candidate, now apparently in good health, Parker pressed for Marcus' selection as being "beyond any . . . doubt."[11] The board's secretary, David Greene, was inclined to look favorably on Marcus' second application, for he was finding that despite the dramatic appeal to save the western Indians, few future missionaries were much interested in the American West. "They had rather learn a language spoken by tens of millions & live among a dense and settled population," he concluded, "than to spend their lives in what they apprehend will be almost fruitless toil in reclaiming small tribes of sparsely settled migrators." The board appointed Marcus to accompany Parker on his exploring trip during the spring of 1835. Although the trip resulted in the eventual establishment of an ABCFM mission in the Oregon country, the board shared the misgivings of many of its own missionaries. It never viewed the missionary activities with the western tribes as important or as worthy of financial support as efforts in more populated parts of the world.[12]

The appointment did lead to Marcus' marriage proposal to Narcissa and provided the means for both of them to undertake the vocation about which they had dreamed for so many years. But dreams nourished by reading, prayers, and inspirational sermons had left much about this vocation ambiguous. While the goal of missionary work was clear to the ABCFM (i.e., "the CONVERSION OF THE WORLD") and the need was pressing ("SIX HUNDRED MILLIONS OF HEATHENS . . . [were] perishing in sin . . . [requiring] *immediate* help"), the means for accomplishing these important goals were far less obvious.[13] The ABCFM's monthly publication, the *Missionary Herald*, and inspirational books about missionaries suggested some of the activities missionaries usually undertook. Wives taught school and sometimes led prayer meetings with native women; husbands preached, cared for the sick if they were medical missionaries, and often farmed. These activities, collectively or individually, supposedly would precipitate far-reaching spiritual and cultural transformations; the acceptance of the Congregational-Presbyterian doctrine of human depravity, a valid spiritual conversion; and ultimately the adoption of the customs and behavior of the missionaries themselves.[14]

If the young missionaries' understanding of the mechanism of conversion had a fanciful quality, their commitment was not tempered by any solid information about the Oregon Indians or Indian culture. The published story of the Flatheads' trip to St. Louis suggested that the western tribes were interested in learning more about Christianity. While it is impossible to know how well Marcus understood the Indians he and Parker met at the fur traders rendezvous of 1835, he reported that the Indians said that white religion had only "reached their ears; they wish it to affect their most vital parts." He judged them, "very much inclined to follow any advice given them by the whites . . . [and] ready to adopt anything that is taught them as religion." His views reaffirmed what he and Narcissa had both read. The *Missionary Herald* pointed out, "probably no heathen nations entertain less definite prejudice against the gospel, or the arts of civilized life" than American Indians. Furthermore, "our western . . . Indians . . . have scarcely anything of their ancient superstitions to oppose the gospel."[15]

The reality of what Narcissa initially called her "pleasing work" could not have departed more radically from the vague missionary scenario suggested by her reading.[16] The story of the Whitman mission at Waiilatpu (1836-47), near present-day Walla Walla, Washington, hardly needs retelling. The varied activities the Whitmans undertook did not lead to conversion. The Cayuse tribe's initial interest in the Christian message faded. As Christianity led to division within the community, opponents became angry and even threatening to the Whitmans themselves. Ultimately some of those who opposed the Whitmans most vociferously killed Narcissa and her husband and several other whites connected with the mission.

Obviously the Cayuse Indians bore little resemblance to the literary descriptions of eager western tribes intent on adopting the white man's religion. Their motives in inviting the Whitmans to settle among them are open to conjecture. But the quarrel between the Nez Perce and the Cayuse about where the missionaries would locate suggests that the Cayuse may have hoped that the missionary presence would strengthen their position relative to other Plateau tribes. Their desire to have the Whitmans act as traders also points to an interest in obtaining white goods, while the effort by some of the men of the tribe to act as religious intermediaries between the missionaries and the tribe highlights the possibility that a few may have hoped to use the missionary presence to enhance their own status in the tribe.[17] It is doubtful that any of the Cayuse, had they known more of the evangelical faith the missionaries wished to impart, would have been so eager to have them settle on the banks of the Walla Walla River.

As the Whitmans eventually discovered, there were many barriers standing in the way of cultural and religious transformation. By the time of the Whitmans' arrival, the Cayuse had adopted some aspects of white civilization; at least a few wore articles of European clothing and raised some crops and cattle as well as horses; and many prayed in the morning and evening and on the Sabbath—observances taught to them either by Hudson's Bay Company traders or by Iroquois in the company's employ. But their cultural borrowing was selective, and their way of life was vigorous enough to withstand the kind of wholesale change the missionaries sought. During the eleven years of the Whitmans' activities, *tewats* or medicine men continued to play an important role in Cayuse life; fields were cultivated by slaves and women, not by the men of the tribe as Marcus wished; and Indians pressed the missionaries to act like their own tribal elders and to tell them marvelous stories (from the Old Testament) rather than to explicate doctrine.[18]

While few primary materials on the Cayuse have survived, some "old stories" transcribed in 1930 by Morris Swadesh, the well-known linguist, suggest the vitality of Cayuse culture. Three of the four stories (one about Coyote, another about buffalo hunting, and the third about digging camas) celebrate the tribe's martial, distinctly unchristian values. My favorite describes the way in which two old Cayuse women kill an enemy from the Snake tribe by scalding him with hot camas root mush. After this feat of valor, they emulate the male warriors of their tribe, "took a knife . . . scalped him and . . . escaped to Walla Walla Valley." There the other Cayuse "shouted with joy" and lauded "the old women brave Cayuse." In recognition of their courageous deed, the tribe named a nearby creek Squaw Creek.[19]

The behavior of Tiloukaikt, who became headman of the band that wintered near the mission, illustrates the uncertain cultural dynamics at

Waiilatpu. At the beginning, Tiloukaikt seemed interested in what the missionaries had to offer. Narcissa identified him as a "friendly Indian"; indeed, it was Tiloukaikt who, in 1837, called their newborn daughter Alice, "Cayuse girl." By 1841, however, Tiloukaikt had become disillusioned with the missionary presence. The friendly Indian had become "most insolent"; he demanded the Whitmans pay for mission lands and, in a direct rejection of white notions of boundaries and trespassing, turned his horses onto the mission fields, and assaulted Marcus. Most likely Tiloukaikt was trying to force the Whitmans to give up the mission. When the Whitmans stayed, Tiloukaikt's attitude wavered; he became one of the few candidates for admission to the church. Whatever interest he felt in the church apparently was not strong enough to allow him to resist those in the tribe who wanted the Whitmans killed in 1847. Some accounts of the massacre suggest he may even have delivered one of the fatal blows to Marcus. Although the evidence about his role in the Whitmans' deaths is inconclusive, Tiloukaikt was one of those convicted and hanged for the crime. He gave his final comment on the Protestant missionary effort by accepting Roman Catholic baptism just before his death.[20]

The character of this cultural encounter between western missionaries and an indigenous people has a kind of timeless quality. Anthropologists and historians have identified similar patterns of interaction in many parts of the world and in many different time periods. One might argue that the Whitman story could be set in Africa, Latin America, or China rather than the Pacific Northwest. If, as one scholar suggests, the Peace Corps is the modern equivalent of the nineteenth-century missionary movement, the same cultural dynamics might be played out today.[21]

A historian cannot rely on general patterns as explanatory devices, however. A close investigation of the Whitmans' work among the Cayuse suggests that as much as their missionary experience may resemble efforts in other times and places, specific social, economic, and religious circumstances in white antebellum culture contributed to their expectations, frustrations, and failures. The role that books and journals, accessible to Americans as never before by the time Narcissa and Marcus were growing up, played in inspiring religious vocations and obscuring realities has already been suggested. Other aspects of the Whitmans' background illuminate the troubled history of the Waiilatpu mission station.[22]

The intensity of religious life in rural New York during the years of the Whitmans' youth and early adulthood left an indelible mark on each of them. Over and over again in letters home, Narcissa and Marcus expressed their desire for a "harvest season" at Waiilatpu. Family and friends knew exactly what the missionaries had in mind: the type of revival which produced so many changes of heart in New York state.

Although conversion had once been a private and individual experience, during the wave of revivals that made up the Second Great Awakening of the 1820s and 1830s, it became a public and collective event in evangelical churches. To some extent conversion demanded awareness of the Calvinist belief that all who had not experienced conversion were destined for hell. But new strategies, played out in a group setting, appealed to the emotions rather than to the intellect as the means for bringing about spiritual change.

A good example of one of the successful "new measures" was the anxious seat. The anxious seat, a special seating area, usually placed between the congregation and the sanctuary, focused group attention on a few selected members of the congregation who were weighed down by the knowledge of their transgressions against God. Separated from family and friends, these sinners expressed their feelings of guilt and dismay while members of the congregation as well as the pastor prayed and wept over them. Urgent personal appeals to repent mingled with cries to heaven for help. Many of those on the anxious seat were eventually overcome by the emotion of the moment and swept into the experience of conversion. Even those who were not ready for the anxious seat might find themselves influenced by the highly charged atmosphere. Even those who were not particularly pious might feel pressures to conform.[23]

Choral music, which had long played a role in Protestant services, now fostered the emotional moods that facilitated conversion. As a young woman, Narcissa proved skilled in using her voice to move the congregation. A family friend remembered that many Prattsburg residents traced "their first serious [religious] impressions to her charming singing and tender appeals to yield to the overtures of mercy." He left a revealing description of her approach. During one of the revivals at Prattsburg, at the conclusion of what was no doubt a graphic and frightening sermon on the final judgement, "by a previous arrangement Miss Narcissa, with two or three leading singers, took their seats near the pulpit and the moment the speaker closed his sermon they struck in and sang the old judgment hymn . . . Christians were melted to tears, and hardened sinners bowed their heads and wept bitterly."[24]

Nineteenth-century revivals worked, as one historian has pointed out, partly because of "the boldness, frenetic activity, emphasis on public [emotional] pressures, and general readiness to experiment." The cultural homogeneity of the areas where the Second Great Awakening ran its course also contributed to the large numbers of conversions during revival time. Perhaps the most important factor in explaining the success of these "harvest seasons" was the community's desire for the revival.[25]

At Waiilatpu, Narcissa and Marcus repeatedly looked forward to a "precious season," when sinners would cry out "What must I do to be saved," and where there would be many a "tearful eye" and heartfelt supplication. They were repeatedly disappointed. The emotional techniques just did not work when there was no collective expectation of, and desire for, change. And while a few might be moved, there were never enough to create the highly charged atmosphere that promoted conversions at home. Moreover, the particular behaviors that evangelical congregations in New York found so necessary and compelling—weeping and shaking, for example—did not have the same meaning for the Cayuse who did not readily respond to them.[26]

A source of continuous tension between the Whitmans and the Cayuse, and surely one of the root causes of the mission's abrupt end, was the particular style of interaction which the Whitmans used with the Indians. Like other evangelical Protestants of the antebellum period, the Whitmans believed it was their duty to draw clear and often public distinctions between nonbelievers and believers and between "sinful" and "Christian" behavior. They felt obliged to chastise rather than to tolerate, to warn rather than to keep silent.[27]

Even among the mission family itself, this kind of behavior caused trouble. Henry Spalding has often been blamed for the bickering in the Oregon mission. A better explanation of the contentiousness which, as unpublished letters show, continued for as long as the mission effort itself, is that all the missionaries felt compelled to point out one another's flaws and weaknesses. While the missionaries eventually learned to live with one another, the Cayuse increasingly indicated their discomfort with this kind of behavior.[28]

As early as 1838, Narcissa noted that some of the Cayuse were blaming the missionaries for pointing out the "eternal realities" of their certain damnation. Despite the "bitter opposition" that emerged to what some of the Cayuse labeled tellingly as "bad talk," Narcissa and Marcus repeatedly singled out as sinners those who followed tribal customs like polygamy, and the couple warned the Indians that they were on the road to hell. Some Cayuse became convinced that the Whitmans were condemning their entire way of life. As Narcissa reported, "One said it was good when they knew nothing but to hunt, eat, drink and sleep; now it was bad." The more the Cayuse demanded that the Whitmans keep silent, the more compelled the Whitmans felt to continue. As Marcus explained, "if he did not tell them plainly of their sins the Lord would be displeased with them . . . it was his duty to tell him that . . . [they] had done wrong." Without greater tolerance, frustrations grew on both sides.[29]

Many of the Whitmans' ideas about privacy, comfort, and style as well as their understanding of gender roles and acceptable behavior also contributed to a problematic relationship with the Cayuse. These notions, so familiar even today that it is tempting to think of them as detached from any particular historical context, resulted from the process of middle-class formation. Although most attention has focused on the development of a self-conscious working class in the early decades of the nineteenth century, an urban middle class was also in the making. Different from middling workers of the previous century because its members did not work with their hands but with their minds, this new class of clerical and professional men and their wives was increasingly differentiating itself by adopting new norms for behavior, family life, leisure time, consumption, and housing. Although Narcissa and Marcus had both grown up in small towns, they shared many of the attitudes, values, and tastes of this new middle class.[30]

Narcissa was, as a member of the Methodist mission in Oregon observed, especially fitted for "*civilized* life . . . a polished & exalted sphere . . . [and] for society, *refined society*." Appreciative of gentility and the society of ladies, Narcissa esteemed "polish," "mental culture," and "tasteful" domestic arrangements.[31] These values not only contributed to her sense of psychological distance from the Cayuse, but also led her to judge Cayuse life harshly. She saw Indian culture as the antithesis of her own, and because she did so, she feared it. The Cayuse, she explained, were savage rather than polished, hypocritical, deceitful, and cunning rather than sincere, dirty rather than clean, and lazy rather than industrious. Instead of devoting themselves to their children, mothers neglected them; they were their husbands' slaves, not their companions. Narcissa felt herself in a "dark and savage" place.[32]

Narcissa's behavior gave the Cayuse many reasons to question her commitment and friendship. During her daughter's infancy, Narcissa kept Alice off the floor because she thought the Indians had made it so dirty. By carrying her child in her arms for months, she must have made her disapproval clear enough. It was no wonder that one of the Methodist missionaries who knew the Whitmans well reported after Narcissa's death that she had maintained "considerable reserve" towards the Cayuse. "Her carriage towards them was always considered haughty. It was the common remark among them that Mrs. Whitman was 'very proud.'"[33]

Like other members of the middle class, Narcissa set a high value on family privacy. She was aggravated by the Cayuses' curiosity and their inclination to peek in her windows. As soon as she could, she secured not only venetian blinds for her windows, but also a fence to make the demarcation between her house and its surroundings clear. She realized that she could not bar the Cayuse from the house altogether, but determined to confine them to one room and one door.[34]

Used to free access to one another's lodges, the Cayuse objected to Narcissa's effort to carve out a private and exclusive space in the house. While this disagreement over space may seem trivial, neither the Whitmans nor the Cayuse considered it as such. In 1840, the Cayuse pressed the Whitmans to hold services in the new mission house. When the missionaries refused, telling them "they would make it so dirty and fill it so full of fleas that we could not live in it," the Indians "murmured" and demanded that the Whitmans pay for the mission land. The following year, a much tenser confrontation occurred over the same issue. One Saturday afternoon, the Indians rushed through several doors into the house, axing one door to pieces along the way. After threatening Marcus with a gun and hitting him in the mouth, they demanded that the Whitmans "not shut any . . . doors against them." When Marcus refused, many stayed away from the Sabbath service the following day. Others broke some of the hated windows in the mission house. Although the crisis passed, due to the intervention of the Hudson's Bay Company trader at Fort Walla Walla, the anger lingered.[35]

Some historians object to using the term cultural clash to describe the relationships between whites and Indians because it minimizes the peaceable exchanges that routinely occurred—such as the transactions between Narcissa and Indian women for berries, or her fan with Indian decorative motifs, or her little daughter lustily singing hymns in Nez Perce. But the term captures an essential truth about relations at Waiilatpu. Both cultures were assertive, willing to accommodate the other only to a limited extent. In 1843, Elijah White noted how "brave, active, tempestuous and warlike" the Cayuse were, how "boisterous, saucy and troublesome." He added that Narcissa's feelings for them resembled those "of a mother towards ungrateful children."[36] Narcissa's comment, "We have come to elevate them and not to suffer ourselves to sink down to their standard," suggests her energetic commitment to her own culture.[37]

Because Narcissa knew that her letters to her family were often shared and that her sister had had her travel journal published, she found it difficult to be candid about the trials of the missionary life when she wrote home. Some members of the ABCFM mission party, however, quite frankly admitted in their correspondence the drastic gap between expectations and reality. Asa Smith told his sisters not to delude themselves, as he had surely done, about missionary work. "You . . . paint scenes which are far different from reality. The heathen are far different from what you imagine & they do not listen to the truth as you suppose . . . Missionary labor viewed from our native land is all poetry, but here it is stern, severe reality."[38]

The Smiths eventually fled from the Oregon mission field, but the Whitmans stayed. Remaining, however, forced them to devise ways for dealing with the disappointments they encountered. Both, for example, eventually blamed the Cayuse for not accepting the Christian message and justified turning their attention to white settlers by pointing out that the Indians were on the way to extinction.[39]

But gender played a role in what strategies were available. A formal structure of support existed for the mission's male appointees. As corresponding secretary for the ABCFM board, David Greene wrote Marcus several times a year to answer questions and to encourage, support, criticize, and advise him. He was able to provide Marcus with a perspective that came from his knowledge of ABCFM efforts around the globe and, to some extent, could serve as a safe sounding board for Marcus' frustrations. But because the ABCFM considered Narcissa only as her husband's assistant, Greene saw no need to write to Narcissa or even to address her problems in his letters to Marcus. His infrequent inquiries about her suggest that the women of the mission were not important enough to warrant more than a passing thought.[40]

The organization of the Oregon mission also provided its male members with regular support. At least once a year, the men from the widespread mission stations gathered for their annual meeting that lasted for several days. While wives often came along, they did not participate in the mission meetings nor did they have the opportunity to debate or vote on mission policy or to decide on what news to send to the board in Boston. The men could take official action to change their realities; their wives could not.

Finally, Marcus as a man and as a physician had a good deal of physical mobility. Although his appointment as a medical missionary suggested that his primary involvement lay with the Cayuse, in fact, he provided medical treatment to the scattered members of the mission family as well as to Methodist missionaries, Hudson's Bay Company employees, and other white settlers in the Oregon country. He could often leave the frustrations at Waiilatpu behind him for weeks at a time. Although his absences caused him some misgivings, he was able to rationalize his choices without too much difficulty. As he told David Greene, it was unfortunate that there was "little room for the more important spiritual part of our duty." He often wished, "to give my whole time to the instruction of the people and resolved to do so more than heretofore, but then a call of sickness [comes] . . . which as a Physician I must regard as superior to any other."[41]

Narcissa's options were more limited than her husband's. Without direct access to the official channels of advice, she had no experienced voice to advise her. Nor could she pour out her frustrations in letters to families and friends. As she knew, her letters were passed around at home and might even be published without her knowledge or consent. As a result, she was extremely careful about what she revealed in her personal correspondence. Nor did she have the freedom to leave the mission as did her husband. Although in the first few years in Oregon she often accompanied Marcus on his trips to other mission stations, she lacked an official excuse to abandon her missionary duties at Waiilatpu.

Unable to escape the physical reality of missionary life, and needing to offset the frustrations she experienced at the mission, Narcissa relied on those powers of imagination that had helped to attract her to missionary work in the first place. Her letters suggest a habit of fantasizing that she was back in Prattsburg. They contain vivid pictures of Prentiss family life, perhaps an image of resting in the cool inner room during a hot summer day or sitting and reading aloud to her mother. Writing these descriptions helped to carry Narcissa back to the safe and predictable world where she had grown up. Her constant pleas for family correspondents to provide her very detailed information ("You cannot be too particular," she told her sister Mary Ann, while she informed her sister Clarissa, "I want to see how you look and how you live") suggest how important it was for her to have enough material to continue to imagine that world even after years had passed. Her moving and oft repeated reminders that "I am still one of your number" make it clear, too, that she was not only seeking the satisfaction of imagining herself in familiar places with familiar people but the sense of emotional sustenance that came from family love and acceptance.[42]

Because letters tied her imaginatively to home and made her life bearable, Narcissa found the first few years at Waiilatpu difficult. "Not a single word has been wafted hence . . . to afford consolation in a desponding hour," she mourned. When letters came, her feelings were of "inexpressible joy." Her description of receiving a letter from her mother suggests the vital role these communications played for her. "We were in bed and had just got to sleep," Narcissa reported, "when [an Indian] . . . announced that letters had come. We could not wait until morning, but lighted a candle to read them . . . It was enough to transport me in imagination to that dear circle I loved so well, and to prevent sleep from returning that night." On another occasion a letter from her sister Jane had her thinking "of nothing else but you [for a whole day] and weeping." When no letters came, Narcissa often "read over old letters and answer[ed] them over again" to assuage her disappointment.[43]

As it had in her youth, reading allowed Narcissa to escape to other worlds. Although Narcissa felt she was in a dark and heathen land far from every civilized influence, she actually had access to the kinds of books and journals she had enjoyed at home: the *New York Observer*, the *New York Evangelist*, missionary biographies, a book entitled *The Pastor's Wife*, and *Mother's Magazine*. While Narcissa's reliance on reading as one means of coping with stress helped her survive at the mission, she paid a great price for those moments of solace. Absorbed in her book on one quiet Sabbath afternoon in June 1839, Narcissa never really comprehended her daughter's little speech that she was going down to the river to get water for dinner. There, while her mother read, the two-year old fell into the water and drowned.[44]

There were limits to how often Narcissa might withdraw from daily reality. She was aware of the need to construct a new world for herself, one with female friends who could provide her with the emotional support she needed. There were, of course, no white women for miles, but Narcissa was not daunted. She began a series of friendships that she nourished through loving and personal letters, exchanges of small presents, and, when possible, occasional visits. Some of the women, like those posted at the ABCFM mission in Hawaii, she never met in person. Others, like the mixed-blood wives of Hudson's Bay Company officials, she probably would never have called her friends in other settings. Even the female members of the Oregon Methodist mission who became her intimates might not have played this part in Prattsburg where sectarian differences loomed large.

In Oregon, Narcissa freed herself from some of the strictures that shaped behavior at home, but never to the extent that she made friends with native women. They were too different, and Narcissa could not "feel a meeting of hearts" with them. But with women like Laura Brewer at The Dalles Methodist station, she could. Two passages from her letters to Laura poignantly suggest the quality and meaning of these ties. "I often think and dream of you" Narcissa wrote on one occasion, while on another she told her friend, "be assured, I shall love you and think of you with increasing interest, and if we meet no more in this world, it gives me joy to think we may meet in Heaven."[45]

Despite the obvious obstacles, Narcissa even tried to replicate the female associational life she had enjoyed in New York. Associational life, of course, was predicated on the idea that the women could gather periodically to discuss business, select projects, and renew friendships. Although regular meetings were out of the question during the first years in Oregon, Narcissa was not discouraged. The constitution of the Maternal Association formed in 1838 called for bimonthly meetings. Even if there was only one other woman at the mission, Narcissa reported that they made "all the effort our times and means will permit." Observing rituals at the same time helped Narcissa feel in touch with the other women, to have that important "meeting of the hearts." "Although we are so widely separated in person," she explained, "yet we . . . feel that our hearts are one for our object is one." In addition, carrying on associational activities like essay writing or fasting on children's birthdays connected Narcissa to "civilization" and imposed a sense of order and significance to her life.[46]

If Narcissa were to compensate for the frustrations of missionary life, she needed to establish an alternative to it—her own sphere of activity, interest, and gratification. From the first days at Waiilatpu, it was clear that she had determined, at the very least, to create a reassuringly familiar physical setting. Marcus devoted two sentences to describing the first mission house, thereby suggesting that home did not play the same psychic function for him as for his wife. Narcissa, on the other hand, filled her early letters with numerous details of her domestic situation, her windows, her furniture, even her washtub and pets. Considering her isolated circumstances, she was amazingly successful at fashioning a cozy haven that shielded her from what she called the "thick darkness of heathendom."[47]

As time passed and the mission station grew, the Whitmans moved into a new mission house. Visitors were surprised at how civilized, even familiar, it was. Whitewashed on the exterior and trimmed in green, the house included a dining room and parlor. The floors were painted yellow and the woodwork was slate colored. There were settees, clothes presses, rocking chairs, and a display cabinet for Narcissa's curiosities. Her family ate off blue and white English china, with the table covered by a table cloth.[48]

This setting testified not only to Narcissa's genteel taste and determination to have comforting physical surroundings, but also to her belief that the proper household arrangements were the necessary underpinnings for meaningful family life. This home circle was to be Narcissa's alternative to missionary work. Her efforts to create it were, of course, sanctioned by nineteenth-century middle-class culture, but her decision to make her family, especially the children, central was her own. Some missionary women felt distracted from their calling by their children, but for Narcissa the children who saved her from many "melancholy hours" became her real work.[49]

Because there was real ambiguity in the role of missionary women—on the one hand, they had made a commitment to Christ, but, on the other, all agreed that women had a sacred responsibility to their children—Narcissa could justify her choice to herself and to others. At times, however, Narcissa suspected that her involvement, especially with her daughter, was excessive. To her Methodist missionary friend, Mrs. Perkins, she wrote: "You like us, are solitary and alone and in almost the dangerous necessity of loving too ardently the precious gift, to the neglect of the giver."[50]

When little Alice drowned, Narcissa was overcome with grief. Face to face with the stark reality that, as a childless missionary, her obvious duty now lay with her "savage" charges, she became depressed and subject to a variety of different ailments. Like many other nineteenth-century women, Narcissa may well have retreated from what she considered an intolerable situation through sickness. Whatever the causes were for her bad health, it severely limited her contact with the Indians. But she was too resilient to resolve her problems by keeping to her room. Unable to conceive again, she began to create a new family by adopting two young mixed-blood girls, then a mixed-blood boy. In 1844, the Sager orphans appeared at the mission and the Whitmans decided to take them all in. Narcissa saw "the hand of the Lord" in their arrival.[51]

Narcissa threw herself into the physical and spiritual care of her large and interesting family. Many of her ailments disappeared or ceased to bother her. The tone of her letters became happy and positive. As she told her sister, Harriet, "we have as happy a family as the world affords." She added, "I do not wish to be in a better situation than this."[52]

Believing that the children would be corrupted by too close an association with the Indians, she prevented them from learning Nez Perce and supervised their activities carefully. As she explained to Mary Walker, "I can not rest to have them out of my sight for a moment unless I know what they are about—but prefer to have their work as well as their play all done in my presence." By the time of the massacre, Narcissa had redefined her mission in a way that excluded most contact with the Cayuse. As she explained to her mother, you "will see that my hands and heart are usefully employed, not so much for the Indians directly, as my own family. When my health failed, I was obliged to withhold my efforts for the natives, but the Lord has since filled my hands with other labors, and I have no reason to complain." If the Cayuse had ever seen her as their friend, few now thought the woman who held herself so aloof still was.[53]

Familiar and even predictable as parts of the Waiilatpu story may be, it still has much to tell us about the racial and cultural dynamics of the nineteenth-century West. On one level, the history of the ABCFM missionary endeavor makes it clear that two vital cultures were confronting one another. As the abrupt end of the Waiilatpu mission suggested, many Cayuse did not undergo the transformations that the Whitmans had in mind. Rather, members of the tribe resisted and rejected white middle-class evangelical values and attitudes. On another level, the mission story points to tensions within white culture. The missionary experience was a gendered one which allotted men and women different responsibilities and resources. Because Narcissa Whitman was only an assistant missionary, the ABCFM board paid little attention to her or her problems. Like many women in the mission field, Narcissa faced up to her failure with little in the way of institutional support. While it is easy to criticize her for not being sensitive to another culture (as presumably we are today), it is important to recognize Narcissa's courage and her success in creating strategies, drawn from the limited number available to women, which allowed her to survive. Women who followed her into the mission field throughout the century would select similar strategies as they confronted similar problems.[54]

Certainly any contemporary biography of Narcissa Whitman pales besides the heroic tale told in the early nineteenth century of the noble Harriet Newell. But Narcissa's life, filled with ambiguities, disappointments, dreams, and satisfactions, surely tells us more about the reality of the missionary outreach of the nineteenth century than does the inspiring but one dimensional story of Harriet Newell.

Notes

1. Jean Comaroff, "Missionaries and Mechanical Clerks: An Essay on Religion and History in South Africa," *The Journal of Religion* 71 (January 1991):1-17, especially pp. 3, 15, 17; William R. Hutchison, *Errand to the World: American Protestant Thought and Foreign Missions* (Chicago: University of Chicago Press, 1987), 1-7.

2. I do not mean to suggest that a similar examination of Catholic missions in Oregon Territory is not important, just that this paper concentrates on the Protestant missions of the American Board of Commissioners for Foreign Missions.

3. *Memoirs of the Life of Mrs. Harriet Newell, Wife of Rev. Samuel Newell . . .* (London: Milner and Sowerby, n.d.), 68, 40, 75, 101. In her unpublished dissertation, "Piety and Play: Young Women's Leisure in an Era of Evangelical Religion, 1790-1840," University of California, Berkeley, 1988, pp. 317-27, Barbara D. Loomis has an interesting discussion of the leisure patterns of evangelical culture and its antipathy to frivolity.

4. Newell, *Memoirs . . . ,* 197, 201.

5. *Oregon Pioneer Association Transactions*, henceforth *O.P.A.*, vol. 19 (1891), p. 147, vol. 21 (1893), p. 138; Lori D. Ginzberg, *Women and the Work of Benevolence: Morality, Politics, and Class in the Nineteenth-Century United States* (New Haven: Yale University Press, 1990), 19-20, discusses the evangelical fear of novel-reading; Rufus Anderson, *Memorial Volume of the First Fifty Years of the American Board of Commissioners for Foreign Missions* (Boston: American Board of Commissioners for Foreign Missions, 1861), 272. For background on the American foreign mission movement, see John A. Andrew III, *Rebuilding the Christian Commonwealth: New England Congregationalists and Foreign Missions, 1800-1830* (Lexington: University Press of Kentucky, 1976); Hutchison, *Errand to the World*; Clifton Jackson Phillips, *Protestant America and the Pagan World: The First Half Century of the American Board of Commissioners for Foreign Missions, 1810-1860* (Cambridge: East Asian Research Center, Harvard University, 1969); for the involvement of women, consult R. Pierce Beaver, *American Protestant Women in World Mission: A History of the First Feminist Movement in North America* (Grand Rapids: William B. Eerdmans, 1980 ed.).

6. Anderson, *Memorial Volume . . . ,* 272; A.T.J. Bullard, *The Wife for a Missionary* (Cincinnati: Truman and Smith, 1835, 3rd ed.), 20. For an analysis of middle-class courtship, see Ellen K. Rothman, *Hands and Hearts: A History of Courtship in America* (Cambridge: Harvard University Press, 1987), and Karen Lystra, *Searching the Heart: Women, Men, and Romantic Love in Nineteenth-Century America* (New York: Oxford University Press, 1989).

7. Clifford M. Drury, *Marcus and Narcissa Whitman, and the Opening of Old Oregon* (Glendale, CA: Arthur H. Clark, 1973), vol. 1, p. 71.

8. The board secretary considered Marcus' early education deficient. In letters to Oregon, Greene chastised both Spalding and Whitman for their bad spelling and poor handwriting. Archer Butler Hulbert and Dorothy Printup Hulbert, *Marcus Whitman: Crusader* (Denver: Stewart Commission of Colorado College and the Denver Public Library, 1936, 1938, 1941), vol. 1, p. 261, vol. 2, p. 263.

9. Drury, *Marcus and Narcissa Whitman . . . ,* vol. 1, p. 91.

10. See Xerox copy, "History of the First Presbyterian Church of Ithaca, 1804-1904," in the author's possession, pp. 27, 29; *Missionary Herald*, June 1834; Samuel Parker, "Article," 1882, Beinecke Library, Yale University; Letter from Parker to David Greene, May 6, 1834, Records of the ABCFM, ABC. 3. 1, vol. 9, Houghton Library, Harvard University. For the famous trip to St. Louis, see Alvin M. Josephy Jr., *The Nez Perce Indians and the Opening of the Northwest* (New Haven: Yale University Press, 1965), 96-101, and Chris-

topher L. Miller, *Prophetic Worlds: Indians and Whites on the Columbia Plateau* (New Brunswick: Rutgers University Press, 1985), 59-61.

11. Letter from Parker to Secretary Greene, November 4, 1834, ABC. 6. 12. 32; December 25, 1824; ABC. 18. 3. 1. vol. 9, Houghton Library, Harvard University; Samuel J. Parker, "The History of Oregon and the Pacific Coast and Its Especial Connection with Ithaca, New York," p. 174; manuscript presented in 1892, Accession #2521, Department of Manuscripts and University Archives, Cornell University Libraries.

12. Quoted in Parker, "The History of Oregon . . . ," pp. 92-93; William G. McLoughlin in *Cherokees and Missionaries, 1789-1839* (New Haven: Yale University Press, 1984), 328, points out that the board was conservative and cost-conscious and saw the salvation of the American Indians as the least important of their missionary endeavors. Rufus Anderson in his celebratory *Memorial Volume . . .* , 379-80, discounted the Oregon mission, writing that "Reverend Samuel Parker's 'Exploring Tour beyond the Rocky Mountains,' made, under the direction of the Board, in 1835, 1836, and 1837, brought to light no field of a great and successful mission; but it added much to the science of geography, and is remarkable as having first made known a practicable route for a railroad from the Mississippi to the Pacific."

13. *Missionary Herald*, October 1834, March 1835.

14. Some idea of the way in which Narcissa conceived of the process of change is suggested by her letter to children of the Ithaca Sabbath school. She wrote, "These [Indian] children do not love the Saviour, because they have no one to teach them." Hulbert, *Marcus Whitman,* vol. 1, p. 239.

15. *Ibid.,* p. 169; *Missionary Herald*, December 1832, January 1833.

16. Clifford M. Drury, *First White Women over the Rockies* (Glendale, CA: Arthur H. Clark, 1963-1966), vol. 1, p. 107.

17. Drury, *First White Women over the Rockies,* vol. 1, p. 110, for Narcissa's account of the quarrel; Hulbert, *Marcus Whitman*, vol. 1, p. 280, for Marcus' comment on trading; *O.P.A.*, vol. 19 (1891), p. 133, for the reference to some men wishing to act as intermediaries. My point about the desire for status was suggested by Harold W. Van Linkhuyzen's fine article, "A Reappraisal of the Praying Indians: Acculturation, Conversion, and Identity at Natick, Massachusetts, 1646-1730," *New England Quarterly* 63 (September 1990):404, 410.

18. John K. Townsend, *Narrative of a Journey across the Rocky Mountains, to the Columbia River, and a Visit to the Sandwich Islands, Chili, &c.* in Rueben Gold Thwaites, ed., *Early Western Travels, 1748-1846* (Cleveland: Arthur H. Clark, 1905), vol. 21, p. 272; Donald W. Meinig, *The Great Columbia Plain: A Historical Geography, 1805-1910* (Seattle: University of Washington Press, 1968), 87; Robert H. Ruby and John A. Brown, *Dreamer-Prophets of the Columbia Plateau: Smohalla and Skolaskin* (Norman: University of Oklahoma Press, 1989), 22. I do not mean to suggest in emphasizing the resilience of Cayuse culture that incremental adaptation would not have important repercussions in the long run. Lawrence E. Dawson, Vera-Mae Frederickson, and Nelson H.H. Graburn in *Traditions in Transition: Cultural Contact and Material Change* (Berkeley, CA: Lowie Museum of Anthropology, 1974), 5, suggest the important and unanticipated cultural effects that new technological items and the new behaviors that they mandate can have.

19. These transcriptions are available in the Boas Collection of American Indian Linguistics at the American Philosophical Society, Philadelphia, Microfilm 372.1, reel 48, Psla.l. The tale of the two old women may date back to the 1840s. The transcription reads, in part, "there a long time ago perhaps 90 years and there lived and there camped for root-digging two old women and the men went hunting." Jarold Ramsey in *Reading the Fire: Essays in the Traditional Indian Literatures of the Far West* (Lincoln: University of Nebraska Press, 1983), 137-51, discusses the Fish-Hawk story and the heroic values of the Cayuse.

20. Drury, *First White Women over the Rockies,* vol. 1, p. 127; Hulbert, *Marcus Whitman,* vol. 2, pp. 238-42, Roderick Sprague, "Plateau Shamanism and Marcus Whitman," *Idaho Yesterdays* 31 (Spring/Summer 1987):56; W.H. Gray, *A History of Oregon, 1792-1849: Drawn from Personal Observation and Authentic Information* (Portland: Harris and Holman, 1870), 492; Mary Saunders, *The Whitman Massacre* (Oakland: privately printed, 1916), 10.

21. Some recent studies of missionary activities in different parts of the world which isolate patterns similar to those explored here include T.O. Beidelman, *Colonial Evangelism: A Socio-Historical Study of an East African Mission* (Bloomington: Indiana University Press, 1982); Mary Taylor Huber, "Constituting the Church: Catholic Missionaries on the Sepik Frontier," *American Ethnologist* 14 (February 1987):107-25; Jane Schneider and Shirley Lindenbaum, "Frontiers of Christian Evangelism: Essays in Honor of Joyce Riegelhaupt," *American Ethnologist* 14 (February 1987):1-8; Judith Shapiro, "From Tupa to the Land without Evil: The Christianization of the Tupi-Guarani Cosmology," *American Ethnologist* 14 (February 1987):126-39; Bernard Porter, *The Lion's Share: A Short History of British Imperialism, 1850-1983* (London: Longman, 1985 ed.), 21-26. For a recent study of seventeenth-century missionary work in Massachusetts, see Linkhuyzen, "A Reappraisal of the Praying Indians," pp. 396-428; Hutchison, *Errand to the World,* 60.

22. Joan Jacobs Brumberg, *Mission for Life: The Story of the Family of Adoniram Judson, the Dramatic Events of the First American Foreign Mission, and the Course of Evangelical Religion in the Nineteenth Century* (New York: Free Press, 1980), 67-68; Richard D. Brown, *Knowledge Is Power: The Diffusion of Information in Early America, 1700-1865* (New York: Oxford University Press, 1989), 218-19, 234-35, 241, 273-74.

23. Donald M. Scott, *From Office to Profession: The New England Ministry, 1750-1850* (Philadelphia: University of Pennsylvania Press, 1978), 37, 81-83; Sandra S. Sizer, *Gospel Hymns and Social Religion: The Rhetoric of Nineteenth-Century Revivalism* (Philadelphia: Temple University Press, 1978), 52. I profited from reading Richard I. Rabinowitz' "Soul, Character and Personality: The Transformation of Religious Experience in New England, 1790-1860," as an unpublished Harvard Ph.D. dissertation in 1977, especially pp. 163-64. The dissertation has since been published.

24. Joel Wakeman, "Articles on Marcus and Narcissa Whitman, Henry Spalding," typescript from the *Prattsburg News*, 1892-98, Northwest and Whitman College Archives, Penrose Memorial Library, Whitman College, Walla Walla, Washington.

25. Richard Carwardine, *Trans-atlantic Revivalism: Popular Evangelicalism in Britain and America, 1790-1665* (Westport, CT: Greenwood Press, 1978), 8, 25, 49, 56.

26. *O.P.A.*, vol. 19 (1891), p. 116; Linkhuyzen, "A Reappraisal of the Praying Indians," p. 418, makes a similar point about the discouragement of weeping in seventeenth century Indian tribes.

27. See Rabinowitz, "Soul, Character and Personality," pp. 188-97.

28. Drury, *First White Women over the Rockies,* vol. 2, p. 303; Hulbert, *Marcus Whitman,* vol. 3, p. 153; Letters to Elkanah Walker, September 28, 1846, May 17, 1847, Beinecke Library, Yale University.

29. *O.P.A.*, vol. 19 (1891), pp. 102, 105, 139, 143, vol. 21 (1893), pp. 121-22, 130-31, 147.

30. For an excellent analysis of the formation of this new urban middle class, see Stuart M. Blumin, *The Emergence of the Middle Class: Social Experience in the American City, 1760-1900* (New York: Cambridge University Press, 1989). For the particular part women played in the creation of the middle class, see Ginzberg, *Women and the Work of Benevolence.*

31. Drury, *Marcus and Narcissa Whitman . . . ,* vol. 2, p. 394, and *First White Women over the Rockies,* vol. 1, pp. 101-02; *O.P.A.*, vol. 19 (1891), p. 147, vol. 21 (1893), p. 162.

32. Gray in his *A History of Oregon* commented on Narcissa's "refined education and manners," p. 123. For examples of her characterization of the Cayuse, see Drury, *First White Women over the Rockies,* vol. 1, pp. 75, 122, 124; *O.P.A.,* vol. 19 (1891), pp. 93-94, 102, 105; for a discussion of the significance the middle class attributed to sincerity, see Karen Halttunen, *Confidence Men and Painted Women: A Study of Middle-class Culture in America, 1830-1870* (New Haven: Yale University Press, 1982), especially pp. 34, 109.

33. *O.P.A.,* vol. 19 (1891), pp. 99-100, 107; Drury, *Marcus and Narcissa Whitman . . . ,* vol. 2, p. 393.

34. *O.P.A.,* vol. 19 (1891), pp. 132, 134.

35. Hulbert, *Marcus Whitman,* vol. 2, pp. 244-45; Drury, *First White Women over the Rockies,* vol. 1, p. 125; *O.P.A.,* vol. 19 (1891), pp. 132, 134-135, 159-160.

36. For an example of cultural interaction drawn from material culture, Paul Kane's depiction of Narcissa's fan is revealing. See J. Russell Harper (ed.), *Paul Kane's Frontier: Including Wanderings of an Artist among the Indians of North America, by Paul Kane* (Austin: University of Texas Press, 1971), 231. Letter from Elijah White to T. Hartley Crawford, April 1, 1843, Oregon Superintendency of Indian Affairs, 1842-1852, Letters Received by the Office of Indian Affairs, 1824-1880, Microfilm 234, # 607, National Archives, Washington, DC.

37. *O.P.A.,* vol. 19 (1891), p. 132.

38. Drury, *First White Women over the Rockies,* vol. 2, p. 194.

39. See *O.P.A.,* vol. 19 (1891), p. 133, for a view that the Indians were on their way to extinction.

40. For this part of the paper, I wish to acknowledge Susan Armitage's suggestive article, "The Challenge of Women's History," in David H. Stratton and George A. Frykman, eds., *The Changing Pacific Northwest: Interpreting Its Past* (Pullman: Washington State University Press, 1988).

41. Hulbert, *Marcus Whitman,* vol. 3, p. 196.

42. Her habit of imagining herself at home or fantasizing home scenes began on her journey west. Drury, *First White Women over the Rockies,* vol. 1, pp. 90-91, 97; *O.P.A.,* vol. 19 (1891), pp. 109, 113, vol. 21 (1893), p. 179.

43. *O.P.A.,* vol. 19 (1891), pp. 97, 106, 130, vol. 21 (1893), pp. 133-34, 205. Patricia Grimshaw makes a similar point about the importance of these emotional links with home in *Paths of Duty: American Missionary Wives in Nineteenth-Century Hawaii* (Honolulu: University of Hawaii Press, 1989), p. 54.

44. *O.P.A.,* vol. 21 (1893), p. 124.

45. *Ibid.,* pp. 110-112, 172, 175-176.

46. *Ibid.,* pp. 149, 155, 172-73. Narcissa told her sister Harriet, "we find it a great comfort to meet together, to pray and sympathize with and for each other in this desert land where we have so few privileges." The Maternal Association was only one of what Scott calls the "dense fabric of groups, societies, and associations" with which Narcissa was involved. She initiated female prayer groups when possible, Sabbath school classes, special meetings with her adopted children, and participated as did the other missionaries in "concerts" of prayer for the success of the missionary effort. Scott, *From Office to Profession,* 43.

47. Drury, *First White Women over the Rockies,* vol. 1, pp. 122-25; Hulbert, *Marcus Whitman,* vol. 1, p. 578.

48. Drury, *Marcus and Narcissa Whitman . . . ,* vol. 1, pp. 421-22; Hulbert, *Marcus Whitman,* vol. 2 , p. 224; *O.P.A.,* vol. 19 (1891), p. 166; "Genteel Background of Mrs. Whitman Shown by Diggings," undated clipping in the Whitman College Library; Robert W. Olsen, "Report and Observation Prepared by Historian Robert W. Olsen," unpublished report, August 1970, at the Whitman Mission National Historical Site.

49. *O.P.A.*, vol. 19 (1891), p. 107.

50. *O.P.A.*, vol. 21 (1893), p. 125.

51. One of the best studies of the psychological function of illness is Jean Strouse's *Alice James: A Biography* (Boston: Houghton Mifflin, 1980); Clifford M. Drury, "The Columbia Maternal Association," *Oregon Historical Quarterly* 39 (June 1933):119-20.

52. *O.P.A.*, vol. 21 (1893), pp. 82, 182.

53. Letter to Mary Walker, June 22, 1846, Beinecke Library, Yale University; *O.P.A.*, vol. 21 (1893), p. 92.

54. See, for example, Patricia R. Hill, *The World Their Household: The American Woman's Foreign Mission Movement and Cultural Transformation, 1870-1920* (Ann Arbor: University of Michigan Press, 1985), and Jane Hunter, *The Gospel of Gentility: American Women Missionaries in Turn-of-the-Century China* (New Haven: Yale University Press, 1984).

VIII
Pacific Northwest Indians and the Bill of Rights

John R. Wunder
(University of Nebraska-Lincoln)

Rainier
Last time around the forest floor
Rain beating on the ferns
Red cedar roots stream with life
Mud puddles reach my shoes
The dust is wet and wind picks up
Country swept of mother guardian earth
Still, I am involved
Searching, searching for my liberty
Sunshine once again
Breathing rays descriptive
Odors of challenge bright motives[1]

"*Searching, searching for my liberty . . .* "These strong words of Port Angeles-born Makah Jim Tollerud are words for all Native Americans. And nowhere has that search been more frustrating than with Indian relationships to the federal Bill of Rights.

The history of Native American relationships with the federal Bill of Rights is a dynamic and confusing one. Change is more often invoked in attempts to restructure these relationships than is continuity. Moreover, most questions involving these relationships have been considered in modern times since World War II, and Pacific Northwest Indians have been at the forefront of making new law.

It should not be too surprising to learn that confusion in these legal relationships prevails. Interpretations of the Bill of Rights by the U.S. Supreme Court have emphasized individual rights, but rights as defined in Native American society are extremely limited. That does not mean that individual rights are not protected and recognized, but consensus is sought to verify a right as one of the group's rights, not just one belonging to a particular individual. Consequently, Indians frequently struggle to obtain legal recognition of collective entitlements rather than individual rights, but cultural ignorance and intolerance, centered in those from the dominant society enforcing the Bill of Rights, makes that recognition difficult to achieve.[2]

Another aspect of this difficulty is conflicting legal interpretations. Federal Indian jurisprudence is in constant conflict, because it acknowledges limited forms of sovereignty within a forced union. In this process, Native American rights have been placed more often at the disposal of Congress than the Supreme Court.[3] Questions of law inherently become questions of politics.

Since World War II, the history of Native Americans and the Bill of Rights has involved Pacific Northwest Indians in prominent roles. Coeur d'Alene Indian writer and poet, Janet Campbell Hale, recently published a novel about a woman named Cecelia Capture and her father Will. At one important juncture in the novel, Cecelia is in jail remembering a childhood event that she suddenly understands. At the time it did not make sense why her father threw away all of his law books. Eagle Capture, the grandfather who her father had told her about with admiration,

> was the one who had brought the white man's system of justice to the tribe. He believed that the key to survival was legal representation. If the Indian people had had adequate legal representation, there would have been no Little Bighorn or Wounded Knee. It wouldn't have been possible for the white-eyes to steal land and murder Indians. Legal representation was the key.

Cecelia, who had shared her father's hopes by the end of the book, also shared her father's doubts.[4] To a great extent this story symbolizes the struggle for rights by Pacific Northwest Indians during the modern era.[5]

Disputes involving Bill of Rights issues and Pacific Northwest native peoples have primarily evolved around questions of sovereignty—from access and protection of natural resources to personal freedoms. At stake was the exercise of hunting, fishing, and water rights by Indian nations. New concerns over nuclear waste disposal on or near reservations have heightened Indian resolve to protect their resources. Also, of considerable sovereign concern for native peoples were questions litigated over the power to tax, and criminal and civil jurisdiction on reservations. Finally, Indians were successful in persuading Congress to act in areas that were to assist in the protection of Indian families and Indian religious freedoms. In all of these crucial legal considerations, Pacific Northwest Indians sought to expand or protect their sovereignty and legal rights by challenging existing rules of law.

Fishing Rights

Beginning in the 1950s and accelerating in the 1970s, significant litigation occurred regarding Indian hunting, fishing, and water rights. This was caused by a combination of factors. Native Americans became much more cognizant of ways to protect their rights. The first Indian law case text, *Law and the American Indian: Readings, Notes and Cases* by Monroe E. Price, was published in 1973;[6] Indian law was taught for the first time at a number of law schools; and programs encouraged Native American students to go to law schools. Legal services, when they represented individual tribal members, took on long established local laws and traditions that discriminated against American Indians. Indians themselves formed cooperative legal rights organizations, such as the Native American Rights Fund, headquartered in Boulder, Colorado. As a result, Native Americans developed new ways to fight for their rights.

At the same time that Native Americans vigorously entered the legal system, states began aggressively to pursue access to reservation resources and started to closely monitor the exercise of Indian rights off and on reservations. The population push to the West resulted in a tremendous demand for water, and states hoped to deny Indian water rights. States and the federal government also became concerned about conservation. State governments tried to regulate hunting and fishing on the grounds that it was necessary to preserve animals and fish from extinction even if Indian treaty rights were violated. Thus, a swirl of litigation surrounded Native American hunting, fishing, and water rights, and the eyes of the nation turned to the Pacific Northwest.

State intervention against Indian hunting and fishing treaty rights on and off reservations, it should be noted, is founded on the notion of a constitutionally protected, inherent, police power left to the states. This runs counter to Indian treaty provisions, the Bill of Rights, and the will of Congress as expressed in modern, federal, self-determination policies for Indian governments.

Many Indian treaties contain provisions protecting traditional Indian fishing and hunting practices. For example, in western Washington Territory in 1854, several Pacific Northwest Indian bands and nations, including the Puyallup and Nisqually, signed the Medicine Creek Treaty. Article 3 of the treaty stated: "The right of taking fish, at all usual and accustomed grounds and stations, is further secured to said Indians in common with all citizens of the Territory."[7]

Congress has reinforced these treaty rights. In Public Law 280, passed in 1953, and otherwise a major assault on Indian sovereignty, Congress stipulated when it gave criminal jurisdiction over Indian lands to six states that,

> Nothing in this section shall authorize the alienation, encumbrance, or taxation of any real or personal property, including water rights, belonging to any Indian or any Indian tribe, band, or community that is held in trust by the United States . . . ; or shall deprive any Indian or any Indian tribe, band, or community of any right, privilege, or immunity afforded under Federal treaty, agreement, or statute with respect to hunting, trapping, or fishing, or the control, licensing, or regulation thereof.[8]

If that language was not comprehensive enough, fifteen years later Congress once again reiterated its protection of Indian treaty rights. With the Indian Bill of Rights signed into law in 1968, under Title IV, "Jurisdiction over Criminal and Civil Actions," Congress listed verbatim the exact protections offered in Public Law 280.[9] Indian hunting, fishing, and water rights were retained.

These acts, however, did not stop states from asserting jurisdiction over fishing and hunting rights or the U.S. Supreme Court from eroding those Indian rights. For 125 years in the rare disputes brought before American courts concerning Indian fishing rights, Native American treaty fishing provisions prevailed. That all changed in 1968 with Justice William O. Douglas's opinion in *Puyallup Tribe v. Department of Game*, now known as *Puyallup I*.[10] In this case, the Treaty of Medicine Creek (1854) was applied to state regulation of off-reservation nets used by Indians. Indians were fishing for their own consumption and commercial sales. Their unrestricted fishing rights ran up against two fierce non-Indian competitors: other commercial fishing interests and sports fishers. They complained because Indians ignored state regulations based upon shortages of particular kinds of salmon. Hostilities and confrontations on the banks of Washington's streams occurred once the state banned the nets Indians were using, and Justice Douglas upheld this ban ostensibly because the treaty did not prevent it. Almost as if to assure extensive future litigation, the majority opinion did not rule on whether Washington state's regulation was "reasonable and necessary." It only speculated that if it were, it was constitutional. Subsequent litigation attempted to define Indian fishing rights in terms of the amount of catch, types of equipment, and place of access, but the bottom line was that states could now question federally protected Indian fishing rights.[11]

One of the first issues to be litigated after *Puyallup I* was how much fish Indians could catch off reservations. The case of *United States v. State of Washington*, begun in 1970, took four years to decide, but the decision was very controversial and led to outbreaks of hostility. Judge George Boldt of the Federal District Court for the Western District of Washington decided that treaties gave Pacific Northwest Indians greater rights to salmon than non-Indians, that off-reservation fishing rights were protected for Indians against state regulation, and that the state could restrain Indian fishing only in so far as to prevent the extinction of fish. Indians, according to Boldt, could exercise a share of up to 50 percent of the fish available, not including fish caught for subsistence or for religious purposes.[12]

Reaction by non-Indians was severe. Judge Boldt was threatened, and a significant backlash in Washington state occurred against Indians, who were confronted when they sought to fish outside their reservations. The state of Washington also refused to enforce the Boldt decision, and this naturally led to more litigation culminating in 1979 with the U.S. Supreme Court upholding most of the Boldt decision.[13]

Fishing rights litigation throughout the Pacific Northwest explored the opening left by both the Douglas and Boldt decisions. For instance, nineteenth-century treaties with the Confederated Tribes of the Warm Springs Reservation in north central Oregon, the Confederated Tribes and Bands of the Yakama Indian Nation in central Washington,[14] the Confederated Tribes of the Umatilla Indian Reservation in northeastern Oregon, and the Nez Perce Tribe of northern Idaho guaranteed to those tribes customary fishing rights on the Columbia River. Nevertheless, both the states of Washington and Oregon tried to close the Columbia to commercial fishing. Indians naturally resisted, and they claimed they had off-reservation rights to any fish. Dams on the Columbia had seriously depleted the number of fish, and the states argued that conservation demanded regulation, even prohibition. Finally, a federal district court ruled in *Sohappy v. Smith*[15] that state fishing regulations were constitutional if they were essential for conservation, and, under those requirements, Oregon's regulations restructuring Indian catches off reservation did not hold up to scrutiny.

Eventually, all of the tribes and the two states agreed on a joint plan for managing the fish harvest on the Columbia, but the litigation leading up to the plan encompassed nearly eight years of court confrontations.[16] New litigation is beginning once again in 1997.

By taking aggressive action, Pacific Northwest states attempted to regulate off-reservation Indian fishing. States were successful against those who did not have specific treaty rights. Moreover, they supervised Indian fishing if there was a clear threat to conservation, necessitating state intervention to protect what they termed the basic Indian treaty right. But the states were not through. New Mexico, in 1983, went to the U.S. Supreme Court hoping to be able to extend its state hunting and fishing regulations onto the Mescalero Apache Reservation. The Court would not allow this, although it tried to weigh the impact of New Mexico's regulations on Indian sovereignty and treaty rights against the need for conservation. The Court's message was that if a state could prove that drastic conservation measures were necessary, then it might be able to regulate fishing on Indian reservations.[17] Such a threat remains to be exercised.

Hunting Rights

Generally, hunting rights are not thought of as legally distinct from fishing rights, but sometimes there are differences. Both states and the federal government became involved in hunting regulations. As with fishing rights, states actively worked to prevent Indian nations from exercising hunting rights guaranteed by treaties. One of the first modern conflicts over hunting rights came in Oregon. The Klamaths were one of the tribes that were the subject of the termination movement in the 1950s and early 1960s. At the time, the U.S. Congress decided to abolish certain Indian groups and nations they thought ready to be assimilated into the general population. Once the Klamath reservation was officially terminated, the state of Oregon attempted to stop the Klamaths from exercising their hunting rights in the forests of their former reservation. Litigation worsened the situation. Courts decided that some Klamaths who willingly resigned their tribal memberships were not allowed to keep their treaty rights, but others could.[18]

Given that termination could not prevent some Pacific Northwest Indians from exercising their hunting rights, might Indian hunting rights be protected even in cases where there was no treaty? The answer was "yes" for the Kootenais of northern Idaho. In *State v. Coffee*, the conviction of a Kootenai for killing a deer out of season was overturned even though the

Kootenais had no treaty with the United States. The court ruled that the Kootenais had been affected by the 1855 Treaty signed at the Hellgate council because as a result of that treaty the Kootenais lost title to lands that they had previously occupied. Since they had some relationship to the treaty, they possessed the hunting rights guaranteed in the treaty.[19]

Indian nations also tried to regulate hunting on their own reservations. In Montana, the Crows prohibited hunting and fishing on their reservation by non-tribal members. Then, the state of Montana tried to assert its power over the reservation by also regulating non-Indian hunters. Thus, both the Crows and the state of Montana sought exclusive jurisdiction over non-Crow hunters. Tribal sovereignty took a blow when the Supreme Court in *Montana v. United States* (1981) held that tribes could regulate non-Indians only on reservation land, but not on the waterways, and only if those non-Indians were threatening the tribe's well-being and political and economic survival. Such limitations made regulation of non-Indians hunting on reservations virtually impossible.[20]

Pacific Northwest Indian hunting rights were also constrained by federal statutes, such as the Endangered Species Act (1973)[21] and the Eagle Protection Act (1940).[22] The Eagle Protection Act was amended in 1962 to prohibit the killing of golden eagles and bald eagles, and to allow Indians, who wished to take eagles, to apply for an eagle hunting license with the Department of Interior.[23] These laws were challenged by Dwight Dion, Sr., a Yankton Sioux, who was convicted of shooting four bald eagles on the Yankton Sioux Reservation in South Dakota. The fundamental question was whether Native Americans had the right to hunt bald or golden eagles on their own reservations for non-commercial purposes. This right, argued Dion, came from treaties, the First Amendment, and the Indian Bill of Rights' free exercise of religion clause. Eagle feathers were an important part of traditional Indian religion, and enforcement of the federal laws, Dion maintained, restricted his free exercise of religious rights.

The courts were confused. The federal district court convicted Dion of violating both the Endangered Species Act and the Eagle Protection Act. The appellate court reversed the convictions based upon the Endangered Species Act, but allowed the others to stand. The Supreme Court then reversed the appellate court and did great damage to Indian treaty rights. In *United States v. Dion* (1986),[24] Justice Thurgood Marshall wrote that the congressional legislation—the Endangered Species Act and the Eagle Protection Act—superceded the Yankton Sioux Treaty of 1858. Consequently, Indians no longer had unrestricted rights to hunt eagles on their own reservations. Marshall refused to consider the religious implications, believing that federal needs to preserve eagles took precedence over Indian needs for eagle feathers to practice their religion. Marshall also refused to recognize the implications of his decision that the right to hunt per se did not stop regulation to prevent the extinction of a species. In essence, Marshall had an opportunity to overrule *Puyallup I*, and he decided not to do so.

By the 1990s, and in spite of the Boldt decision, Indian fishing and hunting rights were greatly weakened. It is now clear that conservation can be used as a concept to overrule treaty rights and, perhaps, even those rights generally guaranteed in the Bill of Rights for all Americans. The courts have determined that reservations are not sanctuaries. The state and federal government can regulate under certain conditions, and this amounts to a direct attack by states on tribal sovereignty. Moreover, *Montana v. United States* made it extremely difficult for tribal governments to regulate even their own reservations.

Water Rights

By the end of World War II, Indian water rights were on a stronger legal footing than fishing and hunting rights, but they too have been weakened during the past twenty years. In 1908, the U.S. Supreme Court articulated the *Winters* doctrine that represents a beginning point for delineating Indian water law.[25] The dispute, *Winters v. United States*, involved the Fort Belknap Reservation of the Gros Ventres, Piegans, Bloods, Blackfeet, and River Crows in Montana. The boundary of the reservation had been placed in the middle of the Milk River. Lands adjacent to the reservation were sold after 1888 to non-Indians who filed for water claims based upon a federal law—the Desert Land Act—that stated all non-navigable waters were available for appropriation depending upon state laws. These land owners began diverting water from the Milk River for irrigation purposes. However, the Fort Belknap Indians' only supply of water was the Milk River, and they sued to prevent its diversion.[26]

Just three years previously, the Supreme Court had decided in another Pacific Northwest dispute, *United States v. Winans* (1905), that Indians could exercise some rights off reservations. This included treaty rights to fish in all customary places. At issue in *Winans* was the state of Washington trying to prevent members of the Yakama nation from setting fish traps in the Columbia River. The state argued that the Yakamas had given up title to the lands surrounding their customary fishing places, and thus they had lost any special treatment reserved in the treaties. The Court rejected this reasoning because it found that treaties were not grants of rights *to* Indians but grants of rights *from* Indians.[27]

The *Winans* court also considered a more basic concept. Justice Joseph McKenna wrote that fishing was essential for the survival of the Yakamas. It was as important as "the atmosphere they breathed."[28] McKenna concluded that Indians have certain fundamental rights to survival reserved under American justice. Those rights included access to food. Another might be access to water.

The *Winters* decision picked up on this theme. Here, the Court held that the Fort Belknap Indians retained their water rights to the Milk River in order to ensure that their tribal lands retained their agricultural value.[29] Montana settlers argued that the Indians deliberately gave up their water rights with their lands, that they had made no effort to reserve any water rights, and that the federal government knew this and understood it. The Court, however, did not care about these arguments. "We realize," said the majority, "that there is a conflict of implications, but that which makes for the retention of the waters is of greater force than that which makes for their cession." The Court then turned the language of water rights appropriation into a right for Native Americans. "The Indians had command of the lands and the waters—command of all their *beneficial use* [emphasis added], whether kept for hunting, 'and grazing roving herds of stock,' or turned to agriculture and the arts of civilization."[30]

There is much in the *Winters* case. One significant implication is that Native American water rights did not accrue from the Fifth Amendment. Nowhere do we see the Constitution or the Bill of Rights used as a foundation for protection of such a valuable resource as water in the arid West. Instead, Indian water rights evolved from the campaign for assimilation. Water was essential to transform Indians into farmers, and for their survival. Because water was essential, it was reserved for Indians for their beneficial use, and such beneficial use could be broadly defined to include the prevention of others from depleting the water supply.

The *Winters* doctrine also established the important concept that the creation of a reservation included not only a "reservation" of land, but a "reservation" of Indian water rights in all waters within or bordering the reservation. These rights to water are held against all competing users except those who had obtained water rights before the creation of the reservation. Indian occupation of some reservation areas, such as in New Mexico, dates back to at least the seventeenth century and virtually had no prior users. Perhaps most important to Native Americans, Indian rights to water had not been lost by not using them. They were retained by the tribes for future uses.

The *Winters* doctrine was a bold declaration, and state governments refused to acknowledge it. Senator William Borah of Idaho exclaimed "The Government of the United States has no control over the water rights of the State of Idaho." Utah's Senator George Sutherland pretended that *Winters* had not happened. He thought it, "one of those unfortunate statements that sometimes courts, and the highest court, lapse into"[31]; in other words they really did not mean it. Western reaction to the assertion of Native American rights outlined in the *Winters* case in 1908 proved to be quite similar to Southern reaction in 1954 to *Brown v. Board of Education*, and analogous to reactions to the 1974 Boldt decision in Washington state. Regarding water rights, it was one thing for Indians to obtain a legal right; it would be quite another to assert it against a hostile world.

Questions still remained after *Winters*. The most significant had to do with how much water could be reserved for Indian use, and this issue was resolved by *Arizona v. California* (1963) in favor of five Indian tribes from California, Arizona, and Nevada. They argued that they needed enough water to irrigate all the "practicably irrigable acreage" on their reservations rather than just the needs of a sparse population.[32] (*Arizona v. California* was the next case litigated before the U.S. Supreme Court concerning Indian water rights after the *Winters* case, which had dated from fifty-five years earlier. The federal government had not actively sought to protect or promote Indian water rights in the intervening five decades.)

In *Arizona v. California*, the Supreme Court upheld the constitutionality of the *Winters* doctrine and elaborated further upon its application. Water rights for Native Americans on reservations, said the Court, stood against all other rights from the time of the creation of the reservation. The Court observed that water was probably more important than food. In addition, the quantity of water reserved was to be based not upon the small number of Indians then living or likely to be residing on a reservation, but upon that needed to irrigate the tillable soils on the entire reservation. This constituted a considerably greater amount of water to be reserved for Indians. The lifeblood of survival on reservations, especially in the arid West, was preserved—for the time being. *Arizona* and *Winters* provided a legal underpinning allowing Native American nations legal alternatives in the competitive battle for scarce water resources.

Courts during the 1970s and 1980s were filled with new disputes directly challenging Indian water rights, the *Winters* doctrine, and the *Arizona* precedent. Slowly, federal and state judiciaries chipped away. The first modification of the *Winters* doctrine came in 1975 when the state of New Mexico sought to define Indian water rights to the San Juan River in its own state courts. The state won, and that litigation is still continuing. State courts are notoriously hostile to Indian water rights, and the Navajos, who have yet to receive their fair share of scarce water in the Four Corners area, must litigate in several state courts.[33]

A dual system of jurisdiction over Indian water rights was accepted by the U.S. Supreme Court beginning in the late 1970s. The Court ruled that the quantity of water reserved for Native Americans could be determined by state courts. Then Wyoming's Supreme Court in 1988 held that Shoshonis and Arapahoes could claim practicably irrigable acreage for agricultural and domestic use only, a new restriction. They could not reserve water for economic development or for sale to non-Indians, and they had no claims to any groundwater under the Wind River Reservation.[34] All of these redefinitions of Indian water rights countered existing U.S. Supreme Court opinions, and the high court allowed the Wyoming case to stand as good law by denying certiorari.[35]

Ironically, the U.S. Congress, normally a leader when it came to taking rights away from Native Americans, was appalled with the actions of the Supreme Court. It began to encourage agreements made by tribes with large users and threw federal financial support behind the development of large water projects that would guarantee water to Indians. These resulted in losses of some Indian water rights, but some agreements protected others, and for the first time since the 1970s Native Americans shifted their legal focus from the courts to the federal legislature.[36]

Indian efforts to exercise their rights to natural resources became a serious battleground. Water, fishing, and hunting rights, so clearly defined in the past by treaties, statutes, and court opinions, began to unravel in this modern era. This was and continues to be a life and death struggle for Pacific Northwest native peoples, for without food and water, the reservation and Indian life itself cannot be sustained.

Mineral and Land Use Rights

Related to hunting, fishing, and water rights is the power of Native Americans to utilize the various other resources of their own reservations.

Exercising this right has taken tribes through a variety of legal disputes over leases, zoning, and taxation powers. The power to tax, as many tribal governments have discovered, is an important, yet controversial power. The ability of tribal governments to exercise civil and criminal jurisdiction on reservations regardless of who is involved, Indian or non-Indian, has proved litigious. These economic and political issues for Pacific Northwest Indians were dramatically addressed during the last two decades.

During the late 1970s and 1980s, Americans learned, often to their surprise, that Indians owned much of the nation's potential energy resources. West of the Mississippi River, 3-5 percent of oil and gas, 30-40 percent of coal, and 25-40 percent of uranium reserves are on Indian reservations. Coal on Montana and North Dakota reservations alone amounts to fifteen times the energy resources of the Alaska North Slope oil and gas fields.[37] Not all tribes, however, have access to these kinds of resources; only approximately 40 out of over 300 federally recognized Native American nations own actual rights to energy reserves. By the end of the 1980s, most of these resources were still untapped and private companies were anxious to capture reservation mineral rights.[38]

Indian reaction to this sudden interest was divided. Some opposed any industrial development and saw their cultures threatened, while others thought mineral exploitation would help provide jobs and a secure economic future. Many Indians were simply cynical. Said one, "Don't tell me about an energy crisis. I don't even have electricity in my village."[39] Indian leadership debated these issues, gathered information, and quickly found that many companies had arranged unfair long-term leases through the Department of Interior, often without tribal knowledge. When tribal governments tried to void leases, they were rebuffed.

Eventually, Native American tribal governments embarked upon a legal strategy. First, they created their own organization, known as CERT (Council of Energy Resource Tribes), and then began monitoring the exploitation of their own natural resources. Through the efforts of Allen Rowland (Northern Cheyenne), Earl Old Person (Blackfeet), and others, CERT evolved into a national energy player.[40]

To combat lease problems, Indians lobbied for new federal laws to address natural resource planning. In 1982, the Indian Mineral Development Act gave native peoples the legal means to allow the extraction of natural resources from their reservations with their own companies. Previously they could only receive royalties from leases.[41]

Just as important as controlling what was being mined on reservations was having some say over various other kinds of projects located on, or near, reservations. Companies and states were attracted to reservation lands for the deposit of wastes, including nuclear wastes. In the same year that Congress passed the Indian Mineral Development Act, it also created the Nuclear Waste Policy Act.[42] This law set up regulatory procedures and standards whereby tribal governments could petition to be classified as "affected." Once a group received this designation, it could participate in decision-making. The Yakamas became the first nation to be defined as "affected." They were invited to review nuclear waste repository activities at the Hanford site near their Washington state reservation.

What the Yakamas found, and what other tribes have subsequently discovered, is that the Department of Energy is more concerned about the actual placing of waste into the ground than where waste should be deposited or its impact on Indian peoples. At Hanford, before 1982 and passage of the Nuclear Waste Policy Act, which gave Indians a voice in the depository process, DOE dug tunnels into Gable Mountain without consulting the Yakama nation or considering First Amendment ramifications. Gable Mountain (though located outside of the Yakama Reservation) is central to Yakama religious beliefs. The tribal council responded with a series of resolutions, but DOE ignored them until the Yakamas banned the transportation of nuclear materials through their reservation. Eventually, the Yakamas were able to stop further desecration of Gable Mountain. Ironically, the states, and in this case the state of Washington, now want to ally with Indian tribal governments to prevent nuclear wastes from being deposited on reservation lands.[43]

Another legal means to protect Indian lands from unacceptable development involved zoning. Indians and local or state governments were frequently in conflict over zoning. At first there was little resistance because tribal governments thought they could not stop local zoning on reservations. However, once Native Americans began to question non-Indian zoning regulations, they created their own zoning laws. Here, Indians at first were successful, but recently they have sustained legal defeats.[44]

Tribal governments in the 1970s and 1980s enacted zoning ordinances covering entire reservations. This power, they argued, was sanctioned by the resolution of an Arizona dispute, *Williams v. Lee*, settled by the U.S. Supreme Court in 1959.[45] This decision preempted states from asserting power over reservations generally and over non-Indians residing on reservations specifically. Since 1958, the *Williams* precedent has eroded until it was constructively overruled in a 1989 decision, *Brendale v. Confederated Tribes and Bands of the Yakima Indian Nation*.[46]

Before *Brendale* and after *Williams*, the Supreme Court had decided that tribal governments could only regulate non-Indians on reservations if they were specifically given that power by the federal government.[47] This represented a departure from *Williams v. Lee*. In *Brendale*, the Yakama Indian Nation passed zoning ordinances regulating the development of reservation lands owned by Yakamas, Indian non-members of the Yakama tribe, and non-Indians—all living on the Yakama Reservation. The tribal council soon found itself in conflict with the Yakima County Planning Department. In the *Brendale* decision, the Supreme Court created a legal test for Indian zoning regulations. Tribal governments could zone reservations only if the ordinances protected the fundamental nature of the tribes. The Court ruled that the Yakamas could not zone areas of the reservation that were under the control of non-Indians, and it could zone mixed use areas only if they were related to Yakama culture.[48] Thus, if a non-Indian bought land on the Yakama Reservation and wanted to build a fast food restaurant, as long as it did not interfere with a sacred site and it met county zoning standards, the Yakamas were powerless to prevent it. *Brendale* seriously compromised Indian sovereignty.

In summary, modern Indians have sought to reclaim control over their lands. They tried to build coalitions and influence national energy policy through CERT. They used tribal ordinances to delay or force enactment of national legislation to guarantee Indian voices in nuclear waste disposal. Zoning regulations became another weapon to prevent unwelcome development. But perhaps the most important power available to tribal governments was the power to tax—especially taxing companies extracting natural resources from Indian lands.

Indians and the Power to Tax

From the 1970s to the 1990s, tribal governments frequently declared their resources to be under the control of tribal authorities, subject only to congressionally mandated restrictions. Tribes, of course, wanted to manage their own reservation resources. Stopping existing leases was nearly impossible because most were long-term arrangements negotiated by the Department of Interior. Not to be denied, however, tribal governments started to tax mining companies. State taxation of reservation resources was generally precluded, so little law had developed regarding any kind of preemption of tribal taxing power. There was a void, and tribal governments filled it.[49]

Three kinds of taxation existed for tribal governments: consumption taxes, property taxes, and income taxes. Consumption taxes typically were sales or use taxes, the most popular being tribal taxes on state tax-free cigarettes. Property taxes were assessed on housing, real estate, and resource production. And, a logical opportunity for Indian governments was applying severance taxes to mineral extraction and oil and gas production.[50]

By 1970, courts had yet to decide whether tribal taxes preempted state taxes or state taxes preempted tribal taxes. Also unclear was whether states could tax Indian or non-Indian income earned on reservations. Congress had not addressed these issues, so it was left to the U.S. Supreme Court to decide. The first case heard originated from an Arizona-Navajo dispute when Rosalind McClanahan, a Navajo who lived on the Navajo Reservation in Arizona, had $16.20 withheld from her paycheck by the state of Arizona. Her income came completely from her work on the reservation. The state of Arizona, however, was attempting to tax the income Navajos made on and off their reservation. The court held in *McClanahan v. State Tax Commission of Arizona* that no state could tax the income that Indians earned on reservations because a state tax interfered with tribal self-government and federal Indian self-determination policies. Open to question was whether the state could tax non-Indians residing and deriving income on the reservation.[51]

In spite of the gray areas and the *McClanahan* decision, tribes were reluctant to adopt tax laws. Indian nations did not want to tax the income of their own people because there was not much Indian income. Imposing sales and property taxes on tribal members also was impractical. The main sources of income on reservations, therefore, became severance taxes on large non-Indian corporations and consumption taxes on goods, usually cigarettes, that non-Indians bought because they were cheaper on reservations without state taxes.

Indian governments moved carefully; they worried that they might be forced to tax Indians and non-Indians alike, and this would cause many problems on the reservation.[52] Another concern was whether states would tax the same products or items that Indians taxed. Dual taxation might drive income-producing developments from a reservation, and this fear was realized as early as 1976 in Montana.

On all tax issues, the Supreme Court allowed states an entry onto reservations. In Montana, Joseph Wheeler, Jr., a Flathead, owned and operated two discount cigarette stores on the Flathead Reservation. He was arrested by Montana authorities for selling cigarettes to non-Indians without a license and not including Montana state tax. Wheeler's case was assumed by the Confederated Salish and Kootenai tribes, who alleged that tribal sovereignty was violated by the state of Montana and its taxing authority. The Supreme Court resolved the dispute with Justice William Rehnquist ruling in favor of Montana. Severely restricting the *McClanahan* holding, *Moe v. Confederated Salish and Kootenai Tribes* (1976)[53] allowed states to tax Indian incomes on reservations that were derived from non-Indian commerce. This decision allowed states to tax Indian income earned exclusively on reservations and seriously eroded Indian taxing powers.[54]

Litigation also included severance taxes. The Jicarilla Apaches won a major victory in 1982 when their tax on oil and gas development in New Mexico was upheld as a crucial part of their sovereign rights and the federal government's policy of encouraging Indian self-determination.[55] The state of New Mexico had argued that only states and municipalities could tax oil and gas production on reservations. Three years later, when the Kerr-McGee Corporation challenged Navajo taxes on their mining activities, Kerr-McGee lost. Certainly, tribal governments could tax non-Indian corporations operating on reservations, but the Supreme Court left open the notion that if Indian taxes were "unfair," they could be struck down.[56]

These early limited tax victories for Native Americans were substantially eroded within a decade. Borrowing from the *Moe* precedent, the state of New Mexico decided, rather than challenge Indian rights to enforce severance taxes, that the state would simply pass its own severence tax. Double taxation would, of course, discourage business development. In *Cotton Petroleum Corp. v. New Mexico*,[57] the Supreme Court ruled that these kinds of state taxes were permissible. This holding threatened the very profitability of the product Indians sought to tax. The only solution for tribes then was to own their own oil, gas, and mineral companies or to enter into taxation agreements with states. In the 1990s, Indian nations began moving in both of these directions.[58]

Tribal Court Jurisdiction

At the same time Indians sought control over reservation taxation and resources, tribal governments attempted to extend tribal sovereignty through tribal courts and their jurisdiction. During the 1970s and 1980s, tribal courts improved in terms of their expertise and availability to reservation residents. By 1975, for example, Navajo tribal council appropriations for courts were over $500,000 per year. Five judges and an appellate tribunal were hired, and tribal criminal and civil codes were adopted. Today, Dinebeiina Nahiilna Be Agaditahe (DNA) ("Lawyers for the Development of the People") or Navajo Legal Services and over fifty Navajo lawyers regularly practice law in Navajo tribal courts.[59]

The Navajo tribal council explicitly limited Navajo court jurisdiction to those criminal and civil disputes where the defendant was an Indian. Many other tribes, however, did not. They included non-Indians within their jurisdiction. Tribal governments reasoned that because reservations were not given much attention by non-Indian law enforcement, justice required that Indian police and courts exercise some means of legal control.[60] Not everyone accepted this development, especially William Rehnquist of the U.S. Supreme Court, who by now was the Court's chief justice.

Mark Oliphant and Daniel Belgarde, non-Indians visiting the Suquamish tribe's Port Madison Reservation during the celebration of Chief Seattle Days, were arrested for reckless driving and assault of an Indian police officer. Oliphant was released after his arraignment in tribal court, and Belgarde posted bail. Prior to their trials both began habeas corpus proceedings in the federal district court for western Washington state. The district court and the federal court of appeals turned down Oliphant and Belgarde, but the U.S. Supreme Court in *Oliphant v. Suquamish Indian Tribe* reversed the decision and held that the Suquamish tribal court did not have criminal jurisdiction to try non-Indians.[61] Justice Rehnquist authored a sweeping opinion that undermined the authority of tribal governments and Indian law enforcement.

Rehnquist held that tribal courts had no power to try non-Indians on reservations because Congress and the federal courts were explicitly granted this power. The presumption was that criminal jurisdiction over non-Indians did not reside in Indian courts, because Indians were allowed to have reservations by the federal government. Therefore Indians had no power to control non-Indians on reservations. Rehnquist concluded that the United States government had the exclusive power to prosecute non-Indians if it wanted to, whether that power had been statutorily mandated or not.[62]

Legalists were stunned by this opinion. Russel Barsh and James Youngblood Henderson wrote that *Oliphant v. Suquamish Indian Tribe* represented, "a carelessness with history, logic, precedent, and statutory construction that is not ordinarily acceptable from so august a tribunal."[63] Rehnquist, argued Barsh and Youngblood Henderson, falsely used history, and as a result of the *Oliphant* opinion, the chief justice had dangerously come close to sharing the mantle with Roger Taney and his pre-Civil War *Dred Scott* opinion as the chief justice most infamous in American legal history when commenting on questions of race and law in American society. The legacy of the *Oliphant* decision was confusion.[64] What might Indian courts do? The Supreme Court had ruled that they did not have criminal jurisdiction over non-Indians. Might that extend to civil jurisdiction?

During the 1980s, issues emerged considering reservation civil jurisdiction. First, in 1985 a Crow child hit by a motorcycle in a school parking lot on the reservation was prevented by federal courts from suing the Lodge Grass School District's insurance company in Crow tribal courts.[65] Then in another insurance case, this time involving the Blackfeet tribal courts, the Supreme Court ruled that all remedies had to be exhausted in non-Indian proceedings.[66]

In 1989, on a North Dakota reservation, a dispute occurred over the water and sewer work done by Parisien Excavation, a company owned by Ernest Parisien, a Turtle Mountain Chippewa. Twin City Construction Company had contracted with the BIA to build a school and subcontracted with Parisien Excavation. According to Twin City, Parisien's company did not do an adequate job. Twin City refused to pay for the work done. Ernest Parisien sued in tribal court, but the Twin City Construction Company went to federal district court where it asked for an injunction to prevent the Turtle Mountain Chippewa tribal court from hearing the case. Twin City argued that Indian tribal courts did not have civil jurisdiction over non-Indians. The federal district court granted the injunction. On appeal to the Eighth Circuit court, after several hearings, the court deadlocked five-to-five, and the U.S. Supreme Court refused to hear the case.[67] Thus, current legal trends suggest that Indian tribal courts soon may not have civil jurisdiction over non-Indians on reservations.

By the 1990s, Native American judicial institutional development was at a crossroads. Indian sovereignty had been reinterpreted by the U.S. Supreme Court and state courts to restrain Indian legal institutions from exercising power over reservations. Indian criminal and civil jurisdiction was fundamentally altered.

Indian Rights to Their Children

Indian families after World War II continued to experience heavy assimilationist pressure from the legal system and social welfare agencies.

Native American mothers and fathers throughout the United States witnessed 25-35 percent of their children being taken from them. For example, in Idaho, out of every 100 children placed in foster care, 78 were Indian children; in some states as many as 40 percent of all adoptions involved Indian children being assigned to non-Indian parents. Seventeen percent of all Indian children in the 1970s lived in federal boarding schools away from their families.[68]

Taking Indian children from their parents defied due process. Charges of physical abuse almost never were made against Native American parents. Violence toward children is seldom a part of Indian culture regardless of the dire poverty many Native American families experience. Social workers used such reasons as social deprivation, emotional damage, or permissiveness for uprooting Indian children. They were bureaucratic excuses for cultural intolerance.[69] Congressional hearings singled out Mormon agencies in Utah, Idaho, and Arizona, Catholic agencies in the Midwest, and state governmental agencies, in states with large Indian populations, with aggressively taking Indian children away from their parents and tribe.

For example, in the early 1970s a two-year-old Indian girl was taken away from her Indian mother by an Oregon state caseworker because the child was "failing to thrive." The child had showed no weight gain or height increase, and the mother told the caseworker her daughter threw up after each feeding. By the time it was learned that a doctor prescribed the wrong formula for the child, Oregon's courts had taken the child away from her Indian mother, and the caseworker refused to tell the mother where her child was. After protests by the Indian Studies Center in Portland, the state was forced to have doctors examine the child. They found that the girl suffered from a hormonal deficiency. Eventually, the Indian girl was reunited with her mother, but she had been physically abused by the non-Indian foster parents.[70] Such scandals cried out for resolution.

Prior to 1978, Indian parents and tribes had no legal recourse to prevent Indian children from being placed in non-Indian families. State courts accepted the "best interests of the child" doctrine if challenges were made in state courts. These courts also did not define Indian families beyond immediate kin. The Indian cultural view of the "extended" family both caring for and raising a child was interpreted by American courts as detrimental. Indian grandparents were treated as legal strangers, and leaving a child with an aunt was construed by non-Indian judges to mean abandonment.[71]

In the 1970s, Indian tribal governments and lawyers made a major effort to save Indian children. It soon because obvious that a federal law rather than a Supreme Court determination was needed.[72] The result, the Indian Child Welfare Act of 1978, was generally satisfying for many Native Americans.

The Indian Child Welfare Act of 1978 (ICWA),[73] signed into law by President Jimmy Carter, contained three sections. The purpose for the act was to, "protect the best interests of Indian children and to promote the stability and security of Indian tribes and families by the establishment of minimum Federal standards for the removal of Indian children from their families."[74] To do so, child custody proceedings involving Indian children on reservations were made the exclusive jurisdiction of Indian courts. If a contested Indian child lived off the reservation, state courts were mandated to transfer jurisdiction to an appropriate Indian court. Tribes were also given the power to intervene in proceedings regarding foster care or adoption.[75]

The ICWA also provided preferences for child placement. A child could be taken from Indian parents, but it must be entrusted first to the child's Indian extended family, second to a foster home licensed by the Indian child's tribe, third to an Indian foster home approved by a non-Indian authority, or fourth to an institution for children approved by the child's tribe. Perhaps most importantly, tribes are guaranteed notice of any proceeding involving their own children.[76]

The Indian Child Welfare Act constituted a beginning of hope for many Native American families. It forced child agencies and state courts to adhere more closely to cultural values. After two decades, the ICWA has worked rather smoothly although there continue to be problems with procedures to identify a child as an Indian, particularly if the child welfare agency does not investigate fully.[77] Also, tribal courts and tribal governments must pass family law codes, develop new family law courts, and train personnel.

Indian Religious Rights

The year 1978 also marked another federal attempt at protecting Indian culture, but it was much less successful than the Indian Child Welfare Act. Congress decided to consider how governmental policies had imposed on Native American religious practices. Testimony before a select committee of Congress chaired by Senator James Abourezk of South Dakota elicited numerous comments concerning the denial of Indian religious freedoms throughout the United States—from not allowing sweat lodge ceremonies in prisons to the U.S. Navy denying access to sacred sites on military property.[78]

At the hearings, Crow leader Barney Old Coyote testified and offered an explanation for why Indian religion was different from Christian religion: "The area of worship cannot be delineated from social, political, culture, and other areas of Indian lifestyle, including his general outlook upon economic and resource development." Worship is, according to Old Coyote, "an integral part of the Indian way of life and culture which cannot be separated from the whole. This oneness of Indian life seems to be the basic difference between the Indian and non-Indians of a dominant society."[79] To Native Americans, their traditional religions are synonymous with their entire being, environment, and culture. American law, judges, and legislators have had a very difficult time grasping this concept, particularly during the 1970s and 1980s.

Congress found serious violations of American Indian First Amendment rights. Indians were being denied access to religious sites, they were not allowed to use certain sacred objects, and their freedom to worship through traditional means was restricted. To help solve this problem, Congress passed, and President Jimmy Carter signed, the American Indian Religious Freedom Act of 1978 (AIRFA).[80]

The Act contained two sections. The first defined the role of the United States government: "[H]enceforth it shall be the policy of the United States to protect and preserve for American Indians their inherent right of freedom to believe, express, and exercise the traditional religions." This section applies to access to, "sacred sites required in their religions, including cemeteries," the use of sacred objects in religious ceremonies, and the practice of traditional Indian rites.[81]

The second section required presidential action. The President was to order federal agencies to evaluate their laws in consultation with traditional native religious leaders, "in order to determine appropriate changes necessary to protect and preserve Native American religious cultural rights and practices." After one year the President was required to issue a report to Congress documenting the policy changes that had been made.[82]

What does this crucial First Amendment reiteration mean? Clearly AIRFA represents a reinstatement of Native American rights to believe, express, and exercise their traditional religions. These rights specifically include access to sacred sites, use and possession of sacred objects such as eagle feathers or peyote, and freedom to worship in traditional ceremonies such as in sweat lodges in prisons. AIRFA also sent an important message to federal agencies. They must consult with practicing Indian religious leaders, rather than BIA bureaucrats or anthropologists. Indians welcomed this new law. They immediately began negotiations with the federal government and other institutions regarding sacred objects. Dialogues started throughout the United States.[83] There was some initial success, but soon tribes met resistance, and AIRFA was not of much legal help.

AIRFA has significant deficiencies. The legislation only applies to *past* religious doctrines and practices, and it only guarantees access to sacred sites. The law does not actually preserve sites. Moreover, AIRFA does not recognize a holistic philosophy; it recognizes only defined doctrine. Indian religion is not perceived as a dynamic, or evolving, aspect of culture, and AIRFA's greatest weakness is that there are no "teeth" in the act. Persons restricting or denying Indians their free exercise of religion cannot be punished.[84]

The Supreme Court first considered the impact of the American Indian Religious Freedom Act in *Lyng v. Northwest Indian Cemetery Protective Ass'n* (1988).[85] For over ten years, the Yurok, Karok, and Tolowa Indian nations tried to prevent the U.S. Forest Service from paving a road and harvesting timber on the Hoopa Valley Indian Reservation and in Six Rivers National Forest in northern California. The Forest Service commissioned a report that recommended not completing the road because it would open up to the general public an area central to private Indian religious practices, but the Forest Service decided to ignore the report. At the federal district court, a judge ruled that the Forest Service could not take action because the results infringed on the Indians' free exercise of their religion. The appellate court affirmed the district court's decision.

However, the Supreme Court overruled, giving the Forest Service permission to pave and harvest. In a 5-3 opinion written by Justice Sandra Day O'Connor, the American Indian Religious Freedom Act was eviscerated. The Court created a two-pronged test in order for AIRFA to apply. Indians must prove: (1) they were coerced into violating their beliefs, or (2) penalized for practicing their beliefs. If neither is proven, then no religious infringement occurred. This is not the same free exercise standard articulated for any other person or groups in the United States. The impact of *Lyng* is significant. Of immediate importance was that the U.S. Forest Service began destruction of a region essential to 5,000 Indians for their religious practices. Native American right of access to sacred sites was obviously not a concept that prevented the destruction of these sites.[86]

By 1990, the protections hinted at by AIRFA and basic rights in the First Amendment were in question for Native Americans, and the Supreme Court made these considerations a legal certainty. The Court placed the legality of the Native American Church and all traditional religious practices in legal limbo. Two Indians living in Portland, Oregon, Alfred Smith and Galen Black, were fired from their jobs with a private drug rehabilitation organization because they used peyote during a Native American Church ceremony. They applied for unemployment benefits, but were denied because the state of Oregon decided they had been discharged for misconduct. After a great deal of litigation in which Oregon's state courts upheld the defendants' right to practice their religion, the Supreme Court heard the case and ruled against Smith and Black and all of Oregon's state courts.[87] In so doing, the Court struck a major blow against First Amendment religious freedoms for Native Americans, and opened the door for state agencies to close the Native American Church.

Five judges, led by Justice Antonin Scalia, voted to accept the notion that peyote usage could be prohibited under a state criminal statute, even though Oregon had not enforced this law. According to the majority of the Court, no persons could hold their religious practices against the state's right to regulate the use of drugs. Even though peyote is recognized as a sacramental element in the Native American Church, that did not matter here. The Court seemed uninformed about the nature of peyote. Moreover, the majority noted that the physical act of drinking wine in a Christian ceremony, presumably even by minors in violation of state alcohol statutes, would be acceptable.[88]

All of the previous tests used for assessing the limits of the free exercise clause and other Indian religion cases were summarily disposed. Some court members appeared unhappy with their colleagues in the making of this decision—justices penned cutting words in their opinions, suggesting some of their colleagues did not know what they were doing. It remains to be seen whether *Employment Division, Department of Human Resources of Oregon v. Smith* (1990) will be the controlling statement on Native American religious freedoms. Indian governments and lawyers have met this setback by making proposals to Congress for revisions of AIRFA.

Conclusion

Native Americans in search of their legal and constitutional rights and liberties found them highly circumscribed during the post–World War II years, especially from the 1970s to the present. Indeed, the Supreme Court along with Pacific Northwest state governments and courts has led the assault on Indian rights.

Hunting, fishing, and water rights were restricted. Attempts to obtain control over reservation resources, whether through taxation, zoning, or extensions of tribal jurisdiction, were contested at every step. Of particular concern were efforts in the 1980s to inhibit Native American social and religious life. Even with Congress attempting to control non-Indian actions, such as through the Indian Child Welfare Act or the American Indian Religious Freedom Act, there were few causes for celebration among Indians seeking to exercise fully what most Americans saw as traditional constitutional rights retained by every person.

By 1991 and the bicentennial of the federal Bill of Rights, Native Americans were poised to move on the offensive. The grounds were shifting once again. Indians wanted desperately to improve their economic lot while retaining their cultural values. The passage of the Indian Gaming Regulatory Act provided what some tribes saw as short-term opportunities. All Pacific Northwest states allowed some kinds of gaming, and under the new federal law they were required to negotiate in good faith with Indian tribal governments for gambling certification. Idaho seems to have resisted the enforcement of the act most strenuously.[89] The federal Gaming Act posed questions and worries along with opportunities. While some tribes near large cities attracted thousands to casinos and enhanced the standard of living for their tribal members, others experienced bankruptcy, such as befell the Yakama Indian Nation's bingo hall.

Also in the 1990s, a new civil rights issue began. Indians demanded recognition of their rights in a form most non-Indians could understand. The legal issue is the repatriation of Indian skeletal remains and burial goods from institutions—universities, historical societies, and even the most revered of museums in the United States, the Smithsonian. Non-Indians identify with Indians in their grief and their resolve. State and federal laws, this time with enforcement provisions, have been passed that give to Native Americans an ability to reclaim their relatives' remains.[90] These laws, however, have yet to be tested at the highest court level, and resistance to their enforcement continues in the Pacific Northwest and other parts of the United States.

♣ ♣ ♣

Returning once again to the writings of Janet Campbell Hale, she tells us in her family history, *Bloodlines: Odyssey of a Native Daughter*, about the warnings her Pacific Northwest people received:

One day in the year 1740, the story goes, a raven, circling in the sky above a Coeur d'Alene village, spoke to the head chief.

"Did you understand?" the chief (who would henceforth be known as Chief Circling Raven) asked the others. No one understood but he. This is what the raven told him:

"A great evil is coming. An enemy more powerful than any of you have ever known will surround you. Even now your enemy has spied you. There will be much bloodshed. Much sorrow. Gather your strength."[91]

"Gather your strength." Hale's words summarize how Pacific Northwest Indians have met the challenge of asserting their legal rights in the last half of the twentieth century. There has been resolve to survive and to exhibit the strength to resist. There has been, as Jim Tollerud has expressed, a continuous search for liberty. And there has been the evolution of a grudging understanding, by Indian and non-Indian alike, that Pacific Northwest Indians have fundamental rights that must be respected and maintained.

Notes

1. Jim Tollerud, "Rainier," in Geary Hobson, ed., *The Remembered Earth: An Anthology of Contemporary Native American Literature* (Albuquerque: University of New Mexico Press, 1991), 397.

2. Burten D. Fretz, "The Bill of Rights and American Indian Tribal Governments," *Natural Resources Journal* 6 (October 1966):613-16.

3. For a brief survey of the historical uniqueness of Indian law, see Wilcomb E. Washburn, "The Historical Context of American Indian Legal Problems," *Law and Contemporary Problems* 40 (Winter 1976):12-24.

4. Janet Campbell Hale, *The Jailing of Cecelia Capture* (Albuquerque: University of New Mexico Press, 1985), 67.

5. For a fuller discussion of these trends and eras, see John R. Wunder, *"Retained by The People": A History of American Indians and the Bill of Rights, 1791-1991* (New York: Oxford University Press, 1994).

6. Monroe E. Price, *Law and the American Indian: Readings, Notes and Cases* (Indianapolis, IN: Bobbs-Merrill, 1973).

7. "Treaty with the Nisqualli, Puyallup, Etc., 1854," *Treaties and Agreements of the Indian Tribes of the Pacific Northwest* (Washington, DC: Institute for the Development of Indian Law, n.d.), 13.

8. U.S., "An Act to confer jurisdiction on the States of California, Minnesota, Nebraska, Oregon, and Wisconsin, with respect to criminal offenses and civil causes of action committed or arising on Indian reservations within such States, and for other purposes [Public Law 280]," *Statutes at Large* 67 (August 15, 1953):589, Section 2b.

9. U.S., *Statutes at Large* 82 (April 11, 1968):73-92.

10. *Puyallup Tribe, Inc. v. Department of Game* 391 US 392 (1968). This case is commonly referred to as *Puyallup I.* Subsequent more complex determinations occurred with *Puyallup Tribe, Inc. v. Department of Game* 414 US 44 (1973) known as *Puyallup II,* and *Puyallup Tribe, Inc. v. Department of Game* 433 US 165 (1977) known as *Puyallup III.*

11. *Ibid.;* Jack L. Landau, "Empty Victories: Indian Treaty Fishing Rights in the Pacific Northwest," *Environmental Law* 10 (Winter 1980):414-37. *Puyallup I* was soundly criticized in the legal profession, and it is blamed for the massive amount of litigation that followed. Litigation in Washington state eventually reached the point where federal judges began to prevent Indian tribes from bringing suits because they no longer were considered federally recognized tribes. See *United States v. Washington* 476 F Supp 1101 (1979); James C. Giudici, "State Regulation of Indian Treaty Fishing Rights: Putting Puyallup III into Perspective," *Gonzaga Law Review* 13 (Fall 1977):140-89; and Sasha Harmon, "Writing History by Litigation: The Legacy and Limitations of Northwest Indian Rights Cases," *Columbia* 3 (Winter 1990/91):5-15.

12. Francis Paul Prucha, *The Great Father: The United States and the American Indians*, 2 vols. (Lincoln: University of Nebraska Press, 1984), II:1184-85.

13. *Ibid.; United States v. State of Washington* 384 Fed Supp 312-423 (1974) and 423 US 1086 (1979).

14. Recently the Confederated Tribes and Bands of the Yakama Indian Nation approved the spelling "Yakama" that corresponds with their 1855 treaty. Previously in many scholarly works and court cases, the Yakamas were referred to as "Yakimas." For this essay, when referring to the Yakamas, the approved tribal spelling will be used except when specifically citing a court case using the old spelling. See Andrew H. Fisher, "The 1932 Handshake Agreement: Yakama Indian Treaty Rights and Forest Service Policy in the Pacific Northwest," *Western Historical Quarterly* 28 (Summer 1997):187, note 1.

15. *Sohappy v. Smith* 302 F Supp 899 (1969).

16. John C. Gartland, "*Sohappy v. Smith*: Eight Years of Litigation over Indian Fishing Rights," *Oregon Law Review* 56 (1977):680-701. For a cogent analysis of *Sohappy,* see "State Power and the Indian Treaty Right to Fish," *California Law Review* 59 (1971):505-9.

17. *New Mexico v. Mescalero Apache Tribe* 462 US 324 (1983). See also David H. Getches and Charles F. Wilkinson, *Federal Indian Law: Cases and Materials*, 2nd ed. (St. Paul, MN: West, 1986), 716-18.

18. *Kimball v. Callahan* 493 F2d 564 (1974). See also Mary Pearson, "Hunting Rights: Retention of Treaty Rights after Termination—*Kimball v. Callahan*," *American Indian Law Review* 4, no. 1 (1976):121-33.

19. *State v. Coffee* 556 P2d 1185 (1976); David H. Getches and Charles F. Wilkinson, *Federal Indian Law: Cases and Materials,* 2nd ed. (St. Paul, MN: West, 1986), 733.

20. *Montana v. United States* 450 US 544 (1981); S. J. Bloxham, "Tribal Sovereignty: An Analysis of *Monta[na] v. United States*," *American Indian Law Review* 8, no. 1 (1980):175-81.

21. U.S., "An Act to provide for the conservation of endangered and threatened species of fish, wildlife, and plants, and for other purposes [Endangered Species Act]," *Statutes at Large* 87 (December 28, 1973):884-903.

22. U.S., "An Act for the protection of the bald eagle [Eagle Protection Act]," *ibid.,* 54 (June 8, 1940):250-51.

23. U.S., "Joint Resolution to provide protection for the golden eagle," *ibid.,* 76 (October 24, 1962):1246.

24. *United States v. Dion* 476 US 734 (1986).

25. *Winters v. United States* 207 US 564 (1908).

26. *Ibid.*

27. *United States v. Winans* 198 US 371 (1905).

28. *Ibid.*

29. *Winters v. United States* 207 US 564 (1908).

30. *Ibid.*

31. Frederick E. Hoxie, *A Final Promise: The Campaign to Assimilate the Indians, 1880-1920* (Lincoln: University of Nebraska Press, 1984), 184-85.

32. *Arizona v. California* 373 US 546 (1963).

33. Lloyd Burton, *American Indian Water Rights and the Limits of Law* (Lawrence: University Press of Kansas, 1991), 31. See also William Douglas Back and Jeffrey S. Saylor, "Navajo Water Rights: Pulling the Plug on the Colorado River?" *Natural Resources Journal* 20 (January 1980):71-90; Robert D. Dellwo, "Recent Developments in the Northwest Regarding Indian Water Rights," *Natural Resources Journal* 20 (January 1980):101-20; Gwendolyn Griffith, "Indian Claims to Groundwater: Reserved Rights or Beneficial Interest?" *Stanford Law Review* 33 (November 1980):103-30; Robert S. Pelcyger, "The *Winters* Doctrine and the Greening of the Reservation," *Journal of Contemporary Law* 4 (Winter 1977):19-37; Robert Isham, Jr., "*Colville Confederated Tribes v. Walton*: Indian Water Rights and Regulation in the Ninth Circuit," *Montana Law Review* 43 (Spring 1982):247-69; Harold A. Ranquist, "The *Winters* Doctrine and How It Grew: Federal Reservation of Rights to the Use of Water," *Brigham Young University Law Review* (1975):639-724; and Kenneth E. Foster, "The *Winters* Doctrine: Historical Perspective and Future Applications of Reserved Water Rights in Arizona," *Ground Water* 16 (May/June 1978):186-88.

34. *In re General Adjudication of All Rights to Use Water in the Big Horn River System* 753 P2d 76 (1988).

35. *Shoshone Tribe v. Wyoming* 753 P2d 76 (1988) *cert. denied* 57 USLW 3860 (1989); *Wyoming v. United States* 488 US 1040 (1989). For a discussion of these confusing and alarming cases, see Burton, *Indian Water Rights*, 38-40. *Cappaert v. United States* 426 US 128 (1976).

36. Burton, *Indian Water Rights*, 69-86. The urge for the Reagan court to return powers to the states went so far as to overrule Indian groundwater rights only recently determined in a 1976 case, *Cappaert v. United States*.

37. Donald L. Fixico, "Tribal Leaders and the Demand for Natural Energy Resources on Reservation Lands," in Peter Iverson, *The Plains Indians of the Twentieth Century* (Norman: University of Oklahoma Press, 1985), 220.

38. Ambler, *Indian Control of Energy*, 29.

39. Fixico, "Energy Resources on Reservations," 222.

40. Ambler, *Indian Control of Energy*, 91-96.

41. U.S., "An Act to permit Indian tribes to enter into certain agreements for the disposition of tribal mineral resources, and other purposes [Indian Mineral Development Act]," *Statutes at Large* 96 (December 22, 1982):1938-40.

42. U.S., "An Act to provide for the development of repositories for the disposal of high-level radioactive waste and spent nuclear fuel, to establish a program of research, development, and demonstration regarding the disposal of high-level radioactive waste and spent nuclear fuel, and for other purposes [Nuclear Waste Policy Act]," *ibid.,* 96 (January 7, 1983):2201-63.

43. Nancy E. Hovis, "Tribal Involvement Under the Nuclear Waste Policy Act of 1982: Education by Participation," *Journal of Environmental Law and Litigation* 3 (1988):45-65.

44. Osborne M. Reynolds, Jr., "*Agua Caliente* Revisited: Recent Developments as to Zoning of Indian Reservations," *American Indian Law Review* 4, no. 2 (1976):249-67.

45. *Williams v. Lee* 358 US 217 (1959).

46. *Brendale v. Confederated Tribes and Bands of the Yakima Indian Nation* 492 US 408 (1989).

47. *United States v. Mazurie* 419 US 544 (1975).

48. Jessica S. Gerrard, "Undermining Tribal Land Use Regulatory Authority: *Brendale v. Confederated Tribes*," *University of Puget Sound Law Review* 13 (Winter 1990):349-75.

49. Daniel H. Israel, "The Reemergence of Tribal Nationalism and Its Impact on Reservation Resource Development," *University of Colorado Law Review* 47 (Summer 1976):617-52.

50. Russel Lawrence Barsh, "Issues in Federal, State, and Tribal Taxation of Reservation Wealth: A Survey and Economic Critique," *Washington Law Review* 54 (June 1979):537-42.

51. *McClanahan v. State Tax Commission of Arizona* 411 US 164 (1973); Russell W. Davisson, "Indian Law—Taxation—Reservation Indian's Income Not Taxable if Derived from Reservation Sources—State Power over Reservation Indians Is Limited," *University of Kansas Law Review* 22 (Spring 1974):471-79. For the history of taxation as applied to the Sioux, see James R. McCurdy, "Federal Income Taxation and the Great Sioux Nation," *South Dakota Law Review* 22 (Spring 1977):296-321.

52. Carole E. Goldberg, "A Dynamic View of Tribal Jurisdiction to Tax Non-Indians," *Law and Contemporary Problems* 40 (Winter 1976):166-89.

53. *Moe v. Confederated Salish and Kootenai Tribes* 425 US 463 (1976).

54. Donald W. Molloy, "'Must the Paleface Pay to Puff?': *Confederation Salish and Kootenai [Tribes] v. Moe*," *Montana Law Review* 36 (Winter 1975):93-102; Russel Lawrence Barsh, "The Omen: *Three Affiliated Tribes v. Moe* and the Future of Tribal Self-Government," *American Indian Law Review* 5, no. 1 (1977):1-73. See also William S. Dockins, "Limitations on State Power to Tax Natural Resource Development on Indian Reservations," *Montana Law Review* 43, no. 2 (1982):217-34.

55. *Merrion v. Jicarilla Apache Tribe* 455 US 130 (1982).

56. *Kerr-McGee Corporation v. Navajo Tribe* 471 US 195 (1985).

57. *Cotton Petroleum Corp. v. New Mexico* 490 US 163 (1989).

58. Ambler, *Indian Control of Energy*, 197-201; Samuel Fabbraio, Jr., "Tribal Severance Taxes: The Uncertain Sovereign Function: *Merrion v. Jicarilla Apache Tribe*," *University of Bridgeport Law Review* 4 (1982):133-51; Katherine B. Crawford, "State Authority to Tax Non-Indian Oil and Gas Production on Reservations: *Cotton Petroleum Corp. v. New Mexico*," *Utah Law Review*, no. 2 (1989):495-519; "BIA Supports Wind River Tax," *American Indian Report* 4 (May 1988):4 and "Senecas and State Reach Tentative Tax Agreement," *American Indian Report* 5 (February 1989):4.

59. Richard P. Fahey, "Native American Justice: The Courts of the Navajo Nation," *Judicature* 59 (June/July 1975):13-15.

60. Richard David Wasserman, "*Oliphant v. Schlie:* Recognition of Tribal Criminal Jurisdiction over Non-Indians," *Utah Law Review* 3 (1976):642-43.

61. *Oliphant v. Suquamish Indian Tribe* 435 US 191 (1978). See also *Oliphant v. Schlie* 544 F2d 1007 (1976); Kyle B. Smith, "*Oliphant v. Suquamish Indian Tribe*: A Restriction of Tribal Sovereignty," *Willamette Law Review* 15 (Winter 1978):128-29; and "Tribal Sovereignty Sustained: *Oliphant v. Schlie* and Indian Court Criminal Jurisdiction," *Iowa Law Review* 63 (October 1977):231.

62. Smith, "*Oliphant*," 127. This was in keeping with recent 1970s federal attacks on Native American sovereignty in the criminal jurisdiction area. See Jo-Nell Silvestro, "Indian Crimes Act of 1976: Another Amendment to the Major Crimes Act—But How Many More to Come?" *South Dakota Law Review* 22 (Spring 1977):407-30; Debra K. Loy, "Criminal Law: Equal Protection and Unequal Punishment under the Major Crimes Act—*United States v. Cleveland*," *American Indian Law Review* 3, no. 1 (1975):103-8; and Russel Lawrence Barsh and James Youngblood Henderson, "Tribal Courts, the Model Code, and the Police Idea in American Indian Policy," *Law and Contemporary Problems* 40 (Winter 1976):25-60.

63. Russel Lawrence Barsh and James Youngblood Henderson, "The Betrayal: *Oliphant v. Suquamish Indian Tribe* and the Hunting of the Snark," *Minnesota Law Review* 63 (April 1978):610.

64. *Ibid.,* 631-32. See also Dario F. Robertson, "A New Constitutional Approach to the Doctrine of Tribal Sovereignty," *American Indian Law Review* 6, no. 2 (1978):371-94; Curtis G. Berkey, "Indian Law—Indian Tribes Have No Inherent Authority to Exercise Criminal Jurisdiction over Non-Indians Violating Criminal Laws within Reservation Boundaries—*Oliphant v. Suquamish Indian Tribe*, 435 US 191 (1978)," *Catholic University Law Review* 28 (Spring 1979):663-87; and Catherine Baker Stetson, "Decriminalizing Tribal Codes: A Response to *Oliphant*," *American Indian Law Review* 9, no. 1 (1981):51-81.

65. *National Farmers Union Insurance Companies v. Crow Tribe* 471 US 845 (1985).

66. *Iowa Mutual Insurance Co. v. LaPlante* 480 US 9 (1987).

67. *Twin City Construction Company v. Turtle Mountain Band of Chippewa Indians* 866 F2d 971 (1989); S. Caroline Malone, "Tribal Power over Non-Indians: Tribal Courts at a Civil Crossroads, *Twin City Construction Company v. Turtle Mountain Band of Chippewa Indians*," *Arkansas Law Review* 42, no. 4 (1989):1027-52.

68. Linda A. Marousek, "The Indian Child Welfare Act of 1978: Provisions and Policy," *South Dakota Law Review* 25 (Winter 1980):99, note 11.

69. William Byler, "The Destruction of American Indian Families," in Steven Unger, ed., *The Destruction of American Indian Families* (New York: Association of American Indian Affairs, 1977), 1-5.

70. Aileen Red Bird and Patrick Melendy, "Indian Child Welfare in Oregon," in *ibid.,* 45.

71. Jane G. Printz, "Navajo Grandparents—'Parent' or 'Stranger'—a Child Custody Determination," *New Mexico Law Review* 9 (Winter 1978-79):187-94; Gaylene J. McCartney, "The American Indian Child-Welfare Crisis: Cultural Genocide or First Amendment Preservation," *Columbia Human Rights Law Review* 7 (Fall/Winter, 1975-76):529-51.

72. David Woodward, "The Rights of Reservation Parents and Children: Cultural Survival or the Final Termination?," *American Indian Law Review* 3, no. 1 (1975):22.

73. U.S., "An Act to establish standards for the placement of Indian children in foster or adoptive homes, to prevent the breakup of Indian families, and for other purposes [Indian Child Welfare Act]," *Statutes at Large* 92 (November 8, 1978):3069-78.

74. *Ibid.,* 3069.

75. *Ibid.,* Title I, Sections 101 a-d, 102 e-f, 3071-72.

76. *Ibid.,* Section 105 b, 3073; Section 102 a, 3071.

77. Joan Heifetz Hollinger, "Beyond the Best Interests of the Tribe: The Indian Child Welfare Act and the Adoption of Indian Children," *University of Detroit Law Review* 66 (Spring 1989):451-501; Manuel P. Guerrero, "Indian Child Welfare Act of 1978: A Response to the Threat to Indian Culture Caused by Foster and Adoptive Placements of Indian Children," *American Indian Law Review* 7, no. 1 (1979):51-77; Marousek, "Indian Child Welfare Act," 105-14. See also Garry Wamser, "Child Welfare under the Indian Child Welfare Act of 1978: A New Mexico Focus," *New Mexico Law Review* 10 (Summer 1980):413-29, and Russel Lawrence Barsh, "The Indian Child Welfare Act of 1978: A Critical Analysis," *Hastings Law Journal* 31 (July 1980):1287-1336. See *Mississippi Band of Choctaw Indians v. Holyfield et al.* 490 US 30 (1989). The Supreme Court upheld the constitutionality of the ICWA, specifically the section of the act that granted the exclusive jurisdiction over Indian children to tribes.

78. U.S., *American Indian Religious Freedom: Hearings on S.J. Res. 102 before the Senate Select Committee on Indian Affairs,* 95th Cong., 2d Sess., 152-53, 193 (1978).

79. *Ibid.,* 86-87, quoted in Howard Stambor, "Manifest Destiny and American Indian Religious Freedom: *Sequoyah, Badoni,* and the Drowned Gods," *American Indian Law Review* 10, no. 1 (1982):59.

80. U.S., "Joint Resolution: American Indian Religious Freedom [American Indian Religious Freedom Act]," *Statutes at Large* 92 (August 11, 1978):469-70.

81. *Ibid.,* 469.

82. *Ibid.,* 470.

83. T. J. Ferguson, "The American Indian Religious Freedom Act and Zuni Pueblo," unpublished manuscript presented at the American Society for Ethnohistory annual meeting, November 1981, Colorado Springs, CO; Dean B. Suagee, "American Indian Religious Freedom and Cultural Resources Management: Protecting Mother Earth's Caretakers," *American Indian Law Review* 10, no. 1 (1982).

84. Kathryn Harris, "The American Indian Religious Freedom Act and Its Promise," *American Indian Journal* 5 (June 1979):7-10; Jill E. Martin, "Constitutional Rights and Indian Rites: An Uneasy Balance," *Western Legal History* 3 (Fall/Winter 1990):245-70; Randolf J. Rice, "Native Americans and the Free Exercise Clause," *Hastings Law Journal* 28 (July 1988):1509-36; Laurie Ensworth, "Native American Free Exercise Rights to the Use of Public Lands," *Boston University Law Review* 63, no. 1 (1983):141-79.

85. *Lyng v. Northwest Indian Cemetery Protective Ass'n* 485 US 439 (1988).

86. Stephen McAndrew, "*Lyng v. Northwest Indian Cemetery Protective Ass'n*: Closing the Door to Indian Religious Sites," *Southwestern University Law Review* 18, no. 4 (1989):603-29.

87. *Employment Division, Department of Human Resources of Oregon, et al. v. Alfred L. Smith et al.*, 494 US 872 (1990); 872-90, Scalia majority opinion; and 890-906, O'Connor concurring opinion; and 907-21, Blackmun dissent.

88. *Ibid.,* 912.

89. U.S., *Statutes at Large* 102 (October 17, 1988):2467-88 [Indian Gaming Regulatory Act]. See also Allen C. Turner "Evolution, Assimilation, and State Control of Gaming in Indian Country: Is *Cabazon v. California* an Assimilationist Wolf in Preemption Clothing?" *Idaho Law Review* 24, no. 2 (1987-88):317-38.

90. Wunder, "*Retained by The People,*" 208-10.

91. Janet Campbell Hale, *Bloodlines: Odyssey of a Native Daughter* (New York: Harper Collins, 1993), xv.

The cover of the promotional leaflet produced by the Twin Falls North Side Land and Water Company correctly promised abundant water to prospective farmers (who could afford it). *Courtesy of University of Idaho Library, Moscow, Idaho.*

IX

"Too Little, Too Late": Annie Pike Greenwood, Failed Sagebrush Pioneer[1]

Susan H. Armitage
(Washington State University)

IN 1913, ANNIE PIKE GREENWOOD and her husband Charles took up a 160 acre homestead in the Twin Falls North Side Irrigation Project in Jerome County on the Snake River in southeast Idaho. When they first moved there, the land supported only sagebrush and vast numbers of jackrabbits. When the Greenwoods left, fifteen years later, the same land grew wheat and sugarbeets; the jackrabbits, although never eliminated, were controlled by fencing and by periodic community hunts that continue to this day. The Greenwoods seemed to have enacted a familiar western story of human triumph over nature, for they had made the sagebrush desert bloom, if not like a rose, at least like a sugarbeet. In reality, after fifteen years of hard labor, the Greenwoods were forced to leave because they had lost their farm and the pioneer dream that had sustained them.

In this essay, I will draw on Annie Greenwood's memoir, *We Sagebrush Folks*, to explore the experience of the Greenwoods and of their fellow settlers in the North Side Irrigation District.[2] The Greenwoods' failure was not unique; indeed it was so common that farmers wryly joked that "the first settlers clear and plow the land for those who are to own it."[3] What *was* unique was Greenwood's bitterly honest memoir, which she herself described as "the first book to be written from the inside by a pioneer farm woman."[4] This unusual perspective allows us to assess the human costs of the larger history of irrigation in southern Idaho.

The Snake River Plain of southern Idaho had long been a locus of irrigation projects, for the stark contrast between the surging river and the surrounding desert fairly begged for reconciliation. American Indians were the first small-scale irrigators, followed in the 1880s by cooperative irrigation projects organized by Mormon settlers in the locality around present-day Idaho Falls. Historian Leonard Arrington, himself raised on a Mormon irrigated farm, tells us that by the end of the 1880s the area between Rexburg and Blackfoot was "literally honeycombed with cooperative canal systems" and that in the 1890s, an even larger Mormon cooperative project, the Great Feeder Dam system, was "the largest single irrigation project in the world."[5] Such success inevitably bred speculative imitations—and failures.

One of the largest and best-documented corporate failures was the New York Canal Project near Boise, whose promising start in the 1880s was aborted in the 1890s as distant investors, impatient for quick returns, failed to provide the money to sustain the project. The well-known author and illustrator Mary Hallock Foote, whose husband was the chief engineer on the project, provided a glimpse of early hopes in her Far West Illustrations for *Century Magazine* in 1889. In the text that accompanied her illustration "The Orchard Windbreak," she quoted a piece of folk wisdom: "He who plants apple trees plants for himself, but 'he who plants pears plants for his heirs.'" She bravely continued, "They are planting pear orchards in the valley of the Boise."[6] Unfortunately, her hopes were misplaced. The New York Canal Project failed and Arthur Foote failed as well, retiring from his engineering career and dragging his wife's hopes down with his own.[7]

The failure of the New York Canal and other private investment projects in the West prompted the entry of the federal government into western irrigation. In 1894 Congress enacted the Carey Act, which offered up to one million acres of arid federal land to any western state that would irrigate it. The state of Idaho pursued this offer more aggressively than any other western state. Indeed, as state historian Carlos Schwantes tells us, "Idaho ultimately contained three-fifths of all land irrigated under the Carey Act and became a national showcase."[8] Idaho turned the actual construction of dams, canals, and ditches on the Carey Act lands over to private companies which made their profits by the sale of homestead entry fees, water rights, and water contracts to would-be farmers. Once the property and water contracts were sold, the original investors sold the irrigation works to newly formed irrigation districts (public corporations formed by the water users) which in turn paid off their indebtedness through tax assessments and user fees charged to district landowners. Thus through the collaboration of federal and state governments and private enterprise, the Carey Act sought to assure financial stability by placing management of

Marry Hallock Foote's engraving, "The Orchard Windbreak," expressed irrigators' dreams of making the desert bloom. From Foote's Far West Series, *Century Magazine,* July 1889.

the irrigation district in the hands of local landowners rather than unpredictable corporate shareholders. The Carey Act's wider intent was firmly rooted in the American agrarian dream: individual ownership of small family farms. [9]

The Twin Falls North Side Irrigation Project, to which the Greenwoods moved in 1913, was a Carey Act project. When Annie Greenwood arrived to join her husband on their homestead, she viewed her new surroundings with alarm and exhilaration:

> Miles and miles of wilderness, and not a sign of habitation: no tree, no green, only the gray of pungent sagebrush. And, everywhere, leaping jack-rabbits. Strange that I should have felt so elated? I was going to live on land untrod by the foot of white woman in all history! I was going to make my home where there had never been a civilized home before! I was to be a living link between the last frontier and civilization! I was a pioneer![10]

Annie Greenwood goes on to tell us: "I loved Idaho. I loved the vast, unspoiled wilderness, the fabulous sunsets, lakes of gold, and the dreamy purple mountains that appeared in the sky along their rims; and when

these gradually dimmed and vanished, a million stars in the dark-blue sky—
a million stars, seen at a breath."[11]

She did not, however, like the wind that "raged for days at a time," and
she had decidedly mixed feelings about the sagebrush that was omnipresent
in her pioneer life. Charley Greenwood arduously cleared the land of sagebrush so that he could grow crops. Annie cooked with it, lived with it:

> A clean kitchen one moment, and bits of sagebrush and dirt from the
> door to the woodbox the next. Bleeding scratches on my arms and
> hands. The smell of sagebrush so constantly throughout the house that
> we can no longer smell it. Cooking with sagebrush. Breaking scraggy,
> scratching sagebrush over my knee, and having it lance my arms with
> its claws.[12]

The Greenwoods and others who settled on southern Idaho irrigated
lands were not the only early twentieth century desert pioneers. At about
the same time, two large dryland homesteading ventures were underway in
the Inland Northwest: 1,200 homesteaders in Lake County in the high
desert country of south-central Oregon in the period 1905-15; and nearly
157,000 homesteaders between 1909 and 1920 in the arid, eastern part of
Montana.[13] In both locations many farmers failed or hung on just long
enough to prove up and sell out. Most were defeated by aridity: they didn't
have enough water to sustain their crops. But the Greenwoods and their
fellow settlers had water. How could they fail?

The Twin Falls North Side Land and Water Company assured them
that they could not fail. In their promotional brochure, "The Land of
Splendid Opportunities" (1907), the company claimed that "irrigation
means quick money," and asserted:

> The soil is rich, so rich that even 40 acres will support a large family,
> make the deferred payments on the water right and leave a bank bal-
> ance . . . All the conditions which surround the settler in this favored
> region are ideal for his success. The climate is perfect. The sun shines at
> least 300 days a year. The rainfall is ten to fifteen inches. The soil is
> rich, deep and mellow, without stones and is easily cultivated . . . The
> market is extensive and . . . the water supply is far in excess of possible
> needs.[14]

The fine print of the brochure told another story. The abundant water promised by the Twin Falls North Side Land and Water Company was
expensive. Water rights cost $40.50 per acre, or $6,480 for a 160 acre
homestead. To "take up" (i.e., move on to) land the prospective farmer was
required to make a minimum payment of $131; he could finance the rest

(the "deferred water right") for a six percent loan guaranteed by the federal government. The cost of land clearing, seed, farm equipment, barns, homes, and hired labor was additional. Yearly taxes on land imposed by local communities and by the irrigation district added to his financial burden. Most farmers on Carey Act lands were never able to work their way free of their original debt. Inexorably, well capitalized large farms became more productive and more profitable than smaller farms and drove the latter out of irrigated agriculture.[15]

In addition to higher costs and ensuing debt, irrigated agriculture imposed another, less quantifiable burden on settlers. Historian Leonard Arrington explains:

> [E]xtensive and complicated irrigation systems depend on an advanced sense of community. The mutual dependencies of all those involved are so crucial that the system will not function unless there is an overriding presiding authority— as in the case of the Mormon settlers in the Upper Snake River Valley—or a predisposed willingness to cooperate—as among the settlers along the river who acknowledged that their own desires must be balanced by the needs of others to achieve desirable and necessary ends.[16]

Annie Pike Greenwood was willing to cooperate. But, apparently from the very beginning, she saw problems inherent in trying to organize her "sagebrush folk" community. To begin with, the community that Annie Greenwood found was unstable. In the fifteen years of the Greenwoods' stay on their homestead, the population turnover was almost complete. The first settlers in the North Side Irrigation District in the early 1900s were "a few scattered Mormons, provident and wise, trusting the Lord and the work of their own hands about equally."[17] Most of these early settlers eventually moved to join larger Mormon communities elsewhere on the Snake River. Next, says Greenwood, after Milner Dam was completed in 1905, came "the city settlers . . . lured by wild dreams of pretty farms on which white peacocks ranged." They were replaced by "both farm and city folks who had just a little money . . . and who were determined to own their own land." Among this group were the Greenwoods themselves, who moved to Idaho from Garden City, Kansas, where Charley had held a management position in a sugarbeet factory. "Practically none of them succeeded," Greenwood says, except the "born farmers" who often remained because "there was no better place to go, and no money with which to go."

As the Greenwoods and other middle class city farmers began to fail in the early 1920s, farmers from Arkansas moved in—"one whole mountain

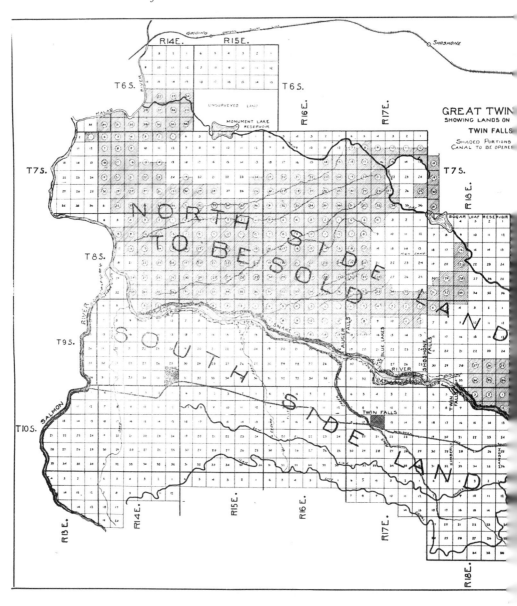

Map of the Great Twin Falls Canal System. The Greenwoods moved to their land, located near Milner in the eastern section of the North Side, in 1912. *Courtesy of University of Idaho Library, Moscow, Idaho.*

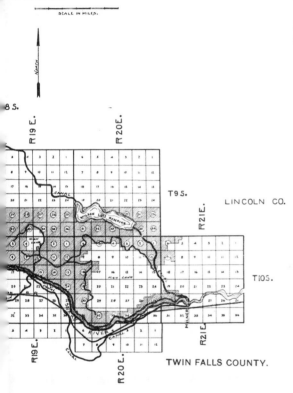

MAP
OF
FALLS CANAL SYSTEM
RTH AND SOUTH SIDE OF SNAKE RIVER.
). AND LINCOLN CO., IDAHO
OW THE LANDS UNDER THE NORTH SIDE
RING 1907 AND 1908.

SCALE IN MILES.

North

8 S.

R 19 E.

R 20 E.

T 9 S.

LINCOLN CO.

R 21 E.

T 10 S.

R 19 E.

R 20 E.

R 21 E.

TWIN FALLS COUNTY.

WHAT THIS MAP SHOWS.

At the extreme right of the map is seen the town of Milner. Here is situated the million dollar dam which diverts the water of the Snake river to the 420,000 acres of irrigable land on both sides of the river. This is the third season of irrigation on that tract where some ten thousand people now live. It was all sage brush and without population in 1904.

The great success of the South Side is to be repeated on the North Side of the river. The shaded portions of the North Side indicate the 180,00 acres of irrigable land open for entry in 1907. Each small square represents a section and each large square a township. The shaded part nearest Milner shows the 30,000 acres opened April 22.

The irregular black line leading northwesterly across the tract from Milner indicates the course of the main canal now being constructed. The three great reservoirs of many hundred acres each are also shown. These will impound enough water to carry the tract through any period of excessive demand. They will give elasticity to the regular supply and furnish places for boating and fishing.

The unshaded portions on the north side indicate lands too high for irrigation by gravity and are not included in the 180,000 acres. An electric road is planned to go through the middle of the North Side Tract, connecting Milner with the Oregon Short Line Railway on the north.

community migrated together" Greenwood tells us. These last, in addition to bringing a distinctive regional culture with them, also differed from former settlers in that many of them rented rather than owned their farms.[18] Finally, although Greenwood mentions them only in passing, as large commercial farms spread in the valley, much of the labor in the sugarbeet fields was supplied by German-Russian families.[19] Thus, in the fifteen years of the Greenwoods' stay, large holdings began to replace small family farms, the numbers of tenant farmers increased, and laborers of a distinctive immigrant ethnicity made up a growing share of the population. The central agrarian ideal of the Carey Act legislation, a cooperative community of small farmers, was giving way to a more economically and ethnically diverse and stratified population.

Nevertheless, the Greenwoods worked diligently to build and maintain community institutions. Annie Greenwood attended church and founded a Sunday School, as did her Mormon neighbors for their co-religionists. The elementary school, in which Annie taught for a year, was the center of local social life: the site of the Literary Society, which she founded, the place where recitations, dances, plays, and the annual Christmas party were held. Both Greenwoods helped to organize the local Grange, and Annie was its first Lecturer. They organized the yearly Fourth of July celebrations too. The men of the neighborhood frequently gathered at the Greenwood home, where they discussed farm problems and politics with Charley Greenwood, who was so well liked that the locals elected him first to the Idaho House of Representatives and later to the state Senate.[20] Annie understood why her husband was so popular. "They could understand him. He managed to be like them. They all fought and growled together, and they all came up smiling together."[21]

Annie, however, was too outspoken an individualist ("Mrs. Bossy," she called herself) to fit in as easily. When asked to join the Ladies Fancywork Improvement Club, which she acknowledged did more good than any other community organization, Annie refused because she knew that many of its members disapproved of her forthright fondness for dancing. She confessed, "So it was again and again: I felt the exclusion of myself from the circle of our sagebrush women by reason of something maverick in my own mind," something that we might today call feminist assertiveness uncommon among the traditional gender role behavior in agricultural communities.[22]

Annie Greenwood had another, less personal reason for her feelings of exclusion: she believed that the sense of community was more real for men than for women.

Men love farming, and one of the reasons is that the normal human being is gregarious. Almost every operation on the farm that is considered men's work requires at some stage a number of men to prosecute it. There is fun in working together, joshing and laughing, but it is a pleasure that the sagebrush women knew very little about.[23]

While some of Greenwood's neighbor women had "good pals" or relatives to work with, many sagebrush women worked within their own homes, as she did, in isolation:

I went absolutely nowhere, and I worked from dawn until dark and was never rested. My finger-nails were broken below the quick, and my heels were cracked and bleeding. I was the Great Beast of Burden of the American nation, the Forgotten Farm Woman—not just then forgotten, but forgotten throughout all history. There were times when it struck me as a terrible way to live.[24]

Greenwood underscores this gendered difference in community experience by describing in detail the activities of men and women at threshing time. Sometimes she had as many as thirty-two men to feed, and no relatives or nearby friends to help her. While the men worked hard but also enjoyed a "grand visiting-time," Annie and one other woman, too busy to talk to each other, prepared and punctually served the large meals. "Probably the earth would change its orbit, and a few planets crash, if it should ever occur that the threshing meal was not exactly ready when the first tableful of men was ready for it." Greenwood goes on to say, "You can never know what it is to be really light-hearted and free until you have endured the galley-slavery of a week or two of cooking for threshers."[25] Her frankness was unusual. Other farm women, in other locations, have commented on their hard and lonely work at threshing time, but rarely with critical intent. Rather, they insist that their work contributed to the communal nature of threshing, which holds a special place in rural community life as the culminating event of the yearly farm cycle.[26]

In the years the Greenwoods lived on their sagebrush farm, American urban culture vastly increased its influence. Improved transportation, such as cars and railroads, made big cities like Boise, with its electric lights, refrigeration, and modern fashions accessible, even as it seemed like another world to farmers. Improved communication—radio, telephones, movies—brought the sounds of the city to the farm. Rural poverty, always a reality of agricultural life, was now accentuated. As Greenwood sarcastically notes, "If you see a man, and he's got a fairly good suit and coat, why, that's a tramp; if you see a man in a ragged coat and worn-out overalls, that's a farmer!"[27]

While both sexes suffered from rural poverty, women suffered doubly, for what little money the farm made had to retire debt or be put into farm improvements, rather than used to raise the family living standard. Annie Greenwood lived for ten years without running water in her house while the canal water rushed past her front yard, an ever-present, ever-attractive danger to her children. Charley fenced his fields with barbed wire within three years but never got around to fencing her garden, leaving it open to the jackrabbits, dogs, and straying burros who ruined her crops on several occasions.

As the agricultural depression of the 1920s bore down upon the Greenwoods and their neighbors, poverty ate away at the trust and cooperation irrigated farmers needed to survive:

> Water among us sagebrush folks was money. When a man stole your water, he committed grand larceny, no matter how much he himself might feel his crime mitigated by the hymns he sang to Jesus a-Sundays. Water in the sagebrush country is not free, as the rain from heaven. Both the just and the unjust have to pay for it, or it is shut off . . . If your head-gate is stuffed with weeds or gunny-sacks, it may mean the loss of all the money you can make that year, for your crop will die . . . When another farmer steals your water, he takes the clothes from your children's backs, robs your wife of the medicine she probably needs, takes every penny out of your own overalls' pocket. It is no wonder that almost every year farmers are killed at the headgates, one discovering another in the act of stealing water.[28]

When their farm was foreclosed by the Federal Land Bank in 1925, Annie first blamed the land: "We all loved the sagebrush country with an unexpressed and inexpressible passion. And, in return, our sagebrush farms were vampires which sucked out blood, and the blood is life."[29] Then she blamed the government for favoring urban consumers rather than rural producers (a complaint that eventually led to the agricultural price support system of the New Deal, too late to save the Greenwoods). She understood the burden imposed by the economics of irrigated land, commenting bitterly, "It is criminal to advise people to try to own land unless they have capital with which to make the start,"[30] yet that was precisely the gamble that previous generations of western homesteaders had made. Like their predecessors, the Greenwoods and other "city dream-farmers" as Annie called them[31] believed that the path to independence was to own a farm of one's own. The faith that a return to the land would bring not only economic independence but the moral regeneration of the country as a whole was a key Progressive Era belief. While famous muckrakers like Lincoln Steffans reformed the cities and Gifford Pinchot conserved forests, forward-thinking people like the Greenwoods brought modern thinking to the nation's rural areas. Indeed, Annie says proudly that Charley Greenwood read every government bulletin and followed all the scientific suggestions of the extension agents.[32] Yet it did him no good, for he lacked the capital to make a success of irrigated farming.

The Greenwoods tried, and failed, to treat their irrigated homestead as no different from other homesteads. But as recent commentators like Donald Worster in *Rivers of Empire*[33] and Marc Reisner in *Cadillac Desert*[34] have pointed out, irrigated lands *are* different. Worster calls irrigated societies "coercive, monolithic, and hierarchical," while Reisner simply calls them expensive. However one analyzes the causes, the fact is that today the irrigated lands of the West are owned by large farmers who often employ migrant labor. There are few small farms maintained only by family labor of the kind the Greenwoods tried to create.

As Worster points out, the history of the West's irrigated lands is the antithesis of what the West has mythically been understood to be: "a saga of individual enterprise, of men and women going out from civilization to carve out with their own hands a livelihood from nature, a tale of release (or attempted release) from eastern form, tradition, and control," and, at the end, the reward of independence.[35] The Greenwoods hoped and expected to live out this myth. Yet, finally, Annie Greenwood acknowledged that times and economic circumstances had changed:

> It was not right that we should fail, Charley and I, yet it was right. It was not our just reward, but it was our best reward . . . Not only did we fail from lack of capital, but we had pioneering problems such as no other frontiersmen ever had. My young mother and father had been Western pioneers, but every one in the whole West was a pioneer then, and the East was a foreign country. We in the sagebrush were surrounded by civilization, touched elbows with it at every turn, yet we lived under conditions much more primitive than those my mother and father endured.[36]

Although she understood the economics of irrigation that cost the Greenwoods their homestead, Annie Pike Greenwood never lost her ideals. She went down fighting: "Pioneers! I was the one who knew what pioneering means!"[37]

Notes

1. The author wishes to thank Corky Bush, with whom I first discovered Annie Pike Greenwood as we researched our unpublished paper, "Pacific Northwest Farm Women and the Frontier Tradition," from which this present article draws in part.

2. Annie Pike Greenwood, *We Sagebrush Folks* (New York: D. Appleton-Century, 1934; reprinted Moscow, ID: University of Idaho Press, 1988).

3. *Ibid.,* 465.

4. *Ibid.,* 319.

5. Leonard Arrington, "Irrigation in the Snake River Valley: An Historical Overview," *Idaho Yesterdays* 30, no. 1-2 (Spring/Summer 1986):4.

6. Mary Hallock Foote, "The Orchard Windbreak," reprinted in Barbara Cragg, Dennis M. Walsh, and Mary Ellen Walsh, *The Idaho Stories and Far West Illustrations of Mary Hallock Foote* (Pocatello: Idaho State University Press, 1988), 276-77.

7. Arthur Foote's failure has been somewhat fictionalized in Wallace Stegner's *Angle of Repose* (Garden City, NY: Doubleday, 1971), the Pulitzer-prize winning novel based on Mary Hallock Foote's life.

8. Carlos Schwantes, *In Mountain Shadows: A History of Idaho* (Lincoln: University of Nebraska Press, 1991), 166.

9. William F. Ringert, "Irrigation Districts: Purpose, History, Funding, and Problems," *Idaho Yesterdays* 30, no.1-2 (Spring/Summer 1986):64-70.

10. Greenwood, *We Sagebrush Folks*, 14.

11. *Ibid.,* 26.

12. *Ibid.,* 25.

13. Barbara Allen, *Homesteading the High Desert* (Salt Lake City: University of Utah Press, 1987), and Daniel N. Vichorek, *Montana's Homestead Era*, vol. 15, *Montana Geographic Series* (Helena: Montana Magazine, 1987). For the hopes and dreams of Montana homesteaders, see also Jonathan Raban, *Bad Land* (New York: Random House, 1996).

14. "Land of Splendid Opportunities," Twin Falls North Side Land and Water Company, 1907 (Special Collections, University of Idaho Library, Moscow, ID).

15. *Ibid.*; for the unintended consequences of the Carey Act, see Donald J. Pisani, *To Reclaim a Divided West: Water, Law, and Public Policy, 1848-1902* (Albuquerque: University of New Mexico Press, 1992), 251-72.

16. Arrington, "Irrigation in the Snake River Valley," 9.

17. Greenwood, *We Sagebrush Folks*, 11.

18. *Ibid.,* 189-90.

19. *Ibid.,* 181.

20. *Ibid.,* 184-224.

21. *Ibid.,* 198.

22. *Ibid.,* 200.

23. *Ibid.,* 51.

24. *Ibid.,* 339.

25. *Ibid.,* 173, 177, 180.

26. Reminiscences of threshing time are common in agricultural communities such as the Palouse region of Washington and Idaho. See the interview with Cora Pierce, Whitman County Oral History Project, Washington State University, 1978, and the article, based on oral histories, by Mary E. Reed and Carol Young, "Rural Women of Latah County: Life and Work with the Harvest and Logging Crews," *Latah Legacy* (Summer 1982):21-27.

27. Greenwood, *We Sagebrush Folks*, 385.

28. *Ibid.,* 380.

29. *Ibid.*

30. *Ibid.,* 453.

31. *Ibid.,* 231.

32. *Ibid.,* 453.

33. Donald Worster, *Rivers of Empire: Water, Aridity, and the Growth of the American West* (New York: Pantheon, 1985).

34. Marc Reisner, *Cadillac Desert: The American West and Its Disappearing Water* (New York: Viking, 1986).

35. Worster, *Rivers of Empire,* 11.

36. Greenwood, *We Sagebrush Folks,* 465-66.

37. *Ibid.,* 466.

X

"There Was No Better Place to Go"—The Transformation Thesis Revisited: African-American Migration to the Pacific Northwest, 1940-1950

Quintard Taylor
(University of Oregon)

For more than a decade a number of historians, including most notably Gerald Nash and Carlos Schwantes, have argued "the transformation thesis," namely that World War II brought overwhelming, permanent change to the West that inevitably ended the region's position as an economic "colony" of eastern capital and established it for the first time as the "pacesetter" for much of the rest of the nation. Recently, however, a smaller group of historians have challenged the idea of sweeping transformation, of the end of "regional" colonialism, and of the West as molder of national social and cultural trends. The second group, which includes among others Roger Lotchin, Albert Broussard, and Stuart McElderry, all argue that continuity rather than change was the watchword for the World War II decade. Indeed Lotchin, the leading "transformation" critic, claims the wartime changes were "remarkably ephemeral."[1]

This essay examines these conflicting visions of the West and World War II through the joint prism of African-American and Pacific Northwest history. I am not so much interested in determining which historians are correct as in using this debate to get a more accurate assessment of African-American life in the Pacific Northwest, and gauge the impact of the presence of black Pacific Northwesterners on the rest of the region's inhabitants.

One point is beyond dispute. African-Americans came to the Pacific Northwest during the 1940s in unprecedented numbers. Drawn by the prospect of employment as defense workers or by assignments as military personnel, the African-American population of Washington, Oregon, and Idaho grew by 309 percent from 10,584 to 43,270, between 1940 and 1950.

The most dramatic change took place in the largest coastal cities of the region. Between 1940 and 1950, Seattle's black population grew 306 percent, from 3,789 to 15,410. The comparable figures for Tacoma were 650 in 1940 and 3,205 in 1950, a 393 percent increase, while African-American Portland grew from 1,931 in 1940 to 9,495 in 1950, a 392 percent increase. Portland's figures are misleading because the city actually had 22,000 African-Americans in 1945 before the population declined to just under 9,500 by the end of the decade. Other cities, especially in Washington, had spectacular increases. Bremerton's black population grew from 77 to 743 in the war decade, an 865 percent increase. Pasco's population grew from 27 to 980, a 3,529 percent increase, and Vancouver, which had 10 African-Americans in 1940, saw its black population explode to 879 in 1950, an 8,690 percent increase.[2]

African-American population increase in selected urban areas, 1940 to 1950.

City	1940	1950	% increase
Seattle	3,789	15,410	306%
Tacoma	650	3,205	393%
Portland	1,931	9,495	392%
Bremerton	77	743	865%
Pasco	27	980	3,529%
Vancouver	10	879	8,690%

The migration of over 30,000 African-Americans primarily to the Pacific Northwest's largest cities, Seattle, Portland, and Tacoma, in the 1940s represented a profound change which made these cities—for good and ill—increasingly similar to the rest of urban America. This migration intensified the concentration of African-Americans in the region's largest cities. By 1950, 74 percent of Washington's blacks lived in the Seattle and Tacoma metropolitan districts while 95 percent of Oregon's blacks resided in one city, Portland. In her study of the East Bay communities in California, Marilynn Johnson concluded that World War II era migration made cities such as Oakland, Berkeley, and Richmond "younger, more southern, more female, and noticeably more black" than ever before.[3] I think that conclusion has equal salience for the cities of the Pacific Northwest.

The concentration of African-Americans in Seattle, Tacoma, and Portland intensified what I call the proletarianization of the black work force in the Pacific Northwest. After decades of labor in menial positions on the periphery of the economy, black workers in the region's cities gained access to employment in the Pacific Northwest's wartime shipyards and aircraft factories, enhancing both their earning potential and their social prestige. Robert C. Weaver, a black World War II-era government economist, concluded that the war generated "more industrial and occupational diversification for Negroes than had occurred in the seventy-five preceding years."[4] However, this industrialization of the African-American work force was far more erratic than most historians have noted. Black access to defense production employment came with setbacks, as occurred immediately after World War II when many African-American workers were quickly dismissed during post-war economic retrenchment. Yet, exposure to defense plant employment, no matter how brief, persuaded many African-Americans to vow never again to be relegated to the kitchen or the porter's station.

African-American employment history from 1940 to 1950, however, illustrates the difficulty of fulfilling that vow. To cite just one example, as late as 1940 only 10 percent of Portland's black men and 3 percent of the city's black women were engaged in industrial work. Conversely 73 percent of the men and 86 percent of the women were domestic servants—chauffeurs, butlers, maids, porters. By 1945, according to one source, 95 percent of black migrants in Portland were engaged in shipyard work for the three Kaiser shipyards (as compared with 77 percent of the white migrants). When the war ended, African-American labor seemed destined to return to its traditional pre-war patterns of employment. Fifty-five hundred black shipyard workers lost their jobs between July and November 1945, with many having no choice but to return to menial work. By 1950, 18 percent of the men and 8 percent of the women were engaged in manufacturing work while 40 percent of the men and 75 percent of the women were again in domestic service.[5]

Seattle's black workers fared slightly better at least in part because of the greater number of industrial facilities in the Washington city and because of the higher numbers of pre-war factory workers. In 1940, 17 percent of the men and 4 percent of the women were factory operatives, while 52 percent of the men and 83 percent of the women were in domestic service. Wartime employment opportunity, of course, quickly changed those

Percentages of Portland's African-American labor force in industrial work and domestic service, 1940 and 1950.

	1940	1950
Men:		
Industrial work	10%	18%
Domestic service	73%	40%
Women:		
Industrial work	3%	8%
Domestic service	86%	75%

percentages. In 1940 there were only a dozen black shipyard workers in Seattle. Yet by 1945, 4,078 worked in that occupation, about 7 percent of the total. In 1940 there were no black aircraft workers; by 1945, 1,233 worked principally at Boeing where they comprised 3 percent of the total. Strikingly, black women led the way in this new employment, an economic development with enormous implications that would be felt far beyond the World War II years. In May 1942, Boeing hired its first black defense production worker—Dorothy West Williams. By July 1943, 329 blacks worked at Boeing, 86 percent of them women. As in the Portland shipyards, many of these jobs did not survive the end of the war. By 1950, 27 percent of the men and 12 percent of the women were engaged in manufacturing work, mainly at Boeing. But 29 percent of the men had returned to domestic service along with 68 percent of the women.

Percentages of Seattle's African-American labor force in industrial work and domestic service, 1940 and 1950.

	1940	1950
Men:		
Industrial work	17%	27%
Domestic service	52%	29%
Women:		
Industrial work	4%	12%
Domestic service	83%	68%

What does this mean? Roger Lotchin and others would probably conclude that World War II gains were temporary. Certainly for black women the argument is persuasive. Hitler may have "gotten black women out of the white folks' kitchen," as one female aircraft worker said in 1943, but, when he was gone, many of them dropped the welder's torch and again picked up the broom.[6]

But one could also argue that certainly not all of the workers became menial servants again. The wages earned during the war and the prestige derived from holding jobs comparable to those of white workers for the first time, or from wearing the uniform of the United States military, would translate into greater demands and bolder action on a number of fronts including civil rights. Even if they no longer held defense jobs, their brief but crucial wartime experience convinced many African-American women and men that they could, and eventually would, return to more lucrative factory employment.

African-American success in the World War II industrial workplace could be measured not only by access to the shipyards and factories, but also by black workers' collective challenge of discriminatory policies and practices of both management and organized labor. By 1942, African-American workers discovered that their pre-war exclusion *from* shipyards and aircraft factories was soon replaced by anti-black discrimination *within* them. Consequently they launched a concerted campaign to end that discrimination which generated consequences felt far beyond the Pacific Northwest. Throughout the World War II years, African-American workers at Boeing challenged the "whites only" clause of the International Association of Machinists (IAM) constitution. The machinists union allowed the entry of black workers into Boeing only as a "temporary concession" to wartime labor shortages. Knowing that their post-war access to Boeing jobs could disappear again if the IAM chose to enforce the ban, black Boeing employees joined sympathetic white and Asian employees to campaign for the clause's removal from the union's constitution. By 1948 the racially integrated delegation from the Pacific Northwest persuaded the union at its national convention in Grand Rapids, Michigan, to remove its nearly century-old ban.[7]

African-American shipyard workers in Portland challenged the discriminatory practices of the International Boilermakers Union which relegated them to segregated "auxiliary" locals. Portland's black workers created the Shipyard Negro Organization for Victory (SNOV) and drew upon the support of a local black newspaper, the Portland *Observer*, the NAACP, and the Fair Employment Practices Committee (FEPC), which in November 1943 held hearings in the city on Boilermaker discrimination. The FEPC ordered the Boilermakers to disband their auxiliary local. Unfortunately the victory came in the spring of 1945, just months before the shipyards would be dismantled and virtually all of the workers, black and white, dismissed. Nonetheless, the post-war Boilermakers union opened its ranks to African-American shipyard workers throughout the nation, in large measure because of the efforts of black workers in Portland.[8]

The African-American migration to the Pacific Northwest permanently altered race relations in Seattle, Portland, and Tacoma as the newcomers demanded the social freedom and political rights denied them in their former Southern homes. But it also made black-white relations the focal point of far more discussion and anxiety than ever before. "WE CATER TO WHITE TRADE ONLY" signs appeared in movie theaters and restaurants in Seattle and Portland, but also in Yakima, Walla Walla, and Pendleton. Interracial tension in the shipyards in Portland and Seattle almost led to riots in 1943 and 1944. Moreover, literally hundreds of minor racial disturbances involving random, senseless attacks perpetuated by blacks and whites throughout the Pacific Northwest exacerbated regional racial tension. The sense of urgency among public officials was best articulated by Seattle Mayor William F. Devin in a July 1944 speech at the University of Washington where he announced:

> The problem of racial tensions is . . . going to affect us not only during the War, but also after the War, and it is our duty to face the problem together. If we do not do that, we shall not exist very long as a civilized city or as a nation.[9]

All of this is not to say that the Pacific Northwest first discovered "race" and racial conflict in the 1940s. Anyone familiar with the history of this region cannot ignore the violence associated with both the century-long contestation between native peoples and European Americans and the numerous attempts in the nineteenth and early twentieth centuries to marginalize Asian-Americans. But what seems striking about the Pacific Northwest's history is how quickly in the 1940s the focus of interracial anxiety and conflict shifted to black-white relations. A 1946 survey of race relations in Spokane conducted by the Sociology Department at Washington State University found that despite the long history of regional anti-Asian sentiment and the recently concluded war with Japan, anti-black prejudice was significantly stronger than anti-Japanese-American sentiment.[10]

But regional race relations were not simply a question of black versus white. Increasingly, African-Americans and Asian-Americans began to eye each other cautiously, alternating between potential alliance and palpable antipathy. The best example of this development can be seen in post-war black-Japanese relations. By 1945 it became evident that the Japanese evacuees would return to the West Coast. The greeting they would receive, however, was in doubt. Thousands of African-American migrants to Seattle had moved into the previously Japanese neighborhood along Jackson Street and seemed unwilling to share it with evacuation returnees.

Many of the African American newcomers harbored little sympathy for the former residents. John Okada's novel, *No-No Boy,* about evacuation returnee Ichiro Yamada, captures this sentiment. When he returned from an Idaho internment camp in 1945, Okada's protagonist Yamada found his old Jackson Street neighborhood filled with recently arrived Southern blacks who failed to recognize him either as an "oppressed minority" or a person displaced from his former neighborhood. When he was scorned and ridiculed by the newcomers, Okada described it as "persecution in the drawl of the persecuted."[11]

Despite the tension Okada described, some concerned Asian-American and African-American citizens attempted to establish the first institutional link between the two communities through the Jackson Street Community Council (JSCC). Formed in 1946 to support neighborhood businesses and voluntary social service agencies, the JSCC quickly became, however inadvertently, a model for inter-ethnic cooperation. Its officers rotated among its Japanese- American, Filipino-American, Chinese-American, and African-American membership as did its "Man of the Year" selection. Moreover, in an early attempt at cultural pluralism and ethnic sensitivity, the council in 1952 selected four queens, Foon Woo, Rosita DeLeon, Adelia Avery, and Sumi Mitsui, to represent the Chinese-American, Filipino-American, African-American, and Japanese-American communities, respectively. Avery was ultimately selected as Miss International Center, entitling her to represent the JSCC in all public functions. The tension between African-Americans and Asian-Americans never disappeared, but the JSCC allowed a forum for public discourse over political conflicts and cultural differences that did not exist in most other West Coast cities, including Portland, during the immediate post-war period.[12]

The increasing influence of African-Americans in the region's politics is also a consequence of World War II migration. Two African-American men, William Owen Bush (1890) and John H. Ryan (1922), had served in the Washington legislature before World War II. Both men represented overwhelmingly white districts and, given their light-skinned complexions, many of their constituents did not realize their racial ancestry. In 1950, however, Charles Stokes, representing the 37th legislative district in central Seattle, became the first African-American to sit in the legislature while representing a heavily black district. Stokes, a Republican attorney, was in fact one of the recent migrants, having arrived from Topeka, Kansas, in 1944. Stokes' election marked the beginning of almost continuous African-American representation for the district. He also served as a model for future black office holding in the region until the late 1980s. Most successful African-American politicians would come from significantly, if not predominately, black districts. The elevation of African-Americans to office in Oregon would lag behind Washington by two decades. In 1972, William McCoy became the first black member of the state legislature. However, the pattern in Oregon would be much the same as north of the Columbia River—African-Americans were elected in significantly black districts.[13]

Moreover, white politicians such as Oregon legislators Richard Neuberger and Mark O. Hatfield, aware of African-American votes, embraced political agendas that promoted black civil rights issues. In 1949, Neuberger, a Democratic state senator from Portland, and Hatfield, a Portland area Republican representative, co-sponsored Oregon's Fair Employment Practices Act. Four years later Hatfield was co-sponsor of the state's first civil rights act. Neuberger and Hatfield (both of whom would eventually be elected U.S. Senators from Oregon) were part of a small but growing group of Oregon and Washington politicians who publicly cultivated support among the Pacific Northwest's African-American voters.[14]

But support for black civil rights stemmed from growing concern about racial injustice as well as political expediency. The response of Oregon Republicans to racial discrimination directed against one of their delegates at the 1949 National Young Republicans Convention in Salt Lake City is one illustration of the changing attitudes. Charles Maxey, a wartime migrant, Portland barber, and NAACP activist, who was selected as a delegate to the convention, found upon reaching Salt Lake City that he was not allowed to stay in the hotel hosting the convention. After making temporary housing accommodations with a local African-American family, Maxey declared he would introduce a resolution condemning his exclusion. The entire state delegation supported his request, modifying it to allow the specific resolution to be introduced by Clay Myers, Vice-Chair of the College Republicans for the state of Oregon. The resolution specifically prohibited the Young Republicans from holding any future conventions in public accommodations that discriminated against blacks. After intense and often emotional debate, the resolution was adopted by the full convention.[15]

The rapid growth of the African-American population in the Pacific Northwest strengthened civil rights organizations in the region, and allowed them to successfully pursue a civil rights agenda for the first time. In the ten year period following the end of World War II, a number of organizations dedicated to pressing for civil rights for people of color or ending the most egregious forms of discrimination emerged in the region's largest cities. Three racially integrated Pacific Northwest organizations—the Oregon Committee for Equal Rights, and the Committee on Inter-racial Principles and Practices, both headquartered in Portland, and the Seattle-based Christian Friends for Racial Equality—were examples of this growing trend toward interracial cooperation. By 1945, an Urban League chapter was formed in Portland, joining the fifteen-year-old chapter in Seattle. However, the most striking example of growing public concern about civil rights was the rise of multiracial NAACP branches in the region. The Seattle NAACP, for example, increased its membership from 85 in 1941 to 1,550 by 1945. Portland's NAACP branch, which was one of the first west of the Mississippi River, doubled from 500 members to 1,000 by the end of the war. Before World War II, these branches were the only ones in the region; by 1950, NAACP branches existed in Tacoma, Spokane, the Tri-Cities of Richland, Kennewick, and Pasco, Bremerton, Walla Walla, and Vancouver. Moreover, representatives from all of the region's branches met annually to discuss civil rights questions affecting blacks throughout the Pacific Northwest.[16]

An alternative way to gauge the success of an organization's civil rights agenda is by observing its ability to influence public policy. In this regard the NAACP branches in Washington and Oregon were remarkably effective. Both forged broadly based political coalitions including progressive labor unions, sympathetic churches, fraternal organizations, as well as the Urban League. Such coalitions constituted a veritable civil rights establishment, which could for the first time in the region's history mobilize financial, legal, and political resources to support civil rights legislation. These coalitions in Oregon and Washington obtained passage of Fair Employment Practices Laws (FEP), allowing these two Pacific Northwest states to join the ranks of only eight states with such laws before 1950. Moreover, the Oregon Committee for Equal Rights (formed in Portland in 1950) was able in 1953 in the wake of the FEP legislation to gain passage of the state's first civil rights statute, a measure which banned discrimination in public accommodations.

The organizational strategy and tactics developed in the immediate post-war period to promote a civil rights agenda served as a model for subsequent efforts well into the 1990s. There is no question, then, that while racial attitudes changed far more slowly in the 1940s than many people of color would have liked, it is seriously misleading to assume, as have some of the critics of the "transformation school," that post-war blacks reverted to the pattern of pre-war obsequiousness in the face of bigotry and discrimination.[17]

Those who posit the wartime "transformation" thesis almost always assume it to mean an improvement in the lives of the region's African-Americans. In many ways they are correct as the examples above attest. However, transformation also resulted in a decline in some aspects of the quality of life. Nowhere is this more evident than in housing. Severe over-crowding, endemic to all of the cities of the region, became especially acute in the black community and accelerated the physical deterioration of pre-dominantly African-American neighborhoods.

African-American newcomers faced a chronic wartime housing short-age which—although a problem shared by white and Asian populations—was exacerbated by a long history of discrimination in residential housing. In Seattle by 1945, over 10,000 blacks occupied virtually the same build-ings that had housed 3,700 African-Americans five years earlier. Most black newcomers in Tacoma were channeled into the Hilltop district, which pro-vided a spectacular view of Puget Sound and little else. Conditions in Port-land were worse than in Washington. Half of the 22,000 wartime migrants remained in the city and the other half took up residence in Vanport, the nation's largest wartime housing project. Whether they lived in Portland proper or Vanport, black residents were racially segregated. In 1945, a Port-land Urban League official publicly articulated a long-standing belief among African-Americans concerning the linkage between segregated housing and societal well-being. He declared: "A Man who must crowd his wife and children into an unsafe and unsanitary home . . . becomes an unstable citizen."[18]

We should be clear about the cause of the deteriorating housing situ-ation. Restrictive covenants, the centerpiece of residential housing discrimi-nation, had a long history in Seattle, Tacoma, and Portland before World War II, ensuring that it was virtually impossible for African-Americans to live outside certain prescribed districts. During World War II, such cov-enants served as invisible walls concentrating the rapidly growing African-American population into single neighborhoods. In Portland, for example, the neighborhood was Albina—a narrow corridor stretching north from downtown toward the Columbia River. In Albina, zoning laws were set aside as homes were transformed into apartments and businesses were built in front yards or occupied converted garages. In spite of this, many newcomers during World War II continued to have to sleep wherever they could find space, including in churches, pool halls, movie theaters, and automobiles.[19]

Not all migrants perceived this transformation of Pacific Northwest cities as a concern. After all, many of the newcomers came from the South where such housing conditions were common. Other workers, who focused on making money quickly and vacating Portland (or Seattle or Tacoma) at the end of the war, cared little about the lasting consequences for neighborhoods. Such apathy caused the Portland *Observer*, the city's black newspaper, to lament in a 1945 editorial:

> The Negro people are passively witnessing the development of a first-rate ghetto with all the potential for squalor, poverty, juvenile delinquency and crime. It is obvious that the herding of Negroes into the [Albina] district portends economic and social problems of far reaching significance for this city.[20]

In Seattle and Tacoma, public housing lessened the burden on the migrants in those cities. Seattle's public housing director, Jesse Epstein, refused to allow racially segregated housing, which had evolved in other cities throughout the region. Said Epstein: "We have an opportunity to prove that Negroes and whites can live side by side in harmony . . . but it's going to require skill and patience to make it work."[21] In Seattle, to a large extent, it did work as African-American and white residents lived side-by-side in Yesler Terrace and other local housing projects.

Portland officials, however, supported by the Chamber of Commerce and other civic groups, discouraged the construction of public housing precisely because they feared the migrants might stay in the region if it were available. In effect, Portland's housing "shortage" was an instrument of public policy. Stuart McElderry has shown that in addition to the usual hostility toward "residential integration" in white neighborhoods from private citizens and real estate or mortgage lending groups, the Housing Authority of Portland (HAP), a government agency appointed specifically to address the wartime housing shortage, actually blocked the construction of badly needed public housing in northeast Portland. HAP even opposed the building of Vanport, although pressure from the Kaiser Company and the federal government eventually garnered HAP's reluctant endorsement. Yet, when the war ended, the agency recommended to the Federal Housing Authority (FHA) the demolition of 484 public housing units in three projects to make room for post-war industrial expansion. Fortunately for many migrant black families who had limited access to private housing, the FHA refused to eliminate these units.[22]

Portland's housing crisis was never resolved. No doubt, African-Americans (as well as other migrants) who slept in automobiles, churches, movie theaters, and on tavern pool tables never knew that this situation was generated by more than "wartime lumber shortages." When one looks at the region as a whole, it becomes apparent that the modern "ghettos" are the result of private and public actions beginning long before World War II, but the long-term consequences first became apparent during the large-scale wartime migration.

The varied impacts of World War II can be seen most graphically in the differing histories of the immediate post-war African-American communities in Seattle and Portland. Unlike most American cities, where economies were buoyed by wartime production followed by post-war economic slumps, Seattle remained prosperous. Seattle's leading employer, Boeing, now received Cold War-inspired military contracts and saw a steady growth in commercial airline orders throughout the late 1940s. Consequently, the city's African-American population grew by 5,000 between 1945 and 1950 as defense industries continued to recruit black workers. The outlook for Seattle blacks in 1950 was so encouraging that the *Chicago Defender*, the nation's largest African-American newspaper, urged in 1951 that they leave the Midwest and East for Seattle.[23]

By contrast Portland's blacks, the vast majority of whom were Kaiser shipyard employees in 1945, had to find new occupations when the yards closed that year. A fortunate minority gained other industrial employment. Others were absorbed into the service industries of the city, and a good number (though not the majority) returned to menial employment. However, what is most striking about Portland's post-war black community is its shrinking size. Between 1945 and 1947 an estimated 11,000 African-Americans, about 50 percent of the 1945 population, simply left the city. Poor job prospects in Portland sent them north to Seattle, south to California, and in some instances back to the South. Yet the flight of thousands of blacks from Portland was not simply due to the closure of the shipyards. As already explained, the intentional housing shortage prompted by city policies had much to do with their departure. After interviewing city leaders in 1950, a Portland *Oregonian* reporter wrote: "City officials are still guided by the wishful thought that most of the Negroes will go back home, leaving the city untouched by racial 'problems.'" The reporter's view was shared by Julius A. Thomas, a Portland Urban League official, who noted in 1947 that many Pacific Coast blacks considered Portland "just like any southern town . . . the most prejudiced city in the West."[24]

The contrasting experiences of African-Americans in Pacific Northwest cities suggest that historians need to examine carefully the growing body of documentary evidence on African-Americans in the region. That evidence illustrates growing black influence in politics in the Pacific Northwest's largest cities, and on public policy in Oregon and Washington. Moreover, blacks gained access to numerous industrial jobs that had been closed to them before World War II. Admittedly some of the spectacular wartime gains were lost in the late 1940s, but the pre-war pattern of menial employment would never completely return. Or, as one postwar observer noted, "the white worker . . . may still come to the table first and take the best seat, but now the Negro sits there too."[25]

But it is equally true that certain prejudicial local government and business policies, as well as public attitudes, toward the newcomers were manifested in greater residential and public school segregation for African-American adults and children. Thus, the Pacific Northwest proved not to be as liberal regarding racial issues as many residents—black and white—had previously believed. Ultimately, that realization prompted African-Americans to generate a protracted civil rights movement in the 1960s. A rationale for that movement can be surmised in the statement by Larry Richardson, who in his 1975 Washington State University dissertation asserted that African-Americans migrated to this region out of the belief that it offered racial equality as well as employment opportunity. Richardson contends that when migrants realized the Pacific Northwest did not fulfill its promise, the newcomers joined with the established black residents in challenging discrimination. That challenge was inevitable, Richardson asserts, because African-Americans "who had migrated West to improve their lot came to realize that [the Pacific Northwest] was the end of the line both socially and geographically. There was no better place to go."[26]

Notes

1. Quoted in Roger W. Lotchin, "The Historians' War or the Home Front's War? Some Thoughts for Western Historians," *Western Historical Quarterly* 26, no. 2 (Summer 1995):195. For the best articulation of the transformation thesis, see Gerald D. Nash, *The American West Transformed: The Impact of the Second World War* (Bloomington: Indiana University Press, 1986), and *World War II and the West: Reshaping the Economy* (Lincoln: University of Nebraska Press, 1990). See also Carlos Schwantes, "The Pacific Northwest in World War II," *Journal of the West* 25, no. 3 (July 1986):4-18. On the critique of the transformation thesis, see Roger W. Lotchin, "California Cities and the Hurricane of Change: World War II in the San Francisco, Los Angeles and San Diego Metropolitan Areas," *Pacific Historical Review* 63, no. 3 (August 1994):393-420, and "The Historian's War or the Home Front's War?" 185-96; Albert S. Broussard, *Black San Francisco: The Struggle for Racial Equality in the West, 1900-1954* (Lawrence: University Press of Kansas, 1993); and Stuart McElderry, "Boundaries and Limits: Housing Segregation and Civil Rights Activism in Portland, Oregon, 1930-1962," *Pacific Historical Review*, forthcoming. Paul Rhode specifically counters the economic arguments of Nash in "The Nash Thesis Revisited: An Economic Historian's View," *Pacific Historical Review* 63, no. 3 (August 1994):363-92.

2. On the 1940 and 1950 population figures, see U.S. Bureau of the Census, *Sixteenth Census of the United States* 1940, *Population* vol. II, *Characteristics of the Population* (Washington: Government Printing Office, 1943), parts 6, 7, tables 31, A-36, C-36; and U.S. Bureau of the Census, *Census of Population* 1950, vol. II, *Characteristics of the Population* (Washington: Government Printing Office, 1952), parts 37, 47, table 34.

3. See Marilynn S. Johnson, *The Second Gold Rush: Oakland and the East Bay in World War II* (Berkeley: University of California Press, 1993), 58.

4. Quoted in Ronald Takaki, *A Different Mirror: A History of Multicultural America* (Boston: Little, Brown, 1993), 398. For a discussion of the proletarianization process among black urban workers, see Joe W. Trotter, *Black Milwaukee: The Making of an Industrial Proletariat, 1915-45* (Urbana: University of Illinois Press, 1985), chapters 2, 7.

5. See U.S. Bureau of the Census, *Sixteenth Census of the United States* 1940, *Population* vols. III, *The Labor Force* (Washington: Government Printing Office, 1943), part 4, table 13, and U.S. Bureau of the Census, *Census of Population* 1950, vol II, *Characteristics of the Population* (Washington: Government Printing Office, 1952), part 37, table 34.

6. The "kitchen" quote appears in Sherna Berger Gluck, *Rosie the Riveter Revisited: Women, the War, and Social Change* (Boston: Twayne, 1987), 42. For the statistics on the Seattle black work force, see U.S. Bureau of the Census, *Sixteenth Census of the United States* 1940, *Population* vol. III, *The Labor Force*, (Washington: Government Printing Office, 1943), part 5, table 13; U.S. Bureau of the Census, *Census of Population* 1950, vol. II, *Characteristics of the Population* (Washington: Government Printing Office, 1952), part 47, table 34, and Quintard Taylor, *The Forging of a Black Community: Seattle's Central District, from 1870 through the Civil Rights Era* (Seattle: University of Washington Press, 1994), 161.

7. For a detailed discussion of the role of black Boeing workers in the integration of the International Association of Machinists, see John McCann, *Blood in the Water: A History of District Lodge 751 of the International Association of Machinists and Aerospace Workers* (Seattle: IAM&AW, 1989), 47-49, and Taylor, *The Forging of a Black Community,* 164-65.

8. On the campaign in Portland, see Alonzo Smith and Quintard Taylor, "Racial Discrimination in the Workplace: A Study of Two West Coast Cities during the 1940s," *Journal of Ethnic Studies* 8, no. 1 (Spring 1980):35-54.

9. Quoted in Taylor, *The Forging of a Black Community*, 167-68.

10. See Tolbert Hall Kennedy, "Racial Survey of the Intermountain Northwest," *Research Studies of the State College of Washington* 14, no. 3 (September 1946):166, 237-42.

11. See John Okada, *No-No Boy* (Seattle: University of Washington Press, 1978), 5.

12. See Taylor, *The Forging of a Black Community*, 174-75.

13. On black officeholders in Washington, see Quintard Taylor, "A History of Blacks in the Pacific Northwest, 1788-1970," Ph.D. dissertation, University of Minnesota, 1977, pp. 187-88, and Taylor, *The Forging of a Black Community*, 176. On William McCoy's election, see Portland *Oregonian*, November 8, 1972, p. 4M, D.

14. See Rudy N. Pearson, "African Americans in Portland, Oregon, 1940-1950: Work and Living Conditions—A Social History," Ph.D. dissertation, Washington State University, 1996, pp. 177-80, 184; and Taylor, "A History of Blacks in the Pacific Northwest," 235.

15. For a full account of this episode, see James Strassmaier, "1949—Oregon Young Republicans Strike Blow for Civil Rights: An Interview with Charles Britton Maxey," *Oregon History* 38, no. 4 (Winter 1994-95):12-15.

16. See McElderry, "Boundaries and Limits," 16-17; Taylor, *The Forging of a Black Community*, 170-71.

17. On anti-discrimination laws in Oregon and Washington, see Taylor, "A History of Blacks in the Pacific Northwest," 233-34, 244.

18. Quoted in Portland *Oregonian*, June 24, 1942, p. 2.

19. See Quintard Taylor, "The Great Migration: The Afro-American Communities of Seattle and Portland during the 1940s," *Arizona and the West* 23, no. 2 (Summer 1981):113-14, 117, 122-23, and McElderry, "Boundaries and Limits," 14.

20. Quoted in *Portland Observer*, July 20, 1945, p. 4.

21. Quoted in Taylor, *The Forging of a Black Community*, 169.

22. For a discussion of the HAP policy on wartime and post-war housing, see McElderry, "Boundaries and Limits," 13-21.

23. See Taylor, *The Forging of a Black Community*, 175.

24. See Portland *Oregonian*, June 17, 1945, p. 8, and April 23, 1947, p. 10. The estimated 11,000 person post-war population decline is reported in the *Oregonian*, June 16, 1947, p. 8. Although Portland lost more people than most West Coast cities, its experience is not unique, nor is the attitude of its public officials. Oakland, Richmond, and shipbuilding centers had staggering unemployment rates. In Vallejo, for example, half of the black population of 4,000 was unemployed in 1947. And it seems Richmond and Vallejo officials made every effort to drive black migrants away. See Cy W. Record, "Willie Stokes at the Golden Gate," *Crisis* 56, no. 6 (June 1949):175-79, and Shirley Ann Moore, "The Black Community in Richmond, California, 1910-1963," Ph.D. dissertation, University of California, Berkeley, 1989, pp. 160-62.

25. Quoted in Katherine Archibald, *Wartime Shipyard: A Study in Cultural Disunity* (Berkeley: University of California Press, 1947), 99.

26. Quoted in Larry S. Richardson, "Civil Rights in Seattle: A Rhetorical Analysis of a Social Movement," Ph.D. dissertation, Washington State University, 1975, p. 32.

Contributors

Susan H. Armitage is a Professor of History at Washington State University, editor of the scholarly journal *Frontiers*, and formerly the director of American Studies at WSU. She is the co-editor of two widely acclaimed books on western women: *The Women's West* (1987), which won the Susan Koppelman Award for American Culture, and *Writing the Range: Race, Class, and Culture in the Women's West* (1997). Professor Armitage also has published numerous articles, served as a commentator on the PBS television special *In Search of the Oregon Trail*, and lectured in Russia as a Fulbright scholar.

Kenneth S. Coates is a Professor of History and Dean of the Faculty of Arts at the University of New Brunswick at Saint John. Prior to holding that position, he was chair of the Department of History at the University of Waikato, Hamilton, New Zealand; and before that he held academic and administrative positions at the University of Victoria, British Columbia, and the University of Northern British Columbia. He is the author of more than four dozen articles and book chapters, and the author or editor of more than two dozen scholarly and trade books, including *Canada's Colonies: A History of the Yukon and Northwest Territories* (1985), *Best Left as Indians: Native-White Relations in the Yukon Territory, 1840-1973* (1991), *The Alaska Highway in World War II: The U.S. Army of Occupation in Canada's Northwest* (1992) co-authored with W.R. Morrison, *Pacific Partners: The Japanese Presence in Canadian Society, Culture, and Business* (1996) co-authored with Carin Holroyd, and *Seizing the Feather: Aboriginal Self-Government in Canada* (1998) co-authored with Greg Poelzer.

Richard W. Etulain is a Professor of History at the University of New Mexico and Director of the Center for the American West. He is the author or editor of more than thirty books and scholarly bibliographies, including *Conversations with Wallace Stegner on Western History and Literature* (1983, 1990), *The American West: A Twentieth-Century History* (1989), which was a History Book Club "main selection," *The Twentieth-Century West: Historical Interpretations* (1989), and *Re-Imagining the Modern American West: A Century of Fiction, History, and Art* (1996). He has served as president of both the Western Literature Association (1978-79) and the Western History Association (1998-99).

Gerald Friesen is a Professor of History at the University of Manitoba in Winnipeg. His book *The Canadian Prairies: A History* (1984) won the prestigious Sir John A. Macdonald Prize of the Canadian Historical Association. He is also author of *River Road: Essays on Manitoba and Prairie History* (1996). For many years he worked on the National Museums of Canada's Visual History Series and a multi-volume history of Manitoba native peoples.

Julie Roy Jeffrey is the Elizabeth Connelly Todd Professor of History at Goucher College in Maryland. She has published on a wide variety of topics, but is best known for her work in women's history. Her books include *Education for Children of the Poor* (1978), *Frontier Women: The Trans-Mississippi West, 1840-1880* (1979), and *Converting the West: A Biography of Narcissa Whitman* (1991), from which her WSU Pettyjohn essay is derived. She is also a co-author of the successful U.S. history textbook *The American People: Creating a Nation and a Society* (1986).

Patricia Nelson Limerick is a Professor of History and American Studies at the University of Colorado in Boulder and chair of the board of the Center of the American West. Professor Limerick is an extremely prolific writer, publishing both in scholarly journals and the popular press (*New York Times, USA Today,* etc.). She is also a popular interview subject and appeared extensively as a commentator in Ken Burns' TV series *The West* and the PBS special *In Search of the Oregon Trail.* Her monograph, *The Legacy of Conquest: The Unbroken Past of the American West* (1987), is the most widely read and influential text of the "New Western History" genre. She is also author of *Desert Passages: Encounters with the American Deserts* (1985), and co-editor of *Trails: Toward a New Western History* (1991). In 1996-97, Professor Limerick served as President of the American Studies Association.

Quintard Taylor, a Professor of History at the University of Oregon, is a specialist in Western history and one of the nation's leading experts on African Americans in the West. He is the author of *A History of Blacks in the Pacific Northwest, 1788-1970* (1977), *The Forging of a Black Community: Seattle's Central District, from 1870 through the Civil Rights Era* (1994), and *In Search of the Racial Frontier: African Americans and the American*

West, 1529-1990 (1998). He is also the author of more than twenty published articles on African American, African, Afro-Brazilian, and comparative ethnic history.

David J. Weber is the Robert and Nancy Dedman Professor of History at Southern Methodist University. He is the author of numerous books on Hispanic culture and history including *Foreigners in Their Native Land: Historical Roots of the Mexican Americans* (1973), *The Mexican Frontier, 1821-1846* (1982), *The Spanish Frontier in North America* (1992), and *Where Cultures Meet: Frontiers in Latin American History* (1994). Professor Weber has been a Fulbright Lecturer and received major grants from the American Council of Learned Societies, the Center for Advanced Study in the Behavioral Sciences, and the National Endowment for the Humanities.

Donald Worster is the Hall Distinguished Professor of History at the University of Kansas. He is the author of numerous monographs and essay collections that have helped define the fields of environmental history and western history. His book, *Dust Bowl: The Southern Plains in the 1930s* (1979) won the prestigious Bancroft Prize in American History. Among his other publications are *Rivers of Empire: Water, Aridity, and the Growth of the American West* (1985), *Nature's Economy: A History of Ecological Ideas* (2nd ed. 1994), *Under Western Skies: Nature and History in the American West* (1992), and *The Wealth of Nature: Environmental History and the Ecological Imagination* (1993). Worster is a past president of the American Society for Environmental History and has won grants and fellowships from the Guggenheim Foundation, the Mellon Foundation, the Rockefeller Foundation, the National Endowment for the Humanities, and others.

John R. Wunder is a Professor of History at the University of Nebraska-Lincoln and served as the Director of the Center for Great Plains Studies. He has degrees in both history and law, and has published extensively on legal history topics. His monographs include *Inferior Courts, Superior Justice: A History of the Justices of the Peace on the Northwest Frontier* (1979), and *"Retained By The People": A History of American Indians and the Bill of Rights* (1994). He is also the editor of ten books including *Native American Cultural and Religious Freedoms* (1996), *Constitutionalism and Native Americans, 1903-1968* (1996), and *Native American Sovereignty* (1996).